SUNY series in the Philosophy of the Social Sciences

Lenore Langsdorf, editor

Ricoeur's Critical Theory

Ricoeur's Critical Theory

David M. Kaplan

State University of New York Press

Published by
State University of New York Press, Albany

© 2003 State University of New York

For information, address State University of New York Press,
90 State Street, Suite 700, Albany, NY, 12207

Production by Judith Block
Marketing by Jennifer Giovani

Library of Congress Control Number

Kaplan, David M.
    Ricoeur's critical theory / David M. Kaplan.
        p. cm. — (SUNY series in the philosophy of the social sciences)
    Includes bibliographical references and index.
    ISBN 0-7914-5695-1 (alk. paper) — ISBN 0-7914-5696-X (pbk. : alk. paper)
    1. Ricoeur, Paul.   2. Critical theory.   I. Title.   II. Series.

B2430.R554 K37 2003
194—dc21

                                                              2002042631

10 9 8 7 6 5 4 3 2 1

For Will Sinda

CONTENTS

ACKNOWLEDGMENTS

I would not have been able to complete this book were it not for the help of several individuals, two public pools, and Roberta. I am grateful to my friends and family for their understanding, loyalty, warmth, and affection. I am grateful to Jim Marsh and Pat Bourgeois, both of whom encouraged and supported me from the very beginning of this project. I am grateful to my chairman at Polytechnic, Harold Sjursen, for reducing my teaching load one year. And I am grateful to my editor, Jane Bunker, who has a been joy to work with. I have profitted immensely from her wisdom and expertise.

My greatest debt is to my friend Michael McGandy. He poured over my manuscript, corrected my awful sentences, questioned me on substantive philosophical issues, and forced me to be more clear. He is a superlative editor and a fine philosopher. No one helped me more with this book than he did.

But I might not have even been in a position to write this book if it weren't for Will Sinda. Will was my Introduction to Philosophy teacher my freshman year at Tulane and he was one of the best teachers I ever had. Because of him, I have devoted my life to studying, writing, and teaching philosophy. It is to him and other exploited adjunct instructors that this book is dedicated.

REFERENCE KEY TO FREQUENTLY CITED TEXTS OF PAUL RICOEUR

CC   *Critique and Conviction*. New York: Columbia University Press, 1998.

CI   *The Conflict of Interpretation: Essays in Hermeneutics*, trans. Willis Domingo et al., ed. Don Ihde. Evanston: Northwestern University Press, 1974.

FM   *Fallible Man*, trans. Charles Kelbley. New York: Fordham University Press, 1986.

FN   *Freedom and Nature: The Voluntary and the Involuntary*, trans. Erazim Kohak. Evanston: Northwestern University Press, 1966.

FP   *Freud and Philosophy: An Essay on Interpretation*, trans. Dennis Savage. New Haven: Yale University Press, 1970.

H   *Husserl: An Analysis of His Phenomenology*, trans. Edward E. Ballard and Lester G. Embree. Evanston: Northwestern University Press, 1967.

HHS   *Hermeneutics and the Human Sciences: Essays on Language, Action, and Interpretation*, ed. and trans. John B. Thompson. Cambridge: Cambridge University Press, 1981.

HT   *History and Truth*, trans. Charles A. Kelbley. Evanston: Northwestern University Press, 1965.

IU   *Lectures on Ideology and Utopia*, ed. George H. Taylor. New York: Columbia University Press, 1986.

INT   *Interpretation Theory: Discourse and the Surplus of Meaning*. Fort Worth: Texas Christian University Press, 1976.

J   *The Just*, trans. David Pellauer. Chicago: University of Chicago Press, 2000.

OA   *Oneself as Another*, trans. Kathleen Blamey. Chicago: University of Chicago Press, 1992.

PS   *Political and Social Essays*, ed. David Stewart and Joseph Bien. Athens: Ohio University Press, 1974.

RM   *The Rule of Metaphor: Multi-Disciplinary Studies of the Creation of Meaning in Language*, trans. Robert Czerny, Kathleen McLaughlin and John Costello, SJ. Toronto: University of Toronto Press, 1977.

SE   *The Symbolism of Evil*, trans. Emerson Buchanan. Boston: Beacon Press, 1967.

TA   *From Text to Action: Essays in Hermeneutics, II*, trans. Kathleen Blamey and John B. Thompson. Evanston: Northwestern University Press, 1991.

TN1   *Time and Narrative*, vol. I, trans. Kathleen McLaughlin and David Pellauer. Chicago: University of Chicago Press, 1984.

TN2   *Time and Narrative*, vol. II, trans. Kathleen McLaughlin and David Pellauer. Chicago: University of Chicago Press, 1985.

TN3   *Time and Narrative*, vol. III, trans. Kathleen McLaughlin and David Pellauer. Chicago: University of Chicago Press, 1988.

INTRODUCTION

Paul Ricoeur is widely regarded as among the most important philosophers of the twentieth century. His ability over the last fifty years to enter into dialogue with a wide range of philosophers and philosophies and to offer even-handed, balanced judgments on the most important debates of the day is nothing less than remarkable. One of Ricoeur's many strengths as a philosopher is his "passion for mediation," an ability to reconcile seemingly antithetical philosophies like phenomenology and structuralism, hermeneutics and phenomenology, narrative theory and hermeneutics, deontological and virtue ethics, liberalism and communitarianism, hermeneutics and the critique of ideology. He tends to think in terms of opposites, pairs, and contrasts juxtaposed in such a way that highlights and preserves differences, while resisting the temptation to synthesize a new unity. Instead he claims only to draw a "hermeneutic arc" between opposites, a metaphor that suggests a chastened, mitigated mediation. A hermeneutic arc, drawn between two antithetical positions, shows how they could go together by linking them together in a way that marks the place of one position in the context of the other. Ricoeur mediates philosophical debates like a good referee calls a game: he does not get in the way of the play and he usually makes the right call. His unique method of nonsynthetic mediation testifies to the uniqueness of his philosophical spirit. He respects the plurality of voices and questions of others while honoring the original philosophical impetus to find unity, reason, and clarity in history. Ricoeur is a thoroughly modernist philosopher for whom philosophy and reason are synonymous. "For my part, I do not in the least abandon the tradition of rationality that has animated philosophy since the Greeks" (CI 296).

Furthermore, the very *telos* of rational, philosophical reflection is a critical philosophy, both in the Kantian sense of identifying the limits of understanding as well as in the Marxist sense of uncovering false consciousness, systematically distorted communication, and social domination, exploitation, and oppression.

1

He is committed to a conception of philosophy as critical theory resulting in personal and social transformation and progressive politics. From his contributions to the leftist journal *Esprit* in the 1950s and 1960s, to his mediation of the Habermas-Gadamer debate and his lectures on ideology and utopia in the 1970s, to his works on ethics, politics, and law in the 1980s and 1990s, philosophical reflection, critique, and liberation are inseparably linked in Ricoeur's works.

Politically he has always considered himself a leftist. While careful to distance himself from Leninism-Stalinism and other versions of political totalitarianism, he nonetheless affirms that a critique of society should be addressed not only to political institutions but to economic institutions as well. Anything less than a democratic economy, in which decisions and actions are undertaken collectively, is exploitative and alienating. In this sense, Ricoeur stands squarely in the Marxist tradition of political philosophy. At the same time, he explains that a democratic economy must also be a democratic society that respects human rights, treats people equally, protects our liberties, and allows for full political participation. In this sense, Ricoeur is a political liberal. But additionally, a democratic society should also aim to foster a good life for communities, emphasize the membership of citizens for whom political participation matters, and recognize the plurality of social goods and historic values that make us who we are. In this sense, Ricoeur is a political communitarian. If we were to reconcile his philosophical-political commitments we could call him a "communitarian-liberal socialist," or "socialist liberal-communitarian," or any ordering of the three terms that does not suggest a privileging of one over the others. A political philosophy should address itself equally to political freedom, economic well-being, and the diversity of social goods. Ricoeur's contribution to political philosophy is to provide (1) a framework for the interpretation, analysis, and criticism of social action and institutions, that is (2) capable of identifying ideological formations and distorted communication that prevent us from living well together in a just society, by (3) highlighting the moral and political character of our decisions, actions, and institutions in the name of democracy, justice, and community. Philosophy is a form of critical pedagogy aiming to bring about a democratic economy, just society, and good life.

Yet for some reason, the critical dimension in Ricoeur's works has been generally overlooked in the secondary literature. Very little attention has been given to his conception of the relationship between hermeneutics and critical theory, his theories of ideology and utopia, and the normative basis for a critique of society. There are several excellent studies of Ricoeur's work, including readings of his early philosophical anthropology and hermeneutic phenomenology,[1] his mature hermeneutic philosophy,[2] his conception of subjectivity,[3] his relationship to Kant,[4] his biblical hermeneutics,[5] his relationship to poststructuralism,[6] deeply sympathetic portraits of his life and works,[7] and other books and collections of essays that address, among other issues, his contributions to theology and literary criticism.[8] But noticeably missing from these otherwise excellent works and collections is any sustained discussion of the critical dimension of Ricoeur's recent thought.

There are, however, two notable exceptions. One is John Thompson's *Critical Hermeneutics*, which attempts to elaborate a critical and rationally justified interpretation of human action for the social sciences geared toward the problems of power and ideology.[9] My work picks up where Thompson's leaves off by considering Ricoeur's works that appeared following the publication of *Critical Hermeneutics*. I hope to show how Ricoeur's more recent studies on narrative, ethics, and law further contribute to the tradition of critical theory. The other notable exception is Bernard Dauenhauer's *Paul Ricoeur: Promise and Risk of Politics*, which develops Ricoeur's political and moral philosophy against the backdrop of his philosophical anthropology.[10] My work intersects with Dauenhauer's by developing a framework for a critical social theory read in light of Ricoeur's hermeneutic philosophy and other recent works. I hope to amplify his voice in the conversation on critical theory by showing how his critical-hermeneutics and moral-political philosophy provide an interpretive, normative, and critical framework that enables us to address social action and institutions in a responsible fashion.

This work can also be seen as a revisitation of Ricoeur's mediation of the Habermas-Gadamer debates in light of his recent works on narrative, ethics, and political theory. He places tremendous emphasis on the Habermas-Gadamer debate or, more generally, on the relationship between hermeneutics and the tradition of critical philosophy.[11] He goes so far as to claim that what is at stake between Habermas and Gadamer is nothing less than "the fundamental gesture of philosophy."

> Is this gesture an avowal of the historical conditions to which all human understanding is subsumed under the reign of finitude? Or rather is it, in the last analysis, an act of defiance, a critical gesture, relentlessly repeated and indefinitely turned against "false consciousness," against the distortions of human communication which conceal the permanent exercise of domination and violence? (HHS 270)

These debates are well known and well rehearsed in recent Continental Philosophy.[12] On one side of the debate is Hans-Georg Gadamer's hermeneutic philosophy, which represents a tradition of modern hermeneutics that stretches back to Heidegger, Dilthey, and Schleiermacher.[13] Hermeneutics is a theory of the operation of understanding in relation to the interpretation of texts. According to this tradition, understanding is always affected by history, prejudice, authority, and tradition. These conditions of understanding inform all interpretation, occur in language, and are constituted by our membership in a historical community. On the other side of the debate is Jürgen Habermas's critique of ideology, which represents a tradition of critical theory stretching back from the Frankfurt School Marxism, Freud, Marx, Hegel, and Kant.[14] This tradition endeavors to uncover the limits, or conditions of possibility of understanding, and to evaluate the justice and well-being of a society. Critical theory is a social philosophy, a social science, a theory of knowledge, and a rationally grounded practical philosophy geared toward overcoming one-sidedness and injustice. Ricoeur argues that the choice between either hermeneutics or the critique of ideology is ultimately a false choice if hermeneutics is reinterpreted in such a way that it honors the fundamental gesture of philosophy, and if the critique of ideology owns up to its own historic conditions of possibility.

Two issues ostensibly divide hermeneutics and the critique of ideology. First is the function of history and tradition in understanding. For Gadamer tradition transmits understanding; for Habermas tradition not only transmits understanding but also violence, domination, and systematically distorted communication. For Gadamer truth is attained by reaching consensus in dialogue; for Habermas the consensus achieved in dialogue may be systematically distorted, and, therefore, truth is never fully attained, but instead violence and domination are perpetuated through false consensus. The second central issue of the Habermas-Gadamer debate is the hermeneutic claim to universality. For Gadamer the hermeneutic claim to universality rests on the premise that all understanding is presented to us through the universal medium of language; for Habermas hermeneutics can claim universality only at the expense of its own limits, which are essentially nonhermeneutic forms of understanding that are able to distinguish between true and false consensus, and genuine and systematically distorted communication.

Ricoeur's proposed reconciliation attempts to recover a transcendental moment of objective reflection and explanation within the hermeneutic circle, thus accounting for the philosophical ends of both hermeneutics and the critique of ideology. He argues that the one philosophical aim of recovering and applying tradition does not necessarily contradict the other philosophical aim of evaluating and criticizing false consciousness and communication on universal grounds. Hermeneutics and the critique of ideology are part of a process of interpretation geared toward enlarging communication by eliminating the systematic distortions that prevent understanding. Ricoeur appropriates from Habermas the a priori necessity of a regulative ideal of unconstrained communication that norms actual communication, while insisting that the rational redemption of the validity basis of communicative can occur through multiple forms of discourse, not just the discourse of rational argumentation. Hermeneutics without the regulative idea of emancipation is blind; the critique of ideology without a concrete content from our practical interest in communication is empty. It is the task of philosophical reflections to show how an interpretation of society is guided by both a retrieval of cultural heritage and a projection of a liberated humanity.

In addition, there is a second aspect of the Habermas-Gadamer debate that Ricoeur addresses in the later chapters of *Oneself as Another*. This debate is also known as the "communicative ethics controversy."[15] On one side is Habermas himself, whose discourse ethics stand in a deontological tradition stretching back to Kant. Discourse ethics affirms the priority of the "right" over the "good" by establishing the universally binding norms of moral justification that are inherent in communication. There is a notion of impartiality connected with the moral point of view that we implicitly rely on every time we try to reach understanding and agreement with each other. The resolution of conflicts is accomplished through a principle of universalization, a dialogical version of the categorical imperative. Discourse ethics is a metaethical reconstruction of the norms that govern impartial, potentially universal, moral reasoning. The antagonist to discourse ethics is the teleological tradition stretching back to Aristotle that affirms the priority of the "good" over the "right" by establishing the relationship between the particular values of a community and the concrete, historical context of their application. From the neo-Aristotelian, communitarian perspective, discourse ethics emphasizes justice and rights at the expense of the substantive bonds and shared convictions of the good that ultimately justify moral life. The search for an impartial point of view that would justify generally binding norms is a quixotic quest. We can never put aside our notions of the goods that constitute us or sever the bonds of our particular attachments in order to achieve universalist neutrality—nor would that be desirable even as an ideal. Instead moral life consists in the habits, practices, and forms of life that enable us to sustain particular interpersonal relationships in concrete situations. Impartial and universal principles are antagonistic to real conflicts and relations, which, because they are historical, are always partial and particular.

Ricoeur, however, claims that the antinomy between the right and good, universal moral norm and particular historical tradition is false. The historical particular is mediated by the abstract universal, which, in turn, is always understood and applied in a particular historical context. His solution to the communicative ethics controversy is to argue that practical reason is tied to both a teleological ethical aim and a deontological moral norm. Deontological norms are ultimately grounded in a teleological conception of ethics but these norms also transcend the historic particular and test it. Ethics has primacy over morality, but morality regulates ethics. When deontological norms produces *aporias* of application—as they inevitably do—we must refer back to the ethical aim of a particular good life in order to mediate conflicting interpretations. Such is the delicate balance of practical wisdom as a non-Hegelian third term that mediates the pair of ethics and morality. But if moral judgment were simply a matter of balancing the ethical aim and moral norm there would be no room for "the tragedy of action," exemplified in stories like that of Antigone. Sometimes there is no right answer to moral problems. It is in these intractable situations that the art of practical wisdom helps us make decisions and act justly and appropriately in the face of tragic situations.

A third set of concerns, somewhat more remotely related to the Habermas-Gadamer debate, is organized around the relation of ethics to politics and the law. Just as the universality of reason in relation to tradition separates hermeneutics and the critique of ideology, the differences that separate political liberals from communitarians hinge on the relationship between universal normative principles and the social bonds that sustain particular historic communities.[16] The communitarian challenge to liberalism questions the primacy of rights and the priority of justice in politics, the thin notion of the self that ostensibly exists prior to and independent of its ends, and the singular principle of justice that distributes a set of basic goods. Communitarians are skeptical about efforts to base social justice on abstract individual rights, the priority of the right over the good, and universal principles of just distribution. Instead they favor a contextualized, historical understanding of the good of persons and of communities. They suggest we cannot understand social justice without understanding the common purposes, ends, and goods that shape and give meaning to our shared life as citizens. We only have rights because of our particular attachments to historic communities, not before them or in spite of them. Social justice then requires that we protect communities, promote a shared vision of the good life, and recognize the plurality of goods and multiple principles of justice and just distribution. After all, liberalism is a tradition like any other, and so political theory should stop abstracting from particularities to construct false universals when, in fact, justice is plural, historical, and particular to membership in cultures.

With typical equanimity Ricoeur mediates the concerns of liberals and communitarians by drawing out the political implications of his theory of practical wisdom and its accompanying notion of moral selfhood. He agrees with communitarian philosophers that the self is an essentially connected self, challenging the liberal ahistorical, atomistic self. We are who we are because of our cultural heritage, shared experiences, and the aims, attachments, and relationships that define us. But the primacy of community values and particular, historical ideals of the good life need not challenge the liberal requirement of social justice that universal rights and liberties be protected. The right and the good in politics as in ethics stand in a dialectical relationship. The practical wisdom exercised at the level of the political resembles the tragedy of action at the level of the ethical. Democracy is a fragile, imperfect attempt to balance social justice and our desire to live well together. The key to Ricoeur's recent political works is the idea of a "contextualized universal" that would lead us beyond the stale debate between liberal universalists and communitarian contextualists. To assert a contradiction between the universal and particular, abstract normative principle and concrete context of action, is to misunderstand both the historic character of reason and the rational character of tradition. Once the contextual character of the universal is understood the communitarian plea for plural spheres of justice becomes far less attractive than Ricoeur's alternative of an institutionalized political body responsible for creating laws, protecting communities, and exercising power in a just and appropriate way.

Taken together, Ricoeur's three mediations of the Habermas-Gadamer debate form the hermeneutic, moral, and political basis of a unique version of critical theory. His hermeneutic philosophy is designed to interpret and diagnose texts and actions as well as criticize distorted communication and false consiousness; his moral philosophy is designed to judge and evaluate social justice and well-being in light of intractable moral and political situations; and his political philosophy is designed to steer a delicate path between legitimate and illegitimate power and authority. It should be noted, however, that the model of critical theory I am proposing to develop from Riceour's works is an interpretive construction; it is not a connection that he makes himself. He has consistently been reluctant to find any common threads running throughout his thirty books and over 500 articles. On his own self-interpretation, each book he has written addresses a different problem, develops in conjunction with different dialogue partners, and is limited in scope. He claims only to deal with particular problems, and refuses to see the relationship between his different books as either continuous or discontinuous.

> After having completed a work, I find myself confronting something that has escaped it, something that flies outside its orbit,

becoming an obsession for me, and forming the next subject to examine. . . . In this way, one can say that the theme of the new book
is off-center in relation to the preceding one, but with a return to
subjects that had already been encountered, touched upon, or anticipated in earlier discussions. What had been a fragment becomes
the new envelope, the totality." (CC 81)

Despite Ricoeur's description of his own work, the model I am proposing re-
considers the problems of false consciousness and distorted communication in
light of Ricoeur's recent philosophy, showing the internal connection between
his hermeneutic, narrative, moral, and political philosophy, in order to transform
the fragments of a critical social theory into a new totality.

There are four prominent themes in Ricoeur's hermeneutic philosophy: the
convergence of language and action, a reflective philosophy of subjectivity, the detour through imaginative and creative expressions, and a post-Hegelian Kantian
methodology. Each theme can be found in both his early hermeneutic philosophy
of the late 1960s and his later narrative-hermeneutic philosophy of the 1980s. Narrative theory connects hermeneutics with moral, political, and legal philosophy.

The first theme is the convergence of language and action. Ricoeur has
used the term *hermeneutics* to describe the kind philosophy he has practiced since
about 1960, with the publication of the *Symbolism of Evil*. It simply means "interpretation," with an emphasis on the interpretation of the symbolic systems
that relate us to the world and impose an indirect or interpretive approach to
knowledge and self-understanding. What distinguishes hermeneutics from phenomenology is the rejection of any claim to immediate, intuitive knowledge of
the world grounded in subjective self-certainty. Hermeneutics distances itself
from the claims of phenomenology to immediacy and full presence. Understanding is always perspectival, limited, prejudiced, linguistic, and historic. By
the late 1960s Ricoeur took a "linguistic turn" by shifting emphasis away from
the problematics of the self and the will in the context of a descriptive philosophy toward the problematics of language and action in the context of an interpretive philosophy. "The question of language . . . is a mode of being, a pole of
existence as fundamental as action itself. A new equilibrium between saying and
doing must be sought."[17]

He achieves such an equilibrium by incorporating the speech act theories
of Austin and Searle into a phenomenological theory of language.[18] Speech act
theory blurs the distinction between saying and doing, speaking and acting. Ricoeur's conception of language as "discourse" is a pragmatic or semantic theory
in which the meaning of an utterance is largely a function of its use in a social

context. The meaning of discourse is also a function of its "sense" and "reference," as those terms are understood by Frege. Discourse, according to Ricoeur, is both an event and a meaning. The distinction between language and action blurs even further when a "work" is considered as an assemblage of written discourse, which nicely displays the double meaning of both labor and writing. "Discourse," "work," and "interpretation" have overlapping meanings as both nouns and verbs; to give an interpretation is not only to understand and explain an experience but also to speak or write and express an understanding or explanation. Hermeneutics is geared toward the interpretation of discourse and other symbolically mediated endeavors, the result of which is are events of understanding, which themselves are actions. Saying and doing, discourse and action, are the two inseparable poles of experience.

The convergence of language and action continues in Ricoeur's later works on narrative theory. The key insight of *Time and Narrative* is that experience has a prenarrative quality that is meaningfully and coherently organized into a story by means of a plot, the function of which is to arrange and structure events and action into a story. An event is meaningless unless it is linked with other events by means of a plot that organizes otherwise random and disparate elements into an intelligible whole. Narrative discourse gives meaning to actions through the writing of history and fiction, transforming thought and behavior when read or heard. Ricoeur proposes a revised conception of the hermeneutical circle based on a model of three stages of the Aristotelian notion of *mimesis*. The first stage represents the temporal, structural, and symbolic dimensions of human action that are "prefigured" by a narrative; the second stage represents the act of emplotment that "configures" and organizes events into a story; the third stage represents the act of reading or listening that "transfigures" experience by connecting the world of the narrative with the world of the reader. Hermeneutics seeks to reconstruct and understand the set of operations by which the experience is configured into a narrative and then transformed by the acts of interpreting and understanding. Hermeneutics is an activity that configures and transfigures actions.

The second theme is a reflective philosophy of subjectivity. Philosophy for Ricoeur is essentially a reflective process of questioning and clarifying the meaning of our existence. He stands in the tradition of reflective philosophy that stretches from Socrates, Descartes, Kant, and Husserl. The goal is to achieve self-understanding while at the same time understanding the world and other people.

A reflective philosophy considers the most radical philosophical problems to be those that concern the possibility of *self-understanding*

> as the subject of the operations of knowing, willing, evaluating, and
> so on. Reflection is that act of turning back upon itself by which a
> subject grasps, in a moment of intellectual clarity and moral respon-
> sibility, the unifying principle of the operations among which it is
> dispersed and forgets itself as subject. (TA 12)

The subject of reflection, however, is not a self-transparent *cogito* that functions
as an ultimate foundation for reason. Self-understanding is mediated by signs,
symbols, and language, and, therefore, requires an indirect method of interpretation—that is, a hermeneutic philosophy. The road to self-understanding must
take a "detour" through language. The idea of a detour as a hermeneutical technique for reading signs of experience through something else is one Ricoeur's
favorite metaphors that reappears throughout his career. "The detour/return,"
he explains "is the rhythm of my philosophical respiration."[19] In contrast to the
tradition of reflective philosophy and the pretensions of the *cogito* to know itself
intuitively, hermeneutics holds that we understand ourselves only by taking a
long detour through the signs, texts, and other repositories of humanity found
in cultural works. Ricoeur considers these written works to be the "very
medium within which we can understand ourselves."[20] Textual interpretation
results in self-interpretation; conversely, self-interpretation is always mediated by
textual interpretation. "The constitution of the *self* is contemporaneous with the
constitution of *meaning*" (TA 119). Hermeneutics is a reflective philosophy
resulting in self-understanding.

   Narrative theory continues the tradition of a reflective philosophy of subjectivity, as well. At the end of volume three of *Time and Narrative*, Ricoeur introduces the concept of "narrative identity" or story of a life that unfolds as we
recount and figure out who we are. Both individuals and communities form their
identities by telling stories about themselves that become their history. Like any
story, a narrative identity has a historical component and fictional component.
The historical component is bound by argument, verification, and fidelity to
what happened; the fictional component utilizes imaginative variations of what
happened to create new interpretations and new ways of seeing things. It is always
possible both to tell another version of what happened and to tell another story
of our lives. In addition to the formation and development of personal and group
identity, narrative discourse mediates the formation of identities based on culture,
nationality, regionality, religion, race, class, gender, and sexuality. Explaining and
understanding identity unfolds in a narrative discourse that creates a new interpretation with each new story. In this way, narrative, identity, and hermeneutics
coincide. Self-knowledge is a self-interpretation, expressed in the story of a life.

A third theme in Ricoeur's works is language as the medium of creative and imagination expression. A basic feature of language is "polysemy," the fact that language at the level of words, sentences, and texts have more than one meaning. Polysemy is the source of not only misunderstanding and miscommunication, but also of the richness and fullness of language. A range of possible meanings accompanies each word, sentence, and text that extends the range of possible experiences. Creative language lets us express aspects of the world and our experience beyond that of ordinary, descriptive language. Poetic and metaphoric language create new ways of seeing the world that effect new ways of being-in-the-world. Ricoeur wants to show

> how human language is *inventive* despite the objective limits and codes which govern it, to reveal the diversity and potentiality of language which the erosion of the everyday, conditioned by technocratic and political interests, never ceases to obscure. To become aware of the metaphorical and narrative resources of language is to recognize that its flattened or diminished powers can always be rejuvenated for the benefit of all forms of language usage.[21]

Although language is constituted, in part, by objective rules, structures and codes, it has the ability to transcend its structure to create and express new meanings. Creative, figurative uses of language have a meaning that is not reducible to literal or descriptive language. The task of hermeneutics is not to discover an unmediated reality, but to continue to mediate reality through new, creative interpretations. The mediating role of creative and imaginative interpretations is always at work in lived experience. In fact, it is not just my lived experience, but our entire social existence that is mediated by language, symbolic representations, and creative interpretations.

The detour through creative discourse will always flirt with ideology and utopia, since they too belong to the realm of figurative language that mediates social existence. Like fiction, ideology and utopia consist of stories and images a group uses to explain and legitimate itself. Ricoeur's thesis is that ideology and utopia form two poles of a single "cultural imagination" that not only distorts consciousness and communication, but also legitimates and integrates power and authority at the level of symbolic action. Consequently, ideology and utopia mediate and integrate human action through interpretive schemas that both constitute and distort us. They are like two opposite images a society has about itself: ideology unifies, consolidates, integrates, and orders a society according to the interests of a dominant group, while utopia calls a society into question, and seeks to shatter a social order for the sake of liberation. Both are ultimately about power: ideology attempts to legitimate power, while utopia attempts to replace power with something else.

The detour through figurative structures links hermeneutics with a critique of ideology. The task for a hermeneutic philosophy is to be able to identify both ideological formations and utopian possibilities of liberation. Ricoeur speaks at length of the critical and subversive force of narrative-utopian discourses because they expand communication, open possibilities, reveal alternatives, and create new ways of seeing the world and being in the world. Any creative discourse can contribute to a critique of society and call the legitimacy of authority into question by showing that a society need not be organized in the way that it is. This critical function can be found not only in works with overtly social and political content but also in the countless works that describe different worlds. Fiction, for example, constructs alternatives that stand in contrast to the reality of the present by acting as models for critique, evaluation, and change. The same is certainly true of nonfiction. The effect of stories in newspapers, radio, television, and magazines are daily reminders of the power of a convincing story. Legal deliberation, political debates, medical evaluations, and religious stories all attest to the transformative power of narrative discourse. To recount the total effect of fiction and nonfiction would be to recount human history.

The fourth theme in Ricoeur's work is the unique and tenuous path he tries to steer between Kant and Hegel. He often describes himself as a "post-Hegelian Kantian," which means that he accepts the Hegelian and post-Hegelian (namely phenomenological) critiques of Kant, yet he retains a Kantian reluctance to reconcile the dualism that haunts our understanding of self, nature, and God.[22] A post-Hegelian Kantian recognizes the importance of the concept of totality but not to the point where social, political, and religious integration become the conditions for rational reflection. At this point, it is important to limit the scope reflection for the sake of critique. Totality, unity, and absolute mediation are only limit ideas that, in principle, cannot be attained. A post-Hegelian Kantian hopes to preserve universal rationality and particular, historic, temporal contingency. On one hand is Kant's dialectics of theoretical and practical reason, on the other is Hegel's dialectic of absolute reason. On one hand is a formal conception of freedom and autonomy in the critical act of reflection, on the other hand is freedom as culturally and historically embodied in concrete reflection. Ultimately, hermeneutic philosophy relativizes both Kantian reflection and Hegelian speculation. Ricoeur explains that "hermeneutic philosophy must place itself at an equal distance from both traditions, accepting as much from one tradition as from the other but opposing each with equal force" (HHS 193). On the one hand,

Hegel adds content to Kantian reflection, transforming a hermeneutics of the *cogito* into a hermeneutics of embodied existence. On the other hand, Kant limits the Hegelian pretensions to absolute knowledge by imposing a series of limits on the scope of reflection. "It is because absolute knowledge is impossible that the conflict of interpretation is insurmountable and inescapable. Between absolute knowledge and hermeneutics, it is necessary to choose" (HHS 193).

Evidence of Ricoeur's post-Hegelian Kantianism appears throughout his career in each of his philosophical mediations. The third term he creates mediates without reconciling. The reason hermeneutics derives equally from Kant and Hegel is because, on one hand, Kant is right that both human experience and philosophy are riddled with *aporias* but, on the other hand, Hegel is right that the very act of understanding is a form of mediation. Ricoeur's "third way" recognizes the aporetic quality of human experience and respects the plurality of voices and conflicting interpretation while at the same time affirming the ability of philosophy to find reason. Instead of resolving an *aporia* or succumbing to it, he proposes another option. "The very act of telling is a kind of response to the *aporia*—not a solution, but a response."[23] What he calls "poetics" is the creative answer of the act of narrating as a response that is in essence limited, incomplete, and imperfect. Each subject he takes up—the will, evil, the subject, meaning, narrative, ethics, politics, the law—he finds *aporias* and creative, practical responses to them. Coping with our limitations, fallibility, and finitude is a profoundly ethical concern.[24] It is to Ricoeur's credit that he recognizes the limits of human understanding but insists on finding ways by which we can act responsibly as ethical and political agents.

Chapter 1 of this book explains the development of the hermeneutic dimension in Ricoeur's critical theory. I begin by tracing the transition he makes from a phenomenology of the will in the 1950s, to a hermeneutics of symbols in the 1960s, finally to the hermeneutics of texts in the 1970s. I then examine argument that phenomenology and hermeneutics are dialectically related: hermeneutics is grounded on phenomenological presuppositions, while phenomenology is grounded on hermeneutical presuppositions. After that I compare his hermeneutics of texts to Gadamer's philosophical hermeneutics. Finally, I give a close reading to his mediation of the Habermas-Gadamer debate. Taken together this chapter unites the critical, interpretive, and phenomenological elements of Ricoeur's works to form a model of a critical hermeneutic philosophy.

Chapter 2 shows how metaphor and narrative contribute to a critical hermeneutics specifically geared toward the interpretation of action. The theories of metaphor and narrative take up and retain the insights of the hermeneutics of texts but add an imaginative, creative, practical, and critical dimension absent from the earlier version. I then examine Ricoeur's theory of truth, which combines elements of a phenomenological-narrative theory of description and a Habermasian theory of argumentation, to show how it functions in a critique of ideology. The resulting hermeneutic conception of truth is both interpretive and argumentative, suggesting a mediation of narrative theory and communicative action.

Chapter 3 examines Ricoeur's early and late philosophical anthropology. Although his thought undergoes significant development from the phenomenology of the will in *Freedom and Nature* to the narrative/semantics of action in *Oneself as Another*, what remains constant is a conception of the self as embodied and constituted by its social-cultural conditions yet autonomous, creative, and capable of initiating something new. I start with a reading of *Freedom and Nature* in order to show how subjectivity is always embodied. I then give a reading of the first three sets of studies in *Oneself as Another*, which answer the questions, respectively, Who is speaking?, Who is acting?, and Who is narrating? After answering those questions we can ask Who is responsible? and Who is the subject of rights? An embodied, communicative, acting, responsible, and political self is the subject of Ricoeur's critical theory.

Chapter 4 is devoted to Ricoeur's "little ethics" in the later chapters of *Oneself as Another*, the part of his book devoted to the ethical and moral determinations of action. I explain his argument showing how the third term in the dialectic between Aristotle and Kant is practical wisdom that mediates conflicts between the ethical aim and moral norm, aiming to live the good life with and for others in just institutions. The similarities between Ricoeur's conception of practical wisdom and Habermas's conception of discourse ethics are striking. However, I argue that Ricoeur's version of discourse ethics incorporates the best of Habermasian discourse ethics without succumbing to its limitations.

Chapter 5 examines the Ricoeur's political and legal philosophies. In this chapter I explain the connection Ricoeur makes between ethics and politics to show how he mediates between the liberal concern for political legitimacy, the communitarian concern for human flourishing and plural spheres of justice, and the Marxist concern for political domination. Next I take up, again, the problem of ideology and utopia. This time the problem is considered in relation to the authority of political institutions with the aim of determining what our responsibilities are as philosophers and citizens in light of the imperative to address ourselves critically to our shared political life. I conclude with a discussion of the relationship between politics and the law in order to understand more about justice in institutions and what our prospects are for what Kant termed "perpetual peace."

Chapter 6 draws out some of the implications of my reading of Ricoeur for three related problematics in contemporary critical theory: identity politics, technology, and economic globalization. First is the politics of identity, also known as the politics of recognition. The recognition of group differences goes to the heart of the problem of political pluralism and multiculturalism. In this part of the chapter I use Ricoeur to answer Charles Taylor and Iris Young on the issue of the formation of individual and group identities in relation to liberal notions of impartial moral reasoning and the rights of individuals. Ricoeur affirms a conception of justice and the rule of law geared toward the recognition of group differences and group oppression in order to promote diversity, multiculturalism, and the good life. Second is the problem of technology. Ricoeur may help us to interpret, evaluate, and criticize how our lives are shaped by technologies and thus overcome the tendency among philosophers of technology to emphasize either the hermeneutic or normative dimensions of it. I hope to find in Ricoeur a model for a "techno-critical-hermeneutics" that would contribute to a critical theory of technology that would show how it can be both an instrument of social control and social cooperation.

Third is the relationship in Ricoeur's work between globalization and democracy. With the collapse of the Soviet Union and development of a truly global capitalist economy, it would appear that capitalist liberalism has triumphed over socialism, in all of its forms, once and for all. Any challenge to the logic that would link free markets with the free societies is now seen as anachronistic or irrational, if one were to believe the typically optimistic accounts of the global economy heralded by our political leaders and championed with equal enthusiasm by the media. Ostensibly we live in an age in which technology has brought transport, communications, and computing costs low enough to make production and capital flows truly global, which will inevitably bring about marvels of progress, freedom, democracy, and prosperity for a new world community. Such enthusiasms, however, are greatly misplaced. Global capitalism has also brought about unparalleled forms of inequality, exploitation, environmental degradation, and poverty. Undemocratic, unaccountable global institutions like the International Monetary Fund and World Trade Organization demand worldwide conformity to laws that ensure the efficient mobility of capital while privileging commercial interests above all, including the interests of labor, public health and safety, national sovereignty, environmental protection, and human rights. In the 1960s Ricoeur wrote that the expansion of global capitalism results in "anonymity," "dehumanization," "barbaric forms of urbanism," and "totalitarian peril" (SP 271–293). Now more than ever it is time to revisit the relationship between globalization and democracy in light of Ricoeur's recent work.

CHAPTER 1

HERMENEUTICS

For Ricoeur, hermeneutics is a version of phenomenology. It is less of a break from phenomenology than an extension and transformation of it. He argues that phenomenology and hermeneutics are dialectically related: hermeneutics is grounded on phenomenological presuppositions, while phenomenology is grounded on hermeneutical presuppositions. A survey of the literature shows that while many recognize how similar and complementary these two seemingly opposed schools of philosophy are, the tendency among commentators is to reduce phenomenology to hermeneutics. The Heideggerian ontological critique of Husserl's epistemological project is generally accepted.[1] Ricoeur, however, is among the few who refuse to subsume Husserlian phenomenology to its Heideggerian reformulation.[2] Instead he maintains that hermeneutics rejects only the idealist interpretation that Husserl later gave to phenomenology; hermeneutics is not at all incompatible with some of the other interpretations Husserl gave to his own work. Hermeneutics "has still not finished 'having it out with' Husserlian phenomenology; hermeneutics comes out of the latter, in the double sense of the expression: phenomenology is the place where hermeneutics originates; phenomenology is also the place it has left behind" (TA xiii). Ricoeur's hermeneutics retains a link to phenomenology in a way that post-Heideggerian hermeneutics does not. This link is decisive not only for his place in the hermeneutic tradition but also for his mediation of the Habermas-Gadamer debate. Phenomenological hermeneutics is a nascent critical theory.

PHENOMENOLOGY AND HERMENEUTICS

Ricoeur retains from Husserl the central insight into the intentionality of consciousness and the methodological technique of bracketing. The well-known doctrine of intentionality asserts that all experience is directed toward some object of reference, while every object of experience is correlated to a particular experience. *What* is experienced is always correlated with *how* it is experienced by someone. The object of consciousness is an entity that can be repeated and signified in a number of ways. Intentionality and meaning are thus coextensive. Husserlian phenomenology can be seen as an answer to the question What does signifying signify? Intentionality is the fundamental, invariant, transcendental condition for the possibility of experience and meaning. The methodological technique of bracketing, or the phenomenological reductions, is a set of rules for directing our attention toward experience. What we bracket is the temptation either to make judgments about the ontological status of an object of experience or to theorize and explain rather than describe experience. Instead we are treat all experience simply as given in consciousness as phenomena, or as meaning presenting itself to consciousness. The goal of a phenomenological description is to explicate experience in terms of the intentional relationship to the world. In phenomenology "our relation to the world becomes apparent as a result of reduction; in and through reduction every being comes to be described as a phenomenon, as appearance, thus as a meaning to be made explicit" (CI 247).

But Ricoeur is critical of the transformation from Husserl's early, descriptive phenomenology to his later, transcendental phenomenology. He says the "logicist" prejudice in transcendental phenomenology is a form of "idealism" that privileges a reflective, representational conception of consciousness over all other forms of it. Husserl overemphasizes the perceptual character of consciousness geared toward establishing the validity of logical and mathematical entities over a broader model of consciousness as a synthesis of experience, speech, and intuition. He also transforms what was originally a methodological program into an ontology of subjectivity. Husserl turns away from a phenomenology of signification to an "egological" ontology in which all meaning is constituted by the activity of the transcendental ego, a notoriously obscure doctrine.[3] Ricoeur concurs with most of Husserl's disciples that the practice of phenomenology does not necessarily coincide with the idealistic interpretation of its method. He thus retains the Husserlian doctrine of intentionality and the methodological techniques of bracketing and eidetic reductions, but rejects the idealist interpretation of transcendental phenomenology in favor of a version that resembles the early, pretranscendental Husserl.

In *Freedom and Nature*, for example, Ricoeur employs the Husserlian method of eidetic analysis to the spheres of the will, affection, and volition, geared toward uncovering our fundamental possibilities of existence through a descriptive, but not a transcendental, version of phenomenology. Unlike Husserl, Ricoeur recognizes the necessity of supplementing phenomenology with "nonphenomenology" given the limits placed on self-understanding by the obscurity of involuntary bodily movement and capacity. The experience of our own bodies is never unmediated and direct; instead we interpret our involuntary movements and functions as signs or symptoms for the will. These signs are read indirectly *through* my will as indications of the involuntary for the voluntary. A purely eidetic phenomenology of the will finds its limits in bodily obscurity that must be explained diagnostically rather than experienced directly in order to be understood. The diagnostic method suggests a "latent hermeneutics" in which understanding is symbolically mediated. Ricoeur begins to make a turn from eidetic, descriptive phenomenology to hermeneutic phenomenology in which signs and symptoms mediate understanding. What he sometimes calls a "hermeneutic variation" of Husserlian phenomenology is a strategy for an indirect reading of experience through language.

> Everything in my first writings which points to an indirect interpretation, applied first to the indices of external objectivities, anticipates the subsequent role of the text as the place for the decentering and dispossession of immediacy. . . . The idea of reading signs . . . is found to be the most fundamental anticipation of a hermeneutic rule for phenomenology.[4]

He replaces an immediate, presuppositionless, intuitive grasping of phenomena by a hermeneutic phenomenology that imposes an indirect, interpretive relationship to any given object of understanding.

In *Freud and Philosophy*, Ricoeur imposes the terms of a second set of limits on phenomenology by psychoanalysis. Through a dialectical confrontation of Husserl and Freud, Ricoeur finds a latent hermeneutics that contrasts to Husserlian idealism and the "transcendental illusion" of a subject that ostensibly is immediately transparent to itself. Freud introduces a science of the dynamics of the relationship between experience and the unconscious and a technique for uncovering the relation of a latent, unconscious meaning to a manifest, conscious meaning. The result is what Ricoeur calls a "semantics of desire." He explains that the importance of Freud is to show that psychoanalysis limits and "falsifies" phenomenology in Popper's sense of falsification (which is ironic given Popper's critique of psychoanalysis as unfalsifiable). Ricoeur writes:

> I have always been very attentive to the idea of "falsification," and I was asking myself what "falsifies" phenomenology. It is the main thrust of my investigation, whereas many people saw it as a sort of

integration of psychoanalysis and phenomenology; on the contrary, I was confirming in my work that this could not be done, that something decidedly resisted it. Phenomenology does indeed have its other. (CC 29–30)

The central Freudian insight into the unconscious is that the play of language and desire reveals and conceals, and therefore shapes and distorts, how we understand ourselves and others. The hermeneutic phenomenology that emerges as a result of such an encounter with Freud is one geared toward unmasking and decoding symbolic expressions as well as restoring and recovering lost and hidden meanings. Dreams and symbols are models of the complexity of language in which meanings are both given and hidden in an immediate meaning. Language and symbolic expressions, instead of perception and experience, are now the primary object of interpretation.

Ricoeur suggests that philosophical reflection begin with the "fullness of language" rather than in a Husserlian search for a presuppositionless origin of all meaning. If language is the medium for thought and experience then it is impossible to think behind language into a prelinguistic and, therefore, presuppositionless realm of consciousness. Symbolic expressions, however, are difficult to interpret given their essentially equivocal nature. Symbols mean more than what is said. A symbolic expression both expresses (signifies) something and indicates (designates) something. "To signify" means both expression and designation; a symbolic expression is a function not only of what the subject intends but also what the symbol designates. And because symbols are public and intersubjective, the *cogito* is mediated and limited by language, shattering the illusion of a self-founding act of consciousness. Symbolism requires hermeneutics because it is a double-meaning expression while hermeneutics is the art of deciphering symbols.

The task of the philosopher guided by symbols would be to break out of the enchanted enclosure of consciousness for oneself, to end the prerogative of self-reflection. The symbol gives reason to think that the *Cogito* is within being, and not vice versa. . . . A philosophy that starts from the fullness of language is a philosophy with presuppositions." (SE 356–357)

A symbol is any double-meaning expression defined by a semantic structure in which the first-order meaning designates a second-order meaning that is attainable only through the first-order meaning. "The fullness of language," refers to the relationship of meaning to meaning in which a second meaning "dwells in" the first meaning. Ricoeur maintains that symbols are "bound to" their primary, literal meanings, which, in turn, are "bound by" their symbols. The "revealing power" of symbols is what binds meaning to meaning, and meaning to me. "The movement that draws me toward the second meaning assimilates me to what is said, makes me participate in what is announced to me" (FP 31). In other words, we believe that a symbol has the ability to communicate something to us because we, in a sense, participate in it when we understand it. Understanding is a form of participation because in order to understand one must already believe. The hermeneutic situation is that we must believe in order to know, yet know in order to believe. "Hermeneutics proceeds from a prior understanding of the very thing that it tries to understand by interpreting it" (SE 352). Hermeneutics is animated by a faith that the symbol has the revealing power to deliver and restore lost or hidden meaning. Interpretation, in this sense, is a recollection of meaning.

Hermeneutics is a contested term. There is no general hermeneutics but multiple hermeneutics, with different rules of interpretation, often competing and even conflicting with one another. At one pole of the hermeneutic field is the "hermeneutics of belief," aimed at recovering a lost message, animated by faith and a willingness to listen; at the other pole is the "hermeneutics of suspicion," aimed at demystification, animated by mistrust and skepticism. The counterpole to a hermeneutics that recovers meaning is a hermeneutics that removes illusions. Symbols not only reveal, but conceal; they manifest as well as mystify meaning. The hermeneutics of suspicion draws on the "masters" Marx, Nietzsche, and Freud, each of whom contests the primacy of consciousness and casts doubt on the validity of our participation in what we ordinarily accept as true and real. Instead the masters posit a false consciousness in place of an immediate, self-transparent consciousness, and deception or delusion in place of the experience of participation. The relationship between the manifest and the latent replaces the traditional distinction between appearance and reality. All three masters create a means to decipher consciousness through a science of meaning, as opposed to an explication of the meaning of immediate consciousness and its sedimented layers of sense. Consciousness not only has hidden, sedimented layers to be either intuitively apprehended or hermeneutically explicated; consciousness is the result of both social and personal guile and deception. Interpretation is the work of deciphering hidden, distorted meaning in apparent meaning, and of unfolding levels of meanings implied in literal meaning. Hermeneutics involves both belief and suspicion.

Hermeneutics rejects any claim of phenomenology to immediate, intuitive knowledge of the world grounded in full presence and subjective self-certainty. It also abandons any notion of a prelinguistic, meaning-conferring realm of consciousness for a philosophy that begins and ends within the fullness of language. But there remains a profound affinity between hermeneutics and phenomenology. Hermeneutics rejects only the idealistic interpretation Husserl gave to phenomenology during the period from *Ideas* to the *Cartesian Mediations*. Nonidealistic interpretations of phenomenology and hermeneutics stand in a relationship of "mutual belonging" and mutual presupposition: hermeneutics presupposes the phenomenological priority of the intentionality of consciousness, and phenomenology presupposes the hermeneutical conception of interpretation as explication (*Auslegung*) in order to fulfill its philosophical project. Ricouer argues that to recognize the relationship of mutual presupposition we must first challenge the idealist interpretation of phenomenology.

He does this by proposing five theses of Husserlian idealism that are opposed, point by point, by post-Heideggerian hermeneutics: (1) Phenomenology must be discontinuous with the naturalism and historicism that typify the physical and social sciences in order to function as their ground and ultimate justification; (2) intuition is the foundation of the sciences; (3) the place of intuition is the subject, for whom only what is immanent is indubitable; (4) transcendental subjectivity is not an empirical subjectivity that is the object of psychology; and (5) the reduction is also an ethical action for which the phenomenologist must take ultimate responsibility.

To the first thesis, Ricoeur replies that the phenomenological, scientific ideal that acts as the ultimate justification is limited by the ontological conditions of understanding, or human finitude, which is better expressed by the Gadamerian concept of "belonging." Before we begin any foundational project of ultimate justification, we belong to and are supported by a relation to a tradition that always precedes us. To be truly radical, one must question back behind the ultimate justification in a sphere of transcendental immanence, back to the ontological conditions of the possibility of phenomenology's foundational project. Belonging is the ontological condition "whereby he who questions shares in the very thing about which he questions" (TA 30). The Gadamerian notion of belonging is similar to the Heideggerian notion of being-in-the-world. Although Heidegger's conception better expresses the primacy of care over perception and the priority of being situated practically in the world over rational reflection, Ricoeur prefers Gadamer's notion of belonging because it better thematizes the epistemological problem of the subject-object relation in terms of each person's participation in a tradition and alienation from that tradition. This relation of distance and belonging sets the terms of Ricoeur's mediation of the Habermas-Gadamer debate.

Hermeneutics counters the second thesis of Husserlian idealism, that is, that intuition grounds the sciences, with the hermeneutic insight that all understanding is mediated by interpretation. As Heidegger explains in section 32 of *Being and Time*, explication is the development of understanding in terms of the structure of the "as."[5] The "hermeneutical as" mediates the explication of our anticipatory preunderstanding of experience. As Heidegger's discussion of fore-having (*Vor-habe*), fore-sight (*Vor-sicht*), and fore-conception (*Vor-Griff*) shows explication is never presuppositionless but always precedes according to how *Dasein* is related to a situation before it begins to interpret itself. The explication of understanding is at the same time an explication of the preunderstanding, or the anticipatory as-structure of experience. The hermeneutic relationship of understanding and interpretation, therefore, radically calls into question the Husserlian demand for presuppositionless and ultimate foundations. Hermeneutics shows us that we never arrive at an origin but are always in the middle of a process without a discernable beginning or an end.

Hermeneutics addresses the third thesis of Husserlian idealism, that is, that the ultimate foundation of knowledge is subjectivity, by showing how the *cogito* itself is susceptible to the same kind of phenomenological critique of appearances as any other object of thought. Unlike an object, a subject participates in its own self-deception, which makes uncovering the truth of consciousness and self-consciousness more difficult than it is for an ordinary object. Heidegger addresses the ruses of self-consciousness in section 25 of *Being and Time*, where he questions the adequacy of understanding Dasein's everydayness in terms of the traditional conception of the self as an object. Ricoeur agrees, but cautions that we should pay attention to how systematically distorted communication affects the constitution of subjectivity. Self-knowledge is as dubious and as presumptive as any other kind of knowledge even if socially constituted and mediated by language. "Insofar as self-knowledge is a dialogue of the soul with itself, and insofar as the dialogue can be systematically distorted by violence and by the intrusion of structures of domination into those of communication, self-knowledge as internalized communication can be as doubtful as knowledge of the object" (TA 34).

The fourth thesis of Husserlian idealism, which asserts the primacy of the subject, is challenged by a theory of the text as the "hermeneutical axis." Following Gadamer, Ricoeur holds that the "matter of the text" is a meaning that is distinct from the intentions of the author. The task of hermeneutics is to understand the matter or issue of the text, which is autonomous with respect to the intentions of the author, its original addressee, and the context in which it was written. Interpretation uncovers the matter of the text as a proposed world in which I could possibly experience, inhabit, verify, criticize, and so on. Ricoeur's the conception of the text is a hermeneutic alternative to the Husserlian claim that the locus of meaning is found in the consciousness of a subject. The text shows that writing communicates without recourse to the subjectivity of the author, contrary to Husserl's insistence in "The Origin of Geometry" that the meaning of writing is a "sedimentation" of the consciousness of the author that the reader must "reactivate" in order to understand.[6]

Finally, hermeneutics counters the fifth thesis of Husserlian idealism, that is, the ultimate responsibility of the constituting subject, by proposing that subjectivity appears at the end, not the beginning, of interpretation as the provisionally final, not the first, principle of a theory of understanding. To read a text is to respond to the proposed world by letting it address me in order to let the matter of the text be. "I exchange the *me, master* of itself, for the *self, disciple* of the text" (TA 37). Subjectivity is the result of understanding, not the condition of understanding. Hermeneutics replaces *self*-responsibility with a self that is a "response to." As opposed to the Husserlian demand for ultimate responsibility for *oneself*, hermeneutics demands ultimate responsibility to *another*.

After completing a hermeneutical critique of Husserlian idealism, Ricoeur argues that phenomenology remains "the unsurpassable presupposition" of hermeneutics. At the same time, phenomenology "cannot carry out its program of *constitution* without constituting itself in the *interpretation* of the experience of the ego" (TA 38). Four theses establish the phenomenological limits to hermeneutical experience. First, hermeneutics shares with phenomenology the presupposition that any question about being is above all a question of the meaning of being. What defines phenomenology is "the choice in favor of meaning." A nonidealist conception of meaning is found in the *Logical Investigations*, before Husserl elaborated the reductions and the field of immanence in which an object is constituted. The idea of a universal conception of meaning, which is a function of the intentionality of consciousness, does not have to lead to a transcendental subjectivity from which meaning originates. It is important not to forget that intentionality signifies a world outside of itself. This aspect of intentionality points to the priority of meaning over self-consciousness.[7]

Second, hermeneutics presupposes phenomenology through the hermeneutical conception of distanciation, the dialectical counterpart to the concept of belonging. As Gadamer says, we belong to a tradition and a history in terms of which we interpret the world. To interpret is to render what is alien, foreign, or distant in terms of our historically inherited preunderstanding. But Gadamer's conception of distanciation in *Truth and Method* is ambiguous; it is both the necessary condition of understanding, as well as what must be overcome in order to understand. The phenomenological correlate to hermeneutical distanciation is the *epoche*, provided that it is interpreted in a nonidealistic manner. The *epoche*, or bracketing, begins phenomenological reflection when we turn our attention away from the natural attitude toward the way in which an experience is intended in consciousness. "Phenomenology begins when, not content to "live" or "relive," we interrupt lived experience in order to signify it" (TA 40). The choice in favor of meaning begins when we break away from the natural attitude and adopt the phenomenological attitude through which experience receives it meaning. It is, however, important to emphasize the exteriority of consciousness is oriented outside of itself, toward a meaning, in order not to slip back into an idealistic interpretation of phenomenology. Then it can be seen how hermeneutical distanciation is similar to the phenomenological *epoche*. Both represent a movement away from experience toward reflection. "Hermeneutics similarly begins when, not content to belong to transmitted tradition, we interrupt the relation of belonging in order to signify it" (TA 41).

Third, hermeneutics presupposes phenomenology through the thesis that language is derivative from experience. Gadamer's thesis that intelligible experience is language comes as a result of a phenomenology of aesthetic and historical experience, neither of which are necessarily linguistic. There must be something that comes to language, even if we can only identify and say what it is by using language. Even historical experience is not completely linguistic. "The interplay of distance and proximity, constitutive of the historical connection is what comes to language rather than what language produces" (TA 41). Similarly, Heidegger's analysis of the assertion (in section 34 of *Being and Time*) shows how it is derivative of the existential structures constitutive of being-in-the-world: discourse, mood, and understanding. Discourse is the capacity to articulate experience in language but it is not itself linguistic. For Ricoeur "the reference of the linguistic order back to the structure of experience (which comes to language in the assertion) constitutes . . . the most important phenomenological presupposition of hermeneutics" (TA 42). Both phenomenology and hermeneutics share the idea that language is derivative of experience.

The fourth phenomenological presupposition of hermeneutics is the relationship between pre-predicative experience and the historicity of human experience. The return to the lifeworld is shared by both phenomenology and hermeneutics. For phenomenology, the lifeworld is the shared, cultural, and historical horizon of experience that grounds the objectifications of math, and the natural and social sciences. For hermeneutics, aesthetic, historical, and linguistic experience grounds and supports the objectifications and explanations of the social sciences. Hermeneutics can be seen as affecting a return to the lifeworld, if the lifeworld is "construed as designating the reservoir of meaning, the surplus of sense in living experience, which renders the objectifying and explanatory attitude possible" (TA 43).

After showing the phenomenological presuppositions of hermeneutics, Ricoeur turns to the hermeneutical presuppositions of phenomenology. Through a sophisticated, deconstructive reading, Ricoeur shows that Husserl's phenomenological method repeatedly has "recourse to *Auslegung*" in the sense of explication, exegesis, and interpretation of experience. Hence something other than intuition is critical to complete Husserl's project. Phenomenological intuition depends on explication and interpretation even though Husserl contrasts the task of hermeneutic explication with phenomenological intuitive self-evidence. "Explication," Ricoeur notes, "is thus midway between a philosophy of construction and a philosophy of description" (TA 50).

In *The Logical Investigations*, Husserl takes recourse in *Auslegung* at the moment in which "signification-conferring acts" are brought to intuition. Ricoeur argues that Husserl conflates logical operations and perceptual operations within intuition by, on one hand, distinguishing between signifying acts and objectifying acts, and yet, on the other hand, suggesting a kinship between them. This ambivalence renders the distinction indeterminate. Furthermore, Husserl claims that the concept of "apperception" is necessary to distinguish between simple acts of perception from sense data, but it too is both an act of perception and interpretation. The result is that the intuitive act that would distinguish between vague, "fluctuating meanings," and fixed, "stable" meaning is, in fact, an interpretive act of elucidation, clarification, and explication.[8]

The Cartesian Meditations, where the development of Husserl's thought culminates in the theory of genetic constitution, has recourse to *Auslegung* in the constitution not only of ideal meanings and articulate expressions but for experience as a whole. The concept of *Auslegung* "intervenes in a decisive manner" in the Fourth Meditation when Husserl shows that the objective world derives its existence, meaning, and validity only in and for an ego. Ricoeur says that Husserl's achievement is at once the "culmination and crisis" of phenomenological idealism. It is the culmination in the sense that "egology" satisfies the demand for apodicticity; it is the crisis in the sense that the question of other egos requires the concept of interpretative explication.[9] In order to show how the other is constituted both in me and as other, Husserl shows how intuition is necessarily accompanied by explication; indeed the phenomenological project as a whole is defined in terms of intentional explication. Ricoeur's claim is that Husserl perceived the coincidence of intuition and explication but failed to recognize all of its consequences. "All phenomenology is an explication of evidence and an evidence of explication. An evidence that is explicated, an explication that unfolds evidence: such is the phenomenological experience. It is in this sense that phenomenology can be grasped only as hermeneutics" (TA 52).

I believe that Ricoeur rightfully appreciates the similarity and complementarity of these two seemingly opposed schools of philosophy. He recognizes that the issue between Husserl and Heidegger has less to do with ontology as it does with genuinely phenomenological considerations. As a result, Ricoeur focuses his mediation on the doctrine of intentionality and the problem of the constitution of meaning. Hermeneutics and phenomenology share the same goal to describe or explicate layers of sense. Both Husserl and Heidegger affirm that experience is intentional, blurring the distinction between phenomenological consciousness and hermeneutical belonging. Phenomenology and hermeneutics maintain that there exists a "correlation-apriori" of subject and object, or *Dasein* and world. However, it is Heidegger who recognizes the ontological character of the correlation-apriori, freeing us from an overly epistemological conception of intentionality by uncovering a more fundamental relationship of being-in-the-world. Phenomenology presupposes the ontological priority of belonging whereby we are always already practically involved in the world before we reflect and make our involvement consciously thematic.

Ricoeur credits Husserl for opening "the field of the meaningful" for Heidegger to perform a phenomenology of care in *Being and Time*. Hermeneutics is not a break with phenomenology but a "broadening of a philosophy of intentionality" as well as a liberation of phenomenology from idealism.[10] Gadamer concurs with Ricoeur's assessment on the similarity and continuity of Husserlian and Heideggerian phenomenology. He notes that when *Being and Time* came out it was quite possible "to see it as simply a new variation and extension within the framework of phenomenology."[11] The anticipatory fore-structure of hermeneutics is itself an intentional relationship. We listen *to* something, we look *for* something, we feel *for* someone. Interpretation is simply the explication of the layers of sense that constitute lived experience; phenomenology and hermeneutics share the insight into the correlation-apriori, which ultimately does not undermine the priority of intentionality.

However, the second thesis of the essay "Phenomenology and Hermeneutics" is considerably less convincing. The claim that phenomenology presupposes hermeneutics is based on an untenable distinction between description and interpretation, or what Ricoeur refers to as the "recourse to *Auslegung*."[12] It is not clear at all what this means. Explication, description, and interpretation are synonymous. They differ only in emphasis: phenomenology is geared to un-covering the structural, universal charater of experience, whereas hermeneutics is geared to uncovering the historic, particular character of experience. Unfor-tunately, Ricoeur's methodological commitment to remain faithful to both Husserlian and Heideggerian orthodoxy obscures what is similar and different between the two. In this case his ethics of method (i.e., respecting the integrity and autonomy of each philosophical position) may have prevented him from more clearly reformulating a nontranscendental, nonidealistic, hermeneutic conception of phenomenology—or rather a conception of hermeneutics that does not forget Husserl. In his subsequent works, however, he develops of ver-sion of hermeneutic-phenomenology that is both descriptive and interpretive, oriented equally to what is universal and particular in experience.

DISCOURSE AND DISTANCIATION

Ricoeur's various conceptions of language—as discourse, text, and narrative—can be seen as an ingredient to an attempt within hermeneutics to retain a phenomenological component of subjective expression and meaning. Around of the time of *Freud and Philosophy*, Ricoeur's conception of language was more phenomenological than hermeneutic. He viewed language as an inter-mediary between an origin and a *telos*; the origin is lived experience, the *telos* an ideal of logicity and ideal entities in terms of which we express ourselves. Language mediates experience and the ideality of meaning. "Language may be reached 'from above,' from its logical limit, or 'from below,' from its limit in mute elemental experience. In itself it is a medium, a mediation, an exchange between *Telos* and *Ursprung*."[13] But contrary to Husserl, Ricoeur clams that an originary, prelinguistic consciousness can never be reached. He affirms that such a thing exists and contributes to the meaning of language, but a regres-sive inquiry (what Husserl calls *Rückfragen*, or back-questioning) into the ori-gin of meaning leads only to a lower limit, not an origin. The putative origins of both absolute subjectivity and the lifeworld are limit ideas that can never be attained, but only approximated. Lived experience "will never be the naked presence of an absolute, but will remain that toward which this regressive questioning points."[14]

Ricoeur distanced himself even further from a Husserlian model of lan-guage following his confrontation with structural semiotics in the 1960s and 1970s. The challenge of structural semiotics to phenomenology is like that of psychoanalysis; both call into question the primacy of consciousness as the priv-ileged, self-evident home of meaning. Both also challenge the claim of Husserlian phenomenology to have discovered, through the reductions, the space of meaning in the intentionality of consciousness in which all phenomenological descriptions about being are descriptions of the meaning, or sense of being. The challenge consists in the notion that "signification is placed in a different field than that of the intentional aimings of a subject" (CI 250).

Ricoeur recognizes the legitimate impetus of a subjectless, structuralist theory of language but wishes to retain what is valid in a subject-centered, phenomenological theory of language. He endeavors to retain the structuralist insight that language has objective characteristics best understood as an empirical science and that meaning is a function of a different agency than consciousness without rejecting the fundamental intentionality of consciousness, or the insight that the activity of the incarnate, speaking, and acting subject is a bearer of meaning. The result of the confrontation with structuralism is a theory of language as "discourse" as a semantic and communicative theory of language. Ricoeur's thought of the 1970s was dominated by an attempt to model a phenomenological-hermeneutics of human action based on the practice of interpreting written discourse.

Language as discourse for Ricoeur is a dialectic of event and meaning, sense and reference. Discourse takes place as an event but has an ideal, repeatable meaning that allows what is said to be repeated, identified, or said differently. Discourse is both the vanishing occurrence that makes language actual and an entity that can be identified and reindentified as such. As an event it is referential (about something), self-referential (said by someone), temporal (said at some moment), and communicative (said to someone). The meaning of an utterance is both what the speaker means and what the sentence means—that is, the utterer's meaning and the utterance meaning. Following Grice, Ricoeur notes that the utterer's meaning is manifested in the utterance meaning.[15] The subjective, utterer's meaning is attested to by the self-referential character of discourse that is displayed by grammatical devices that indicate who is speaking. Discourse is, therefore, a subjective expression that has objective properties independent of the intentions of the speaker. Both event and meaning constitute the other and neither is fully intelligible without reference to the other.

> The suppressing and the surpassing of the event in the meaning is a characteristic of discourse itself. It attests to the intentionality of language, the relation of noesis and noema in it. If language is a *meinen*, an intending, it is so precisely due to this *Aufhebung* through which the event is canceled as something merely transient and retained as the same meaning. (INT 12)

Meaning, then, is both noetic and noematic. Discourse is the medium of understanding into which the event and meaning as well as the subjective and objective poles of language become articulated.

The fundamental feature of discourse is its constitution by a series of sentences whereby someone says something to someone about something. Discourse is a communicative, signifying intention, or a willing to say, that ends in a meaning, outstripping the event of its production. In order to show that discourse is a communicative act, Ricoeur draws on Austin's analysis of the classes of speech acts, the "locutionary act" (the act of saying), the "illocutionary act" (the doing in saying) and the "perlocutionary act" (what we do by saying). Austin's contribution to a theory of discourse is to show that language does more than describe and report facts; people do things with language. Speakers use language, following the customary rules of appropriate application, in order to achieve goals and to accomplish tasks. Even the locutionary act is a speech act and is, therefore, less of a statement that describes or reports some state of affairs than a use of language that accomplishes something. Speaking is an action, the validity of which has more to do with success and failure than truth and falsehood. The criteria for the successful use of language are prescribed by context and custom. This shifts our orientation away from the consciousness of the subject, who represents the world inside her head, out toward a context of shared practices, which ultimately confers meaning and evaluates successful uses of language.[16]

Speech act theory also specifies the conditions for successful communication. One condition is the reciprocal recognition of intentions by both speaker and hearer. If the relationship of a speaker to a hearer constitutes discourse as communication, then dialogue must be an essential structure of discourse. It is here that Ricoeur introduces the "interlocutionary act," or the "allocutionary act," which is the kind of speech act that functions to establish mutual understanding. "Each illocutionary act is a kind of question. To assert something is to expect agreement, just as to give an order is to expect obedience" (INT 15). Discourse is a dialogical, communicative speech performance whereby a speaker and hearer use language to achieve any number or goals, ends, and tasks. The event of discourse is the shared experience of dialogue. At the same time, the communication of meaning transcends the event of its production. The surpassing of the event in the meaning is what Ricoeur calls the "intentional exteriorization" of discourse. In discourse something is expressed and communicated to another. What makes a performative utterance unique is the intention of the speaker that the hearer will recognize his intention. It is always the intention of a speaker to assume that his intention will be understood by the hearer. The orientation of dialogue is toward mutual understanding and reciprocal recognition, which means that a speaker tries to produce an experience by the hearer in which the latter recognizes the intentions of the former.

> Their intention implies the intention of being recognized, therefore the intention of the other's intention. This intention of being identified, acknowledged, and recognized as such by the other is part of the intention itself. In the vocabulary of Husserl, we could say that it is the *noetic* in the psychic. The criterion of the *noetic* is the intention of communicability, the expectation of recognition in the intentional act itself. The *noetic* is the soul of discourse as dialogue. (INT 18)

The claim is that not only my statements have a sense that refers but also as a speaker I intend to do something in speaking that I also intend to be recognized by my interlocutor. Therefore, all illocution is allocution. An utterance simultaneously implies an "I" that speaks and a "you" to whom the former addresses itself. Discourse is a communicative act that presupposes a reciprocal recognition of intentions. This is an insight shared by Habermas as well.

Ricoeur adds complexity of the meaning pole of discourse by drawing on Frege's distinction between sense and reference.[17] The objective side of discourse can be either what a sentence means or about that to which a sentence refers. The "what" of discourse is its sense, the "about what" is its reference. The meaning of discourse has a sense that is immanent to it, that points beyond itself to a referent in the world, through which a referent is given. "The speaker refers to something on the basis of, or through, the ideal structure of the sense. The sense, so to speak, is traversed by the referring intention of the speaker" (INT 20). The dialectic of sense and reference describes the relationship between language and our being-in-the-world. The idea of bringing an experience to language does not suggest that an experience is fully comprehended without language. On the contrary, language raises experience to intelligibility. The claim is that having experiences in the world is the ontological condition of having and using a language. The further claim is that language points not only to ideal meanings but also refers to what exists. Because the theory of discourse is a semantic theory that is communicative and pragmatic, there should be no concern that Ricoeur has adopted an ostensive definition of language.

The double dialectic of event and meaning, sense and reference constitutes not only spoken discourse but written discourse as well. The central feature of written discourse is the exteriority of discourse to itself shown in the surpassing of the event in the meaning. The need for interpreting writing is more clear because its meaning is further detached from the event of its production. The meaning of written discourse must be interpreted in the absence of a speaking subject who can explain himself, or a shared dialogical situation that acts as a common reference. In dialogue we do not have to construe a hidden meaning to understanding the meaning of a speaker; the intentions of the speaker coincide with the meaning of the message. Putting aside for the moment the problem of unconscious motivations and distortions, to understand what the discourse means is the same as to understand what the speaker means. The ordinary language usage of "to mean" suggests that understanding what a speaker means also means understanding what the speaker says. At very least, speaker and hearer can question each other or refer to a shared dialogal situation to mediate misunderstandings. In writing, however, the meaning of the author and the meaning of the text may or may not coincide.[18] It is here that even the term *fixation* becomes misleading because writing does more than just fix speech. The inscription of spoken language changes the meaning of discourse by dissociating the meaning of the text from the meaning of the author.

> Inscription becomes synonymous with the semantic autonomy of the text, which results from the disconnection of the mental intention of the author from the verbal meaning of the text, of what the author meant and what the text means. The text's career escapes the finite horizon lived by its author. What the text means now matters more than what the author meant when he wrote it. (INT 29–30)

The semantic autonomy of the text also affects the other side of communication, that of the hearer or addressee. Whereas spoken discourse is addressed to someone, in a particular dialogical situation, written discourse is addressed to an indefinite number of absent readers. Writing opens up the possibility of enlarging circles of communication by initiating new modes of communication. At the same time, writing creates the more obvious need for hermeneutics. A text must be interpreted over and over as each reader construes a meaning without being able to question the author. Writing refers differently in the absence of a speaking face, with eyes that look back at you, a body that gestures, and a voice that carries meaning. However, the absence of a speaker and a common dialogical situation does not mean that the referential capacity of writing is either limited or defective. What it does mean is that the reference of writing extends beyond the shared situation to a descriptive account of a possible world. A text must be able to "decontextualize" itself so that it may be "recontextualized" in the act of reading. The liberation of writing from the author, his or her audience, and his or her situation open up possible worlds to be interpreted by an indefinite number of readers. Such interpretation presupposes literacy, the absence of censorship, the accessibility and availability of works, and other social conditions that allow for free interpretation and for a text to reach its indefinite audience. Although the audience of a text is potentially universal, addressed to whomever knows how to read, in fact, reading and writing are significant political and economic issues, subject to rules of admission, exclusion and systematic distortion like any other social phenomenon. Its universality, is, therefore, a limit idea that guides any discussion of who, in fact, reads what, why, and how.

A new dialectic emerges in reading and writing, which Ricoeur calls "distanciation and appropriation." Distanciation refers to the intentional exteriorization or semantic autonomy of the text to bear meaning apart from the intentions of the author; appropriation refers to the hermeneutic act to make what was foreign familiar and one's own. The hermeneutical situation is constituted by a play of distanciation and appropriation. "Interpretation, philosophically understood, is nothing else than an attempt to make estrangement and distanciation productive" (INT 44). The dialectic of distanciation and appropriation is Ricoeur's alternative to the disjunction between the two attitudes taken in the Romanticist hermeneutic tradition and the semiological sciences, between understanding and explanation, truth and method. Distanciation and appropriation are dialectical counterparts of "a struggle between the otherness that transforms all spatial and temporal distance into cultural estrangement and the ownness by which all understanding aims at the extension of self-understanding" (INT 43). The play of estrangement and retrieval, distanciation and appropriation, is what constitutes the transmittal of a cultural heritage. Written discourse, particularly texts, sustain a heritage and tradition through the detachment of writing from its original author, context, and addressee, and the appropriating act of reading that rescues writing from the estrangement.

According to Ricoeur, Gadamer's philosophical hermeneutics is guilty of maintaining this antinomy between belonging and estrangement, while privileging the former over the latter, appropriation over distanciation. The fundamental hermeneutical act of making the foreign familiar is achieved by overcoming an alienating distance to form a new relationship in which our horizons belong together. Although Ricoeur is very close to Gadamer in this respect, he is concerned that by maintaining this dichotomy Gadamerian hermeneutics moves too quickly to overcome the very distance that enables understanding. In so doing, Gadamer not only misunderstands the nature of discourse but also he precludes the possibility of gaining critical distance from a tradition. Although the dialectic of alienating distanciation and the experience of belonging constitutes hermeneutical experience, Gadamer unnecessarily forces us to choose between either participatory belonging to a tradition, or the detached attitude of methodological explanation. The problem becomes a false choice between truth or method. His conception of alienating distanciation makes it seems that the kind of objectification that we find in the human sciences is at the same time that which destroys the fundamental relation whereby we belong to and participate in our historical reality. We must either "adopt the methodological attitude and lose the ontological density of the reality we study, or we adopt the attitude of truth and must then renounce the objectivity of the human sciences" (TA 75).

Ricoeur, however, rejects the Gadamerian alternative between alienating distance and participatory belonging, and suggests that a positive and productive notion of distanciation exists in discourse that enables communication in and through distance. Because discourse is always distanced from itself, the difference between ordinary language and the empirical sciences is not as great as Gadamer would have us believe. Distanciation can never be overcome, nor should it be. Distanciation is a moment of belonging, which allows for a critique of ideology to be incorporated, as an objective and explanatory segment, in the process of communication and self-understanding.

> The extension of understanding through textual exegesis and its constant rectification through the critique of ideology are properly part of the process of *Auslegung*. Textual exegesis and critique of ideology are the two privileged routes along which understanding is developed into interpretation and thus becomes itself. (TA 35)

Given the shared recourse to *Auslegung*, critique of ideology is internal to phenomenology as well as hermeneutics. The key is the common notion of distanciation that is both the condition for understanding and critique. "Distanciation, dialectically opposed to belonging, is the condition of possibility of the critique of ideology, not outside or against hermeneutics, but within hermeneutics" (TA 268).

Three different forms of distanciation correspond to each of the constitutive parts of a text. A text is a work of discourse that communicates through a distance, projects a possible world, and mediates self-understanding. Spoken discourse displays a "primitive type" of distanciation in the surpassing of the event by the meaning. This primitive distanciation is the "distanciation of the saying in the said." The intentional exteriorization of discourse is transformed into the semantic autonomy of the text when discourse is fixed in writing. With the inscription of spoken language, meaning is dissociated from the meaning of the original author. The text also separates the writer from the reader and thus distances the act of writing from the act of reading. The reader is absent when the text is written and the writer is absent when the text is read. The text produces a "double eclipse" of the reader and the writer thereby replacing the immediately dialogical situation with the more complex author-reader relationship. Discourse realized as text maintains a distanciation in relation to both the author and the reader. The distanciation of a work from its author, it original readers, and original situation is constitutive of discourse as a text. The relationship between objectification and interpretation is dialectical; interpretation must overcome objectification, but objectification conditions and gives rise to interpretation. This first form of distanciation may be called "the distanciation of the world of the work."

A second form of distanciation occurs within the world of the text. "The distanciation of the real from itself" is the distanciation that fiction, poetic, and historical discourses inserts into our everyday experience. The metaphoric and symbolic expressions that constitute creative, imaginative discourses open up a referential capacity absent in ostensive and descriptive discourse. They refer to a world "as if" we could be there. The reference is "divided" or "split," meaning that such writing points to some aspect of the world that cannot be described but only suggested and referred to indirectly. The referent in such creative discourse is "discontinuous" with that of ordinary language, although it refers to "another level" that is "more fundamental" than that attained by descriptive language. Creative discourse reaches the world at the level of the lifeworld.

Creative language is often more revealing than descriptive language; some things are best said or described creatively or metaphorically. The world of the text is distanced from the everyday world. But by pointing beyond the everyday world by projecting new possibilities, the text points back to the everyday world and presents new ways to be in the world. History, like fiction, similarly projects an absent world that invites us to question our present world. Therein lies the critical dimension of poetic and fictional discourse that is unavailable to descriptive discourse. The critical power of poetic discourse is made possible by its referential capacity to point beyond the world, which is another name for the distanciation of the real from itself. Poetic discourse opens up a distance between the everyday world and the world of the text, allowing us to step back and reflect on our world in light of a different, possibly better world.

With the second form of distanciation, we begin to turn from the production of discourse to the interpretation of discourse. If distanciation is communication in and through a distance, appropriation is understanding in and through a distance. The aim of hermeneutics is to make the foreign familiar in terms of my horizon of existence, which is an act of appropriation much like the kind Gadamer describes. What is appropriated in a text is its sense, or its meaning, as well as the reference, or the world that unfolds before the reader. The acts of reading and writing transform the subjectivity of both author and reader.

The third form of distanciation is what Ricoeur calls the "distanciation of self from itself," for the text is the medium of self-understanding.

> To understand oneself is to understand oneself as one confronts the text and to receive from the conditions for a self other than that which first undertakes the reading. Neither of the two subjectivities, neither that of the author nor that of the reader, is thus primary in the sense of an originary presence of the self to itself. (TA 17)

Reading transforms us as the result of the appropriated meaning of a text. When I "lose myself" in a good book, I really do lose my self in an important way. "It is in allowing itself to be carried off towards the reference of the text that the ego divests itself of itself" (HHS 191). To appropriate the meaning of a text we must first let go and relinquish the illusion that subjectivity alone confers meaning. Reading is a transformative experience in which we gain ourselves as we lose ourselves. Appropriation, then, is not only the dialectical counterpart to distanciation but also the transformation of the self and of self-understanding.

Reading serves a potentially critical function by displacing the illusions of subjectivity and by transforming the experience of the reader who encounters new, different, possibly better worlds. By linking the revelatory power of the text with the critique of subjectivity, Ricoeur integrates the hermeneutics of suspicion with the hermeneutics of the text. The appropriating act of interpreting texts, not just symbols, helps to overcome the illusions of subjectivity. Self-understanding is mediated by the text just like for Freud consciousness is mediated by the unconscious. Interpreting texts may broaden our horizon of experience, change our self-understanding, and transform who we are, how we live, and how we act in the world.

> A critique of the illusions of the subject, in a Marxist or Freudian manner, therefore can and must be incorporated into self-understanding. The consequence for hermeneutics is important: we can no longer oppose hermeneutics and the critique of ideology. The critique of ideology is the necessary detour that self-understanding must take if the latter is to be formed by the matter of the text and not by the prejudices of the reader. (TA 88)

What is at stake in preserving alienating distanciation is a matter of preserving the possibility of achieving distance, or perspective on oneself and one's culture in order to be able to evaluate it critically. These are the terms of the Habermas-Gadamer debate, as well as the universalism-communitarianism debate. Ostensibly one must choose between hermeneutical consciousness or critical consciousness, particular experiences or universal principles. What Ricoeur wants to show is that hermeneutics, properly conceived, is also critical and evaluative. By limiting hermeneutics to the problem of understanding mediated by texts and text analogs, we can see that distanciation belongs to the mediation itself, and the critical instance that is supposedly overcome in Gadamer's hermeneutics is preserved in Ricoeur's. Distanciation opens the possibility of achieving critical distance from one's self and one's tradition, because the medium of understanding itself is distanced from itself. Critique can be raised from within Ricoeur's hermeneutic circle because distanciation is never fully overcome. Distanciation is "the soul of every critical philosophy" (PS 249).

HERMENEUTICS AND IDEOLOGY CRITIQUE

Ricoeur claims that what is at stake in the Habermas-Gadamer debate is the fundamental gesture of philosophy: submission to finitude or defiance against domination. Rather than articulate a perspective that reconciles hermeneutics and the critique of ideology, he claims that he is merely trying to show how each can recognize the universality of the other. He claims not to fuse "a supersystem which would encompass both," but instead to let each "recognize the other, not as a position which is foreign and purely hostile, but as one which raises in its own way a legitimate claim" (TA 271). His goal is to eliminate any false antinomies between the two and to recognize their different concerns and orientations, namely a rehabilitation of tradition and historical understanding in the case of hermeneutics, and a theory of the intersection of institutions with language, labor, and power in the case of the critique of ideology.

The following four issues form the basic differences between Habermasian critique of ideology and Gadamerian philosophical hermeneutics: (1) Where Gadamer rehabilitates the concepts of prejudice, tradition, and authority by linking them with Heidegger's fore-structures of understanding, Habermas develops the concept of interest that stems from the Western Marxist tradition; (2) where Gadamer appeals to the human sciences to reinterpret and to overcome distanciation from cultural traditions, Habermas focuses on the critical social sciences in order to locate the emancipatory possibilities of critical reflection on institutional reifications; (3) where Gadamer takes misunderstanding to be the obstacle to understanding, for Habermas the obstacle is ideology, or systematically distorted communication that gives rise to false consensus and pseudo-communication; and (4) where Gadamer bases the task of hermeneutics on an ontology of language, Habermas links a theory of communicative competence with the regulative principle of unconstrained communication. The contrast, then, is between the humility of philosophical hermeneutics and the defiance of the critique of ideology. The former emphasizes our finitude and the historical conditions to which we belong, while the latter opposes hidden, systematic distortions of self-understanding guided by the limit idea of an ideal community of unconstrained communication.

Ricoeur offers four themes that would constitute a critical supplement to the hermeneutics of tradition. First, the task is to substitute discourse for dialogue as the model of communicative understanding. The crucial quality of distance is more clearly seen in discourse than in dialogue, making it impossible to overcome distanciation completely because the medium of understanding is always distanced from itself. In discourse the saying is distanced from the said, the text is distanced from the author, reader, and original context, and the world of the text is distanced from the lifeworld. "The emancipation of the text constitutes the most fundamental condition for the recognition of a critical instance at the heart of interpretation; for distanciation now belongs to the mediation itself" (TA 298). Distance opens the possibility for critique within hermeneutics. We never belong to our horizon and tradition to the extent that we cannot reflect on the limits of our understanding.

Second, hermeneutics must overcome the dichotomy between explanation and understanding in order to account for our capacity for criticism. The opposition of explanation and understanding goes back to Dilthey, who argued that there are two modes of intelligibility that correspond to two spheres of reality, the physical and the psychic.[19] One can either "explain" as the scientist does, or "understand" as does the historian. For Ricoeur, interpretation overcomes the Dilthey's dichotomy. The task is to bring to understanding the underlying structures of discourse. Objectified, sedimented structures within speech and writing must be explained as well as described in order to be understood. All explanations, however, are not necessarily critical. They are critical only if they uncover the conditions for the possibility for meaningful discourse and action, or if they disclose false consciousness, domination, and illegitimate authority. A hermeneutical theory that incorporates methodological explanations into the heart of the interpretive process is a "transcendental hermeneutics." Such a hermeneutic theory overcomes the claim to universality of

Gadamerian hermeneutics by providing a means of understanding what occurs "behind the back" of language.

Third, the world of the text, the referential dimension opened for the reader, contains a potentially subversive force in the imagination. All kinds of discourse, even fiction and poetry, have the power to reinterpret reality in such a way that challenges and undermines authority. "The power of the text to open a dimension of reality implies in principle a recourse against any given reality and thereby the possibility of a critique of the real" (TA 300). Fiction helps determine what's real and valid by performing imaginative variations on reality in order to distinguish between what is the case, what could or should be the case, and what has to be the case. We must know what a thing is before we can know what it is not. We must be able to intuit what is essential and inessential, contingent and necessary, the same and different before we can identify something as distorted, inadequate, irrational, or unjust. Both fiction and nonfiction may serve a critical function by proposing alternative interpretations that explain why things are the way they are.

Fourth, a thematic connection exists between the transformation of subjectivity in interpretation and the critique of false consciousness. As we interpret, we learn, we develop, and we transform ourselves. Corresponding to the appropriation of proposed worlds offered by the text is the "disappropriation" of the self. Interpretation implies self-interpretation, thus any discourse that challenges authority may also challenge one's self-understanding. Self-reflection turns into critical reflection when it identifies the limits of understanding in order to determine legitimate and illegitimate prejudices and authority. Any interpretation that exposes the illusions of the subject functions in the same way as a critique of ideology.

Ricoeur next offers four themes that constitute a hermeneutical reflection on critique. First, the Habermasian theory of interests function like Heideggerian existentiales. As quasi-transcendental categories they are neither empirically justifiable nor theoretically posited. Instead they are anthropological structures that link knowledge with interest. A hermeneutical preunderstanding and a knowledge-constitutive interest share a common ground in human finitude "which secures *apriori* the correlation between the concept of prejudice and that of ideology" (TA 303). Prejudice and ideology both presuppose our belonging to a tradition and are understood on the basis of a motivated interpretation. Although ideology functions differently from a prejudice, it is recognized as such in a similar way through a dialectic of explanation and understanding. In this respect there is no difference between an interest and prejudice. However, the concept of a prejudice is preferable to that of an interest because its epistemological and ontological status is more clear and more consistent. Habermas himself eventually abandons the concept of the knowledge-constitutive interest.[20]

Second, the distinction between an interest in emancipation to the interest in communication is illegitimate. Habermas later abandons this distinction as well.[21] The critique of distortions is always linked to communicative experience, thus collapsing the distinction between an interest in emancipation and interest in communication. Any critique is raised from someplace and must be expressed in language, that is, in terms of a concrete, historical context. The critique of ideology is made on the basis of a creative interpretation of a cultural heritage. It is an interpretation prejudiced by the idea that domination and exploitation are unjust and unacceptable. Hermeneutics presupposes something different and better in terms of which the object of interpretation is explained and understood. Without such regulative ideals hermeneutics is not as revelatory and disclosive as its proponents would have us believe. In turn, a critique of ideology that is motivated by an interest in liberation and a concern for the oppressed is sustained and enabled by the very language and tradition it criticizes. Hermeneutics without a project of liberation is blind; a project of liberation without historical experience is empty. We must be able to interpret our past in order to project our emancipation in a historical context.

> Distortions can be criticized only in the name of a *consensus* which we cannot anticipate merely emptily, in the manner of a regulative idea, unless that idea is exemplified; and one of the very few places of exemplification of the ideal of communication is precisely our capacity to overcome cultural distance in the interpretation of works received from the past. (TA 304)

Third, the practical task of the critique of ideology is identical to the goal of hermeneutics: to enlarge and restore communication and self-understanding. A critique of society must be expressed in language, supported by the creative interpretation a of cultural heritage. An interest in emancipation is nothing but a "pious vow" unless it is embodied in communicative action itself, which, in turn, depends on the creative renewal of cultural heritage if it is to be understood. The ideal of unconstrained communication must be historically situated and applied in a particular situation in order to function as a regulative ideal and achieve any critical force. No theoretical solution exists to the antinomy of reason and tradition. Instead there is only the practical mediation geared to recovering the past and projecting a better future.

Fourth, no antimony exists between the prior consensus to which we belong and an anticipation of freedom in an ideal of unconstrained communication, or between an ontology of understanding and an "eschatology of freedom." We are at the same time preceded by a consensus yet oriented futurally toward the anticipation of an ideal conversation in which a consensus could be reached. We have a communicative ideal only because dialogue is constitutive of who we are; conversely, we can only understand the dialogue that we are through an ideal of unlimited communication. Herein lies the circle of hermeneutics and critique. On one hand, any critique is raised on the basis of a preunderstanding and a tradition. No one is ever in a position to create new values *ex nihilo*. "We can perhaps 'transvaluate' values, but can never create them beginning from zero" (PS 269). On the other hand, we distinguish true and false communication on the basis of an anticipated ideal of unconstrained communication. "It is only under the aegis of our interest in emancipation that we are stirred to transvaluate what has already been evaluated" (PS 269). Hermeneutics and critique each presupposes the other.

In addition to the hermeneutic claim to universality, the Habermas-Gadamer debate also centers on the meaning and function of tradition. If hermeneutical philosophy sees tradition as the source of historical consciousness that enables understanding, the critique of ideology sees tradition as the source systematic distortions that perpetuates domination. Habermas claims that Gadamer rightly ties understanding to historical consciousness but offers no possibility of transcendence in order to evaluate our historically effected consciousness. If there is no transcendental perspective on history, then there is no way to recognize if my tradition is ideologically distorted. If there is no way to recognize ideological distortions, then there is no way to criticize the domination and injustice tradition may conceal. Gadamer concedes to Habermas that language is not only a place of rationality and consensus but also a place of coercion and domination. Nevertheless, it is impossible for anything that can be understood to happen behind the back of language if everything comprehensible that happens *is* the event of language. Hermeneutics is, therefore, already a critique of consciousness and communication and an appeal to any extrahermeneutic entity is illegitimate.

Ricoeur believes that much of the Habermas-Gadamer debate hinges on a confusion over the meaning of the notion of tradition. In *Time and Narrative*, he distinguishes between "traditionality," "traditions," and "tradition," in order to clarify the different ways we are affected by history. "Traditionality" refers to the transmission of a past heritage, including the beliefs, practices, and prejudices affecting its creation and interpretation. Traditionality is a dialectic of innovation and sedimentation. It consists of an interplay of new creative interpretations of objects and events in the past, which themselves were once new creative interpretations of a previous heritage. It is a dialectic of creativity governed by paradigms, themselves the result of previous innovation. Paradigms furnish the models, forms, genres, or individual works that pattern subsequent innovation. The result is a singular work created from a sedimented paradigm that may, in turn, itself become typical and sediment into tradition, furnishing a paradigm for another creation. It is not unlike what Gadamer calls a "fusion of horizon," or the process of making the foreign familiar by reawakening and applying the past in terms of the present. But the difference is that Ricoeur leaves no impression of conservatism in his description of cultural transmission. He notes the range of possible permutations in between "servile application and calculated deviation, passing through every degree of rule-governed deformation" (TN1 69). In other words, a tradition is never a static repository of the past, transmitted conservatively; instead it is a living tension of both innovation and sedimentation, old and new, progressive and traditional interpretations.

"Traditions" refers to the particular content of what is handed down from the past, including all of the linguistic and symbolic elements that can be transmitted. Traditionality is a formal concept, whereas traditions is a material concept of the content of a tradition. It represents the language that precedes us that is the medium of understanding. We are always heirs to traditions; we are always preceded by things already said and already understood. Traditions are bearers of meaning—or better, proposals of meaning to be interpreted. Following Gadamer, Ricoeur affirms the logic of question and answer as key to the art of interpretation, noting that "the past puts us into question before we put it into question" (TN3 222). The past and its contents are as open to being questioned and interpreted as we are to questioning and interpreting. This is what Ricoeur means when he say that "the text and the reader are each in their turn familiarized and defamiliarized" (TN3 222). Interpretation results in self-interpretation and a reinterpretation of traditions because to question a text is also to question traditions and question oneself.

"Tradition" refers to an orthodoxy that claims historical authority. The contested issue in the Habermas-Gadamer debate has to do with the legitimacy of the authority of tradition, not with traditionality or traditions. Tradition is like custom, or *Sittlichkeit* for Hegel, for we are always situated in a historical order of meaning before we reflect back on it—which is precisely the problem. Just because tradition precedes us and is a necessary condition for reflection does not legitimate its authority. Our finitude is unavoidable, but that does not make our situation right or just, or in itself legitimate the truth claim of a tradition. The

Gadamerian notion of a prejudice, which is a necessary condition for interpretation, is a prejudgment, and thus open to critical questioning. A prejudice "makes its plea before the tribunal of reason" (TN3 225). Like any judgment before this tribunal, the claims of tradition must submit to the law of the better argument. It cannot "set itself up as an authority without behaving like someone accused who refuses to accept the judge without becoming its own tribunal" (TN3 225). Tradition, in the sense of an authoritative source that always makes a claim on us simply because it is a part of our past, is something that can and should be questioned and judged in terms of something other than tradition.

Ricoeur's position on the relationship between reason and tradition is to seek a middle ground between a Gadamerian receptivity to the truth that tradition reveals and a Habermasian suspicion of the domination that tradition conceals. His conception of the "presumption of truth" refers to the attitude we assume toward the validity of the claim to legitimacy and truth made by tradition. We should accept the truth claim made by tradition or authority as putatively true until a better argument shows otherwise. In hermeneutical experience the moment of openness and receptivity precedes the moment of critique and explanation. A presumption of truth means "that confident reception by which we respond, in an initial move preceding all criticism, to any proposition of meaning, any claim to truth, because we are never at the beginning of the process of truth and because we belong, before any critical gesture, to a domain of presumed truth" (TN3 227). Ultimately what validates the authority of tradition is a process of communication and discursive argumentation.

The notion of a presumption of truth bridges the distance between the dialogue that we are and the dialogue that we ought to be, forming a transition between the necessity of the hermeneutical situation and the absolute validity of the idea of communicative truth. In the notion of a presumption of truth "the inevitable and the valuable asymptotically rejoin each other" (TN3 227). Ricoeur's mediating position is a model of presumed truth submitted to rational validation. It is a practical, not a theoretical mediation.

> The transcendence of the idea of truth, inasmuch as it is immediately a dialogical idea, has to been seen as already at work in the practice of communication. When so reinstalled in the horizon of expectation, this dialogical idea cannot fail to rejoin those anticipations buried in tradition per se. Taken as such, the pure transcendental quite legitimately assumes the negative status of a limit-idea as regards many of our determined expectations as well as our hypostatized traditions. However, at the risk of remaining alien to effective-history, this limit-idea has to become a regulative one,

orienting the concrete dialectic between our horizon of expectation and our space of experience. (TN3 226)

Ricoeur agrees with Habermas that it is necessary to anticipate an ideal speech situation where absolute freedom and equality exists in order for participants to reach a rational and binding consensus. Any critique of tradition is mediated by a regulative ideal of unconstrained communication, which, in turn, remains historically situated in order to be applied in a particular context. The regulative ideal of unconstrained communication mediates our consciousness of effective history.

But like Habermas himself, Ricoeur prefers to emphasize the validity basis of communication more than the ideal it entails. He agrees with Habermas that in order to able to establish understanding through communication, we tacitly presuppose the ability to explain ourselves if necessary. That is, we can clarify what we are talking about and we can justify what we say if challenged. Every time I say something to someone else I implicitly claim that what I say is intelligible, its contents are true, I am justified in saying it, and I am speaking sincerely. According to Habermas, "The goal of coming to an understanding is to bring about an agreement that terminates in the intersubjective mutuality of reciprocal understanding, shared knowledge, mutual trust, and accord with one another. Agreement is based on recognition of the corresponding validity claims of comprehensibility, truth, truthfulness [sincerity] and rightness."[22] The practical activity of reaching understanding or enlarging communication implies the ability of speakers to raise and test validity claims inherent in discourse. Ricoeur accepts this claim as internal to communicative action.

Thompson claims that Ricoeur never takes on the status of communicative competence as such in his mediations of the Habermas-Gadamer debate.[23] According to Thompson, Ricoeur misses the point when he claim that the critique of ideology itself stands in a tradition of Western Marxism and therefore its authority is no different from any other traditionally inherited prejudice. The issue is not whether the notion of communicative competence and an ideal speech situation are related to a tradition of Marxism or the Enlightenment; Habermas never appeals to the authority of these traditions for the justification of these ideals. In fact, the authority of the validity basis of discourse derives from precisely what is not bound exclusively to tradition, namely the validity basis of discourse. Although Thompson's critique of Ricoeur is valid with respect to the arguments found in in several essays from the 1970s, including "Hermeneutics and the Critique of Ideology," "Ethics and Culture," and *The Lectures on Ideology and Utopia*, elsewhere Ricoeur explicitly appropriates and incorporates the Habermasian validity basis for speech within hermeneutic reflection as transcendental, regulative ideals of rationality.

In both *Time and Narrative* and *Oneself as Another* Ricoeur attempts to contextualize the transcendental component of Habermasian pragmatics into a hermeneutic philosophy and a theory of practical reason. He explains that the "entire question is then whether one can contextualize the universal while keeping it as a regulative idea" (CC 61). I read his claim to imply that the critique of ideology—and the validity basis of communication—is internal and necessary to hermeneutical understanding. Ricoeur's hermeneutic philosophy and, as I argue later, theory of practical reason incorporate Habermas's theory of universal pragmatics. Like Habermas, Ricoeur adopts a less rigorously transcendental version of speech pragmatics than Apel's version.[24] Apel argues that one commits a performative contradiction by arguing against the validity of the universally binding rules of communication because in order to deny their validity one must argue, and to argue is to communicate. A person performs in speech, and, therefore, presupposes and implicitly accepts, the norms of communication while explicitly denying their validity. But because Ricoeur is more concerned with questions of practical application than those of ultimate justification, he is able to appropriate the validity basis of discourse into a hermeneutic-phenomenology without having to evoke necessary, regulative ideals in order to mediate conflicting interpretation. I read Ricoeur's mediation of Habermas and Gadamer as precisely the fusion into a "supersystem" he claims he avoids. He is neither closer to one than the other. Instead his version of critical hermeneutics is a unique, fragile balance between Gadamerian hermeneutics and Habermasian critique of ideology that retains the best of both. It raises its claim to universality by evoking a contextualized notion of the universal as the practical activity of interpretation and argumentation—without forgetting Husserl!

CHAPTER 2

NARRATIVE

One of the central themes in Ricoeur's hermeneutic philosophy is the creative capacity of language, especially metaphoric and narrative language. Creative language expresses aspects of reality that would otherwise remain hidden from ordinary language. By describing the world in new ways metaphors and narratives creates new interpretations and experiences of the world. Creative language broadens the scope of hermeneutics. With the publication of *Time and Narrative*, Ricoeur's work shifts away from questions of textual interpretation to questions of human action, in particular human temporal and historic experience. He maintains the thesis that written works mediate interpretation but now he reformulates the hermeneutic circle in terms of the circularity of narrative prefiguration, configuration, and refiguration. Our lives are inchoate stories with a prenarrative structure that only becomes fully intelligible when transformed into a narrative. Reading completes the course of a narrative. It is the final act of the activity of narration. Narrative discourse configures human actions, already prefigured like a narrative, into a coherent whole that is then refigured by the reader. The most important insight of *Time and Narrative* for hermeneutic philosophy is that the narrative function is indispensable in articulating the intelligibility of human action. Anything that is recounted unfolds in time, and anything that occurs in time can be recounted. To describe and to explain the genesis and development of an event or object is to narrate. One of the vexing problems for a critical theory, however, results from the internal connection between creative, narrative discourses and ideology, utopia, and other distortions of reality. The same medium that configures human action also distorts it. How can we tell the difference between an ideological and non-ideological narrative? Another vexing problem for narrative theory is how to distinguish between fiction and history if they share a common narrative structure. And if there is no certain way to distinguish between the two, what are the prospects for a critical theory that depends on our ability to distinguish between true and false consciousness, genuine and false communication? I believe Ricoeur has answers for both problems.

METAPHOR AND NARRATIVE

The problem of metaphor is to describe and explain how creative and imaginative uses of language refer to reality in such a way that produces new interpretations of the world. In *The Rule of Metaphor* Ricoeur develops his thesis that the split-reference of creative discourse discloses a possible way of being-in-the-world that remains hidden from ordinary language and first-order reference. The world of the work that unfolds in reading opens up nonsituational references revealing new possibilities of existence. A metaphor is a "heuristic fiction" that "redescribes" reality by referring to it in terms of something imaginative or fictional, allowing us to learn something about reality from fiction. Heuristic fictions help us to perceive new relations and new connections among things, broadening our ability to express ourselves, interpret ourselves, and transform ourselves. The "strategy of discourse" in metaphorical language is not necessarily to improve communication or argumentation but "to shatter and to increase our sense of reality by shattering and increasing our language."[1]

Like any form of discourse, a metaphor communicates something to someone about something—produced as event, understood as meaning. Only "living metaphors" are at the same time both event and meaning. A "dead metaphor" has lost its event character when it becomes sedimented into a traditional stock of expressions adopted by a community, like, for example, to call a left-handed person a "southpaw," or to describe someone who is nervous as having "butterflies in his stomach." A live metaphor, on the other hand, is a truly novel expression in the sense of a "metaphorical twist" that produces a new, surprising meaning.[2] In a live metaphor there is tension in the way something is described metaphorically and how we normally understand it to be. In order to grasp the differences and resemblance that constitute a metaphor we must see-through the first-order, ostensive reference to the second-order, creative reference to understand how it redescribes the world. To understand what a metaphor means is to see that it is similar to and different from an ordinary description. For example, when I read in the sports page that "Patrick Ewing is a warrior" I understand that he is still a basketball player and not literally a warrior but somehow like a warrior, and, in some sense, he truly is both a warrior and not a warrior at the same time. I "get it" when I both "see-as" and "see-not-as." The tension in a living metaphor between literal and imaginative must be preserved, not overcome to be understood. There is no tension in dead metaphors.

After developing a theory of metaphoric reference in great detail, *The Rule of Metaphor* concludes with a rather truncated discussion of the relationship between speculative thought and poetic discourse. Metaphysics needs metaphors to describe our being-in-the-world. The tensional theory of truth produced in the interpretation of the split reference of metaphor "articulates and preserves the experience of belonging that places man in discourse and discourse in being" (RM 313). At the same time, the moment of distanciation of discourse opens the possibility of speculative discourse which, in turn, "reflects" and "rearticulates" the splitting of reference and redescription of reality achieved by metaphoric discourse. A dialectic exists between "the experience of belonging as a whole and the power of distanciation that opens up the space of speculative thought" (RM 313).

Ricoeur, however, quickly grew dissatisfied with his theory of metaphorical reference. It lacked any account of the reader who connects the metaphorical utterance with its interpretation, transforming the new way of "seeing-as" with my new experience of "being-as." For what is redescribed is, after all, the reader's experience of belonging to the world. He also abandoned the Fregean conception of the linguistic reference because it appeared to be too direct and unmediated, suggesting a kind of referential realism. *The Rule of Metaphor* is, therefore, best seen as a transitional work between the hermeneutics of texts of the 1970s and the hermeneutics of action of the 1980s. In *Time and Narrative* he reformulates the hermeneutic circle in terms of a "narrative refiguration of experience" in order to account for the act of interpretation connecting texts and actions, and to overcome the perception of realism. He explains that the term *refiguration* is more appropriate than the term "reference" because of "its derivation from the term *figure*, it recalls the belongingness of the whole problematic of configuration and refiguration to the preconceptual order of the schematism of the productive imagination."[3] *Time and Narrative* continues to develop the themes of semantic innovation and the ability of poetic discourse to disclose new ways to see and to be in the world, but in a far more thorough and convincing fashion than *The Rule of Metaphor*.

The key to understanding the connection between metaphor and narrative is Kant's conception of the productive imagination. The productive imagination schematizes synthetic operations, meaning that it synthesizes differences according to rules. For Kant, the imagination is not psychological but transcendental, and thus it constitutes the matrix of rules as such. It synthesizes the categories of understanding by connecting understanding and intuition; the resulting synthesis is both intellectual and intuitive. Imagination is this "*ability* to produce new kinds by assimilation and to produce them not *above* the differences, as in the concept, but in spite of and through the differences."[4] The productive imagination at work in the metaphorical process is our ability to create new meanings by the synthetic act of understanding to see similarities in difference. Semantic innovation occurs in a metaphor through an unusual predication that is understood when we follow the split-reference and grasp together the figurative and literal meanings. Semantic innovation occurs in a narrative through a similar synthesis of heterogeneous parts. The basic unit of a narrative is a plot, which unifies the elements of a story including the reasons, motives, and actions of characters with events, accidents, and circumstances together into a coherent unity. A plot synthesizes, integrates, and schematizes actions, events, and, ultimately, time into a unified whole that says something new and different than the sum of its parts. Both metaphor and narrative involve a synthesis of the heterogeneous. In metaphor it is the ability to perceive resemblance in difference; in narrative it is the ability to construct a meaningful organization of otherwise unrelated events.

> This parallel between *Time and Narrative* and *The Rule of Metaphor*, considered from the perspective of semantic innovation, is pursued in a complementary sphere: in both instances, the task of hermeneutics is to bring to light a type of intelligibility precisely compatible with this work of schematization on the plane of the imagination and to establish its primacy in relation to simulations stemming from a logic of transformations.[5]

The thesis of *Time and Narrative* is the essential connection between the temporal character of human experience and the act of narrating a story. "Time becomes human time to the extent that it is organized after the manner of a narrative; narrative, in turn, is meaningful to the extent that it portrays the features of temporal experience" (TN1 3). Temporal experience is expressed in the form of a narrative, while a narrative is able to reflect our social reality (in large part) because it expresses temporal experience. The circularity of time and narrative is mediated by three senses of representation: $mimesis_1$, $mimesis_2$, and $mimesis_3$. $Mimesis_1$, or prefiguration, represents the aspect of the imitation of action that draws on our preunderstanding of the difference between human action and physical activity. $Mimesis_2$, or configuration, is the "pivot" of the analysis of the relationship between time and narrative in which events are configured into a story. $Mimesis_3$, or refiguration, refers to the act of reading that changes our practical understanding according to the configuration of the story. Mimetic activity presupposes, represents, and reinterprets human action. Each stage and form of configuration is also an interpretation and transformation of action. Narratives share a common form with action; they configure what is already a figure in action. Mimesis is the ordering and structuring activity that duplicates the order and structure of human activity. The implications of the threefold mimetic activity for hermeneutics is that it is now seen as the reconstruction of the actions of authors, works, and readers regarding human acting and suffering. "What is at stake, therefore, is the concrete process by which the textual configuration mediates between the prefiguration of the practical field and its refiguration through the reception of the work" (TN1 53).

Mimesis$_1$ describes the basic preunderstanding of human temporality one must have in order to imitate or represent action. It has three aspects—structural, symbolic, and temporal—that form the cognitive and practical background that determines how we interpret human action. The structural dimension refers to our understanding of the conceptual network of the semantics of action that is the necessary competence a speaker or narrator must have in order to identify the domain of human action and distinguish it from mere physical movement. We must understand how to use words like "motive," "reason," "intention," "agency," and so on, to be able to grasp the connection between agents and actions, actors, and patients. The ability to answer questions about "who," "what," "why," "how," and "with whom" regarding an action is to understand that the domain of meaningful action refers to a conceptual network different from that of mere physical movement. Narrative discourse presupposes our ability to tell the difference between the perspective of a subject and the perspective of others, as well as the difference between the predicates attributed to humans and those attributed to objects.[6]

The second feature of mimesis$_1$ is our preunderstanding of the symbolic character of narrative understanding. Human actions can be narrated because they are already articulated by the kinds of things that narrating picks out and organizes. Narrative shares a common form with action; it configures what is already a figure in action. Ricoeur adopts Geertz's notion that actions are symbolically mediated by the signs, rules, and norms of a culture.[7] Because meaning is public so is culture. Just as there are no private meanings, there is no such thing as a culture that is not open to interpretation. Cultural meanings are incorporated into action, conferring intelligibility and normativity. The symbolic mediation of action refers to systems of symbols and patterns of meanings that provide the background and context for describing, interpreting, and judging actions. We must have a preunderstanding of what is a relevant feature in human action before we interpret it in speech or writing. This symbolic mediation shapes actions into the things we interpret.

The third feature of mimesis$_1$ reflects a preunderstanding of the temporality of action. Human time and narrative time share so many common elements that Ricoeur often speaks of the "prenarrative" structure of temporal experience. Heidegger's analysis of temporality in the second division of *Being and Time*, particularly his discussion of "within-time-ness," characterizes the temporality of action reflected in mimesis$_1$.[8] Temporality is tied to care, which means that we describe time in terms of the way we care about things. The time kept by clocks and watches is an abstract representation derivative of the existential meaning of time, which is something we reckon with. We "take time for," "make time for," "don't have enough time to," and so on. Our language expresses the datable and public character of time through the use of adverbs like "then," "since," "during," and "until." These adverbs express the different ways we can be preoccupied by thoughts of something that will happen or has happened, all of which involves an orientation toward a different temporal dimension than the present. Such abstract concepts of time as a linear succession of "nows" or as the duration of elapsed time are derivative of our within-time-ness. Time is based on the time it takes for what we reckon with, what we care about, and what preoccupies us. What occurs happens "in" time.[9]

Mimesis$_2$ is configurative operation of "emplotment" that mediates between a preunderstanding of action and a "postunderstanding" of action. All narratives, fictional and historic, share a form or configuration that brings to expression the semantic, symbolic, and temporal structures embodied in human action. Mimesis$_2$ is the configurational act of emplotment that picks out, interprets, and articulates our preunderstanding of action. It does so in three ways: (1) A plot mediates between the parts of a story and the story taken as a whole. It brings together events and transforms them into a story. An event is only an event in relation to a plot of a story. In turn, a story is more than a succession of events but is an organization of events into an intelligible whole. (2) Emplotment brings together multiple elements like agents, events, goals, means, interactions, circumstances, consequences, reversals of fortune, and unexpected results. It synthesizes heterogeneous, disparate parts into a whole. (3) A plot mediates a story by synthesizing temporal characteristics into a unified whole. Emplotment leads the reader along by expectations, guided by a "sense of an ending," to a conclusion, or end point that provides of perspective from which the story can be seen as a unity. The configuration of actions in a narrative is able to create new meanings in part through its ability to arrange events and time into meaningful organizations. Mimesis$_2$ "opens the kingdom of the *as if*" (TN1 64).

Ricoeur describes the configurational act that joins mimesis$_1$ and mimesis$_2$ as in an interplay of innovation and sedimentation. A narrative configuration retains a link to the past while at the same time creating a new way of interpreting the world. The process is Kantian in the sense that the configuration organizes heterogeneous elements into an intelligible unity according to a schema but one that is constituted within a particular history. The act of emplotment is a creative interpretation of events within an established framework, inherited from the past. The interplay of innovation and sedimentation is also known as "traditionality." Narrating constitutes a living tradition by moving forward and backward from what is new based on what is old. New interpretations are linked to the past, which itself was formed by new interpretations. To narrate is also to transmit a tradition.

Mimesis$_3$ is the act of reading that links the world of the work with the world of the reader. It completes the passage from mimesis$_1$ to mimesis$_3$ through mimesis$_2$ that is, "from a prefigured world to a transfigured world through the mediation of a configured world."[10] The prenarrative structure of action, imitated in narrative by means of emplotment, is then unfolded in the act of reading, itself an action that imitates a narrative. What is signified in a narrative is what was already "presignified" in human action, and what is then "resignified" when understood. The act of telling and interpreting stories links narration with the practical transformation of the world.

> The distinction between the inside and the outside of the text is created by a methodological decision, that of considering texts only as closed on themselves. I think that it is a task of hermeneutics to reopen this closure and to reinsert the world of literature between what precedes it, let us say a kind of naive experience, and what succeeds it, that is to say, a learned experience. So, in a sense, the act of reading has this wonderful quality of interpolating the world of literature between the stage of unlearned experience to a stage of learned experience and praxis.[11]

Reading completes the hermeneutic circle of prefiguration, configuration, and refiguration. It is what Gadamer calls "application," or what Ricoeur elsewhere calls "appropriation." The act of reading performs the critical function of bridging the world of the text with the world of the reading and thus inaugurates the reconfiguration of life by narrative. Ricoeur maintains that the act of interpretation institutes a break, like an *epoche*, in my world of experience and action, inviting me to reflect on the putative truth of the proposed world of the work. In this way narrative theory retains the notion of distanciation that is central to both hermeneutics and phenomenology.

The superiority of narrative over nonnarrative discourse is the more dynamic account of the relationship between experience and writing. In a narrative, the subject is action, as are the configurational and reconfigurational acts of telling a story and following a story. As a modified version of the hermeneutic circle, the threefold conception of mimesis overcomes the awkward language of "reference" and "redescription" of the hermeneutics of texts. *Time and Narrative* repeats the argument for the referentiality of discourse found in *The Rule of Metaphor* but subsumes the referential dimension to the configurative act, which implies all three moments of mimesis and thus better retains its dynamic, practical character. Narrative theory is a better model of the way discourse, action, and interpretation are connected.

NARRATIVE AND HISTORY

The second part of volume I of *Time and Narrative* explores the relationship between historical explanation and narrative understanding. Ricoeur defends two theses. First, the narrative character of history in no way conflates narrative with fiction. It is one thing to claim that narrative discourse clarifies, organizes, and configures the temporal and historical dimensions of human experience into meaningful episodes; it is another to claim that there is no difference between a true story and an imagined one. Second, the intelligibility of history is tied to our ability to follow a story. That competence is made possible by the prenarrative character of human experience that becomes configured and refigured when understood. The essential difference between fiction and history is the latter's claim to be true, which must be established if narrative theory is to have any relevance for a critical social theory. After he establishes the narrative character of historical understanding, Ricoeur continues the argument in volume 2 of *Time and Narrative* that storytelling of all kinds, in the sense of recounting, is grounded in the temporality of human action. Storytelling (*raconter*) transforms "natural time" into "human time" while it creates new interpretations and new meanings. Time, narrative, history, and hermeneutics are interrelated parts of a whole.

To show the connection between narrative and history, Ricoeur takes Hempel's deductive-nomological (DN) model to be paradigmatic of explanation in both the natural and human sciences.[12] Hempel's claim is that deductive explanations are arguments. What we explain (the "explanandum") is the conclusion of an argument, the premises of which (the "explanans") lead to rational and justifiable conclusions. Any event can be deduced from two premises. The first describes the initial conditions, antecedents, or prior conditions; the second are general laws asserting a regularity of some kind. At least one of the premises must be nomological—a general statement of lawful or causal regularities. If the two premises are established, then the event can be said to be deduced, and therefore explained by some form of regularity that exists between an individual event and the assertion of a universal hypothesis. The explanandum must be a logical consequence of the explanans. In addition, the explanans must be empirical and capable of being tested by observation or experimentation. If the empirical and logical conditions are satisfied, then the DN model can explain any phenomenon and any historic event. Even teleological explanations can be understood as asserting general laws that yield deductive conclusions.

Ricoeur contends that the DN model of explanation fails to account for the activity of the historian who deals not only with events but also with documents and texts, as well as with events that receive their historical status by being recounted. Choosing which events are significant is an interpretive act. Even determining what would count as an initial condition, or antecedent state of affairs, presupposes an interpretive framework in terms of which we see something as an event, condition, or state of affairs. If there were no interpretive framework that picks out aspects and assigns significance, it would be impossible to determine what in experience is relevant, or even what counts as an event. Ricoeur proposes that we instead think of historical explanations as true stories, rather than causal explanations. Deducing historical events from initial conditions and general laws can only occur within the context of a narrative. Events are historical occurrences that take place in time, meaningful only in relation to a narrative configuration of statements and sentences that interprets, orders, and represents what happened. A historical explanation occurs within "a prior narrative organization that has already characterized events as contributing to the development of a plot" (TA 5). A historical explanation is a "narrative explanation" that shows how an action or event is involved in a story. Ricoeur does not so much argue against the DN model as show how it must be situated within a broader interpretive framework. In this way, he retains a dialectic of explanation and understanding similar to the one found in his hermeneutics of texts, which incorporated a moment of methodological understanding within a broader framework of hermeneutic understanding.

Ricoeur appropriates Gallie's phenomenology of the act of following a story in order to show the similarity between reading a historical narrative and a fictional narrative, and hence the similarity in the way we comprehend them.[13]

According to Gallie, the ability to follow a story is what unifies history and fiction at the level of the refiguration of mimesis$_3$, or reading. We could not understand either if we did not know how to follow a story, which requires that we suspend judgment in order to be lead along in anticipation of a coherent, meaningful conclusion.

> To follow a story is to understand something as a succession of actions, faults, and feelings that present coherent direction as well as surprises. The conclusion of a story is accordingly not something deducible, or predictable, but it does have to be both consistent and acceptable. Without this basis there is no story and no history. The interests of the hearer, or the reader, is not the underlying laws but in following the plot as unfolded in a story.[14]

We are motivated to follow a story based on the expectation that obstacles will be overcome and predicaments resolved. The *telos* of a story is an acceptable conclusion that makes sense from the perspective of the end. If in retrospect the conclusion squares with the events that lead up to it, then we consider the story acceptable.

Narratives establish the history of action by linking together a succession of events into meaningful episodes, understood from the perspective of an anticipated end. A narrative is like a long memory that orders and repeats sequences of events from beginning to end. With memory comes a retrieval of our past. For Heidegger, such a retrieval is a repetition of our potentialities of being-in-the-world as inherited from our personal and collective past. We derive our historicity from our temporality. For Ricoeur, the retrieval of one's destiny and fate occurs only in the repetition of action in a narrative. We can only understanding the temporality and historicity of experience—the stretching along of life from birth to death—when it is marked, organized, and clarified in a narrative. Time is meaningful only as human time, when it becomes refashioned and turned into the kind of public, social thing that can be understood when expressed in a fictional or historical narrative.[15]

Both history and fiction are narrative configurations of events interpreted to contribute to the development of a plot, which unifies and organizes sequences of actions, events, and circumstances, with the experiences of actors or characters (real or imaginary). History and fiction "interweave," thanks to a fundamental ontological and epistemological structure "by virtue of which history and fiction each concretize their respective intentionalities only by borrowing from the intentionality of the other" (TN3 181). The interweaving of fiction and history occurs at the level of mimesis$_2$ and works in two directions. First is the "fictionalization of history," or the narrative mediation of lived time and objective time. The mediation of time and narrative occurs through three "connectors."

The first connector is calendar time. Calendars, along with clocks and watches, join together astronomical time, tied to the rotation of the planet, with public, datable time. A calendar is both an astronomical and a social-political instrument. It unites workdays, holidays, significant events, and dates with seasons and years, integrating human time with cosmic time. "It cosmologizes lived time, it humanizes cosmic time" (TA 214). A second connector is the notion of a succession of generations, or a biological time that underlies human time. Belonging to the same generation and the coexistence of different generations are ways that biological time marks and organizes lived time. A culture is linked together by the contemporaneity of predecessors, successors, and contemporaries. We are constantly reminded of our connection to the past through the presence of generations. The social bond is woven with a biological texture that assures a continuity of life among the living.

The third connector is the document, or the historian's evidence of the past. A trace of the past is a vestige left behind, a remnant, or relic that provides clues of what the past was like. A trace is a physical entity that exists in the present but refers to the past, which itself exists and persists through the trace. At the same time, a trace is only a trace for someone who knows how to read it as a sign of something absent. A trace is a present remnant of an absent past that simultaneously belongs to both the past and the present.[16] It is a stand-in for the past, as Heidegger says. It connects lived time with the time of history, just like a calendar connects lived time with cosmic time, and the presence of generations connects lived time with biological time. The fictionalization of history is another name for the way that a narrative configures the signs of the past with the present to create an intelligible experience of human time.

The second interweaving of history and fiction is the "historization of fiction," which occurs whenever something is recounted. Usually the voice of a narrator is in the past tense, or it speaks of events as past facts recounted in the present. As we read we believe that the events reported by the narrator "belong to the past of that voice" (TN3 190). We assume the narrator is in a position to know. This common structure lets us see all recounting as a form of narrative; fiction can be seen as "quasi-historical" and history is "quasi-fictive."

> History is quasi-fictive once the quasi-presence of events placed "before the eyes of" the reader by a lively narrative supplements through its intuitiveness, its vividness, the elusive character of the

> pastness of the past. . . . Fictional narrative is quasi-historical to the
> extent that the unreal events that it relates are past facts for the nar-
> rative voice that addresses itself to the reader. It is in this that they
> resemble past events and that fiction resembles history. (TN3 190)

Both history and fiction take place "as if past." History takes place in the real
past, fiction in the possible past. The "past-like" character of both history and
fiction is reflected in the shared, interweaving referential intentions (TN3 192).

The only difference, then, between fiction and history is that only the latter are explanations raising truth claims. Fictional stories must only satisfy the requirements of narrative acceptability, and coherence, not rational proof,
validation, or falsification. Historians, however, are not simply narrators; they
must also argue, give reasons, and explain by offering evidence. The fact that
historical explanations take place within a narrative should not suggest that history is simply a genre of narrative. The claim that history has a narrative character asserts only that history and fiction share a common form. Recalling the
development of his thought, Ricoeur notes that he never intended to conflate
the truth claims of fiction and history, only to compare the commonalities in
their structure.

> Concerning the historical narrative, I can say that I did not give in
> to the temptation to which certain English-language "narrativist"
> theorists have, in my opinion, too readily succumbed, that of taking
> historical explanation as simply the province of narrative intelligi-
> bility, as if *history* were a species of the genus *story*. . . . If it seemed
> to me legitimate to see in narrative intelligence, considered the un-
> derstanding of plots, the matrix for historical explanation, it also
> seemed to me necessary to take into account the features by which
> historical explanation, through an epistemological break, distin-
> guished itself from simple narrativity. (TN1 79)

The narrative function of an historical explanation is to help the reader makes
sense of a story; it helps us follow a story if we know why events and actions oc-
curred. Such explanations, however, must not only satisfy the requirement of a
coherent story, but also the requirements of intersubjective validation. They are
at least potentially true.

A hermeneutic conception of narrative truth can be found in *Time and
Narrative* in the conception of mimesis$_3$. A narrative truth is like a metaphorical
truth, which is the ability of poetic discourse to bring to language hidden aspects of reality. It is a hermeneutic conception of truth as manifestation. A

reader or hearer experiences a new way of seeing-as through the referential dimension opened up by a use of language, including symbols, words, metaphors, sentences, or narratives. Any form of discourse may introduce new interpretations and new experiences of the world, affecting me at the level of the life-world that I inhabit and presuppose prior to reflection. Reading and hearing a discourse leads me to the (real or imaginary) reference through the sense of that discourse. "What a reader receives is not just the sense of the word, but, through its sense, its reference, that is, the experience it brings to language and, in the last analysis, the world and the temporality it unfolds in the face of this experience" (TN1 79). I experience the world through my experience of listening and reading. Similarly, I experience the world through the unfolding of a narrative.

> Reference and horizon are correlative as are figure and ground. All experience both possesses a contour that circumscribes it and distinguishes it, and arises against a horizon of potentialities that constitutes at once and internal and an external horizon of experience: internal in the sense that it is always possible to give more details and be more precise about whatever is considered within some stable contour; external in the sense that the intended thing stands in potential relationships to everything else within the horizon of a total world, which itself never figures as the object of discourse. (TN1 78)

The movement from prefiguration to configuration to refiguration describes how narrative discourse refers to the world and mediates experience. Reading transfigures my experience through a fusion of my horizon and the horizon of the world of the work.

Ricoeur employs a narrative theory of truth to show how the criteria of verification and falsification operate in the truth claims made in Freudian analysis. The proof for truth claims are found in psychoanalytic case histories that consist of narrative configurations of utterances, memories, actions, events, theories, and interpretations. As a patient recounts events, the analyst reinterprets them in order to offer insight and plans of action geared toward overcoming the psychological barriers preventing the patient from living well—or to put it in a more Freudian-Marxists language, to overcome the systematic distortions that are the source of misunderstanding and neurosis. The truth claims of psychoanalysis take the form of a coherent story that makes sense. A psychoanalytic explanation is a narrative configuration that incorporates lawlike statements and theories into a case history. The nonnarrative elements of a case may include data collected from clinical experimentation, medical explanations of symptoms, and other various theories, laws, generalizations, and axioms. When incorporated into the case history, psychoanalytic explanations provide underlying consistency, coherence, and clarity to help make sense of one's life as a whole. A case history provides intelligibility and coherence to an otherwise unintelligible and disconnected course of events. Truth claims are intertwined with narrative criteria of unity, consistency, and congruity. But if the truth claim resides in a case history, the proof of the truth claim resides in the entire network of narrative configurations, including theories, explanations, lawlike regularities, and narrative coherence. Truth in the social sciences involves both narration and argumentation (HHS 247–273).

Herein lies the importance of narrative discourse and narrative truth for a critical theory. If anything recounted unfolds in time and anything occurring in time can be recounted, then any description and explanation of the genesis, development, or history of an event or object also unfolds in a narrative. It is indispensable to understanding past actions or for a complete understanding of present actions. Ricoeur believes that the implications of narration as a retelling and reinterpretation of history are considerable.

> For history is not only the story (*histoire*) of triumphant kings and heroes, of the powerful; it is also the story of the powerless and dispossessed. The history of the vanquished dead crying out for justice demands to be told. As Hannah Arendt points out, the meaning of human existence is not just the power to change or master the world, but also the ability to be remembered and recollected in narrative discourse, to be *memorable*. These existential and historical implications of narrativity are very far-reaching, for they determine what is to be "preserved" and rendered "permanent" in culture's sense of it's own past, of its own "identity."[17]

Narratives not only constitute history and tradition but determine who we are, what we are, and what our prospects for the future are. The political implications of narration cannot be overstated, if an interpretation of history is a retelling of what happened. What stories are told, how they are told, who or what is the subject, how events are organized and assigned significance, to whom and what responsibility is attributed, and to whom stories are told—all of these elements determine what will be preserved, remembered, and taken as true.

Any critical interpretation of society must first show that the present could be different by providing an alternative historical explanation of events—unearthing the "unfulfilled future of the past" (TN1 80). For example, a Marxist interpretation of history is a retelling of events geared toward revealing what would otherwise have remained hidden in a conventional version of history. If instead of reading history as "the plot of kings, battles, treaties, and the rise and fall of empires," it is read as "the plot of suffering rather than that of power and glory," then an entirely different and influential story emerges.[18] Previously invisible forces and actors, like class struggle and oppressed workers, appear as central historical agents. In a Marxist interpretation

> the normal narrative ordering of history is reversed and the hero is now the "slave" rather than the "master" as before; a new set of events and facts are deemed to be relevant and claim our attention; the relations of labour and production take precedence over the relations between kings and queens.[19]

Or, in more conventionally Marxist terms, if we interpret "free market societies" as "capitalist modes of production" then we are able to see through any number of conventional interpretations of the workings of markets and politics as mystifying ideology. What is a radical discourse other than a conflicting interpretation that challenges ruling-class authority?

Not only history but also fiction, poetry, film, music, and the various visual and performance arts can also contribute to a critique of society by suggesting new, different, and possibly better ways to be in world. All creative discourses harbor utopian possibilities of new worlds, new figures of speech, new interpretations, and new ways to be in the world. Anything that enlarges communication, opens possibilities, and creates new ways of seeing the world and being in the world are all potentially subversive forces that can challenge the legitimacy of authority.

> If it is true that one of the functions of fiction bound with history is to free, retrospectively, certain possibilities that were not actualized in the historical past, it is owing to its quasi-historical character that fiction itself is able, after the fact, to perform its liberating function. The quasi-past of fiction in this way becomes the detector of possibilities buried in the actual past. What "might have been" . . . includes both the potentialities of the "real" past and the "unreal" possibilities of pure fiction. (TN3 192)

Disclosing alternate possibilities is a necessary moment in calling into question seemingly unchanging and timeless social relations. We must first uncover frozen social relations and perceived necessity to show that such ahistorical notions are false universals that need not be the case. Any such doctrine or belief purporting to justify domination and authority can be called into question by a narrative that shows how things could be different.

But creative, narrative discourses are both the cure and the poison. As imaginative interpretations of the world that mediate understanding, they have the capacity to shape social relations for better or worse. Ideology and utopia, the pair Ricoeur insists remain together, are like other metaphoric and narrative discourse in that they project new ways of seeing and being in the world based on creative configurations of human action. Ideology and utopia are polar opposites of a single "cultural imagination" that mediates and integrates human action through interpretive schemas that both constitute and distort a society. It is the same symbolic structure that is prefigured in narrative discourse that also constitutes social life as the cultural imagination. "Unless social life has a symbolic structure, there is no way to understand how we live, do things, and project these activities in ideas, no way to understand how reality can become an idea or how real life can produce illusions" (IU 8). His thesis is that ideology and utopia are operative but never totally thematic; we think and act from them rather than about them.

Ideology and utopia are forms of "noncongruence" with social reality that represent deviant attitudes of individuals and groups. Ideology is noncongruent from social reality in the sense that it distorts and dissimulates; utopia is noncongruent in the sense that it projects a possible world that makes the existing world appear imperfect, inadequate, and unjust. Or utopia may function as an escape from social reality by suggesting a possible world that is unfeasible, impractical, and nonsensical. From a Marxist perspective, the noncongruence of utopia with reality makes the concept itself ideological. From the perspective of the cultural imagination, both ideology and utopia are simply imaginative variations of a broader, symbolic structure of social life. They are among the creative interpretations that constitute of historical belonging, yet offer an alternative, noncongruent way to interpret and be-in-the-world.

What distinguishes ideology and utopia from other creative discourses is their function. Ideology functions by coordinating social integration through an interpretive schema that distorts, dissimulates, integrates, but most important legitimates power, authority, and domination. Utopia functions by challenging and questioning power and authority. Ideology attempts to legitimate power, while utopia attempts to replace power with something else. Both have a positive, constitutive dimension, and a negative, pathological dimension: each has a constructive and a destructive function. The positive function of ideology is to constitute and preserve social relations; the negative function is to resist the transformation of an order that has frozen social relations in such a way that sustains domination. Ideology is always conservative. It preserves order by patterning, organizing, and ensuring the stable functioning of a community as it distorts, legitimates, and integrates. As Ricoeur notes, there is "no social integration without social subversion" (IU 16), thus pathology is a condition of community, as such. The pathology of ideology is its conservative role in preserving and conserving social relations of domination that should be changed.

The positive function of utopia is its ability to call a society into question from an imagined, possibly critical, vantage point; the negative function is to provide an escape and retreat from social reality, which then leaves everything as it is. A utopia is a view from "nowhere" in terms of which we experience and rethink our social reality. "Utopia is the mode in which we radically rethink the nature of family, consumption, government, religion, and so on. From 'nowhere' emerges the most formidable challenge to what-is" (TA 184). Utopias offer other ways of life based on imaginative variations of power relations, like Husserl's imaginative variations concerning an essence. Usually the utopian ideal is either a better political structure or no political structure at all, or a choice between being governed by good rulers or by no rulers at all. Ricoeur is very attentive to the function of power, authority, and domination in utopia, questioning "who has power in a given utopia and how the problem of power is subverted by the utopia" (IU 17).

Ricoeur's conception of the cultural imagination is a properly hermeneutic concept. No transcendental entity is posited as the basis for critique. Just as creative discourse is neither derivative nor parasitic of literal discourse, neither ideology nor utopia are derivative of reality. Just as no social life exists apart from the underlying symbolic structure of action, no vantage point exists that is entirely free from either ideology or utopia. The problem is this: if we can never achieve a perspective on social reality that is able to penetrate behind the level of symbolic action, is there such thing as a perspective that is entirely free from ideology or utopia? Ricoeur claims that "a non-ideological discourse on ideology" cannot never reach "a social reality prior to symbolization" (TA 261). It is impossible to exercise a critique that would be absolutely radical "because a radically critical consciousness would require a total reflection" (TA 261). If we reject the possibility of total reflection, how is any critique of ideology possible if ideological formations are also constitutive of our language and interpretive schemas? How can we be sure that we support ideology and utopia in the good sense, not the bad sense? How can we be sure what we are supporting is even ideological or utopian in the first place?

Ricoeur never tells us how we can tell the difference between an ideological and nonideological interpretation. He never explains why we should prefer the projected utopian image of society over either the ideological interpretation or another alternative interpretation. If all creative discourses open up a distance between the everyday world and the world of the text, allowing us to step back and reflect on our world in light a different, possibly better world, what makes one possible world more or less preferable to another? What is it about the utopia, or world of the text that is better—and why is it better? The claim that a utopia or the projected world of the text provides any kind of normative basis for critique is woefully inadequate. The proposed world must be *demonstrably* better for it to justify a normative claim, not just *possibly* better. In order to demonstrate that it is better, one must offer relevant reasons to support that judgment.

Ricoeur gives two answers to the problem of finding a nonideological perspective for a critique of distorted consciousness and communication. First, ideology can be identified and criticized by a hermeneutic philosophy, if properly conceived to preserve a critical moment of distanciation. In his mediation of Habermas and Gadamer, he argues that no antimony exists between our historical belonging to a tradition and our interest in emancipation based on the anticipation of a communicative ideal. This is because hermeneutics and critique each presuppose the other in order to be what they are. It is in the practical activity of recovering the past and projecting a better future that we creatively interpret ourselves on the basis of a communicative ideal. There is no other way around the antinomy of reason and tradition. If looked at from a theoretical perspective, it would appear that hermeneutics and the critique of ideology are antagonistic. But from a practical perspective, a critique of false consciousness and distorted communication is inseparable from the acts of self-understanding, interpreting our cultural belonging, and communicating with others.

Second, ideology can be identified and criticized on the basis of utopia, and utopia on the basis of ideology. They form a circle. Each is not only inescapable, but inexorably connected to the other. We can never be sure that we are free from the effects of ideology; if we are, we inevitably raise the specter of utopianism, itself a dangerous, imaginative construct. The cultural imagination is not something we can stand outside of and evaluate. Instead we criticize the negative dimensions of ideology and utopia in terms of the positive dimensions of the other. In other words, we criticize conservative social relations in terms of a utopian possibility, and utopian escapism by what is "wholesome" in ideology namely the social bonds that hold a society together. The only way out is to try "to make the circle a spiral" through the practical activity of engaging in a critique of ideology (IU 312). The critique of ideology—or utopia—occurs within hermeneutics as creative discourses enter into interpretation as the distanced moment of reflection and critique. Just as critical distance is a part of hermeneutics, so is the critique of ideology carried out by utopia and utopia by ideology. Narrative discourse only explains what happens when we create and interpret written works; it offers little that would help resolve the antinomies of the Habermas-Gadamer debate. Whatever Ricoeur says about the critical function of narrative discourse could also be said of Gadamer's hermeneutic philosophy. The more promising approach is to follow Ricoeur's notion that truth claims involve both narration and argumentation. That way we can retain the insights of narrative theory in which truth claims reside without conflating truth claims with narration. That would dangerously blur history and fiction. Something other than narrative is required for the proof of truth claims raised in and by narration.

INTERPRETATION AND ARGUMENTATION

A critical social theory needs a strong theory of truth to be able to vindicate the claims made by historians and social scientists, to identify true from false consciousness, to provide a methodological basis for the interpretation of human actions, and to retain a meaningful distinction between reason and tradition. Ricoeur is considerably more sensitive to the epistemological concerns of the social sciences and ideology critique than other hermeneutic philosophers. Neither Heidegger nor Gadamer, for example, have much to say about basic epistemological concerns, much less the specific requirements of ideology critique. Hermeneutics fails to answer questions about the conditions that must be satisfied for an interpretation to be valid (or at least more probable than another), how conflicting interpretations are mediated, what the role of evidence is in interpretation, how are claims justified, and by what criteria. Heidegger and Gadamer instead speak of the "truth event," which is ostensibly the ground or condition of possibility of truth in the ordinary sense. The hermeneutic conception of truth as revelation or disclosure of being forms the ontological condition of truth in the sense of a theory of correspondence, coherence, or consensus. The truth or falsity of any particular assertion or state of affairs presupposes and is derivative of a truth event, which lets us see something as either true or false. It is, however, far from clear what the difference is between the meaning of the word *true* in the ordinary and hermeneutic senses. The same truth event can give rise to both true and false propositions, in which case the notion itself is at best problematic and at worst contradictory.

In contrast, Ricoeur's hermeneutics is geared equally to the interpretation of texts and actions, and as a result is more attuned to the needs of both literary criticism and the social sciences. In the 1970s he described interpretation as a movement from guess to validation and from explanation to comprehension. Interpretation consists of a guess based on experiences resulting in explanations that must be validated by others, terminating in comprehension, which is another name for understanding that is informed and enriched by an objective process of validation (INT 71–88). Although he eventually drops a number of the dichotomies of this period (sense and reference, distanciation and appropriation, explanation and understanding) in favor of the narrative reconfiguration of experience, he is committed to a model of interpretation that consists of description, explanation, argumentation, and intersubjective validation. Determining which interpretations are more plausible than others requires that we argue for our descriptions and explanations by offering relevant reasons in order to convince another of the superiority of one interpretation over another. Given the range of interpretations, often conflicting and contradictory, Ricoeur echoes Habermas, claiming that "the question of criteria belongs to a certain kind of interpretation itself, that is to say, to a coming to an agreement between arguments. So it presupposes a certain model of rationality where universality, verification, and so on are compelling."[20]

In the hermeneutics of texts of the 1970s, Ricoeur took over Dilthey's well-known distinction between explanation and understanding but he refused to treat each as a form of knowledge restricted to mutually exclusive domains of inquiry: explanation to the causal world of facts and laws, understanding to the human world of intentions and desires.[21] Instead he maintains that the opposing attitudes of explanation and understanding must be integrated into a general theory of interpretation. Explanation and understanding are two moments in a dialectical unity. The type of knowledge characteristic of the human sciences consists of objective structures and theories that must be explained, while the type of knowledge characteristic of the natural sciences is not simply objective but has a history and preunderstanding like any other interpretation. Explanation and understanding are moments in a broader theory of interpretation. Together they form the hermeneutic circle. Recalling the development of his thought at the time, Ricoeur says he believed that the nature of the text itself as a structured work is coextensive with the problem of writing and therefore required a moment of explanation to be integrated into a theory of understanding.

> The sciences of the text imposed an explanatory phase at the very heart of understanding. Here, explanation was not reduced to implementing Humean causation but contained a diversity of forms,

among these genetic explanation, explanation in terms of the underlying material, structural explanation, and explanation by optimal
convergence. On this new level, I discovered once again the mediating role already acknowledged in semiotics in the semantic analysis of
simple discourse. What was new in this had to do with the rules of
composition proper to the text. In other words, it was the very texture of texts which authorized and even required this detour through
the procedures belonging to objective analysis and to explication in
the sense of explanation and of clarification.[22]

Explanation explicates the objective moment of discourse; understanding grasps
the whole. To read is to interpret and to interpret is to understand and explain.

The process of interpretation begins with a guess because the reader has
no access to the intentions of the absent author. Once meaning is freed from the
psychology of an author, nothing can stand outside of the text as a privileged authority to mediate conflicting interpretations. The only choice we have is to
guess at a meaning and then compare and validate guesses until we decide on the
superiority or preferability of one interpretation over another. Following
Hirsch, Ricoeur offers three rules for validating guesses of the meaning of a
text.[23] First is the rule of hermeneutic holism, where the meaning of the text is
construed as a whole with a meaning greater than the meaning of its constitutive sentences. Guessing the meaning of a work is a circular process, in the sense
that the presupposition of a certain kind of whole is implied in the recognition
of the parts, and it is through the parts that we construe the whole. The rule of
hermeneutic holism is fundamental: we understand the whole in terms of the
detail and the detail in terms of the whole.

The second rule of validation is to construe a text as an individual. Although a work belongs to a genre, we can determine its individuality by pro-
gressively eliminating generic concepts to find what belongs uniquely to it. Here
Ricoeur draws on the Husserlian conception of genetic constitution for the
constitution of the text as an object. Like any object, a text can only be perceived from a particular perspective but never from all perspectives at once. Just
as objects are given to us in profiles but constituted as a whole in a synthetic act,
similarly the text is always perceived from a perspective but each view is understood to be a part of a whole. More precisely, we read sentence by sentence but
the discrete sentences lose their meaning if we lose sight of the fact that these are
sentences of an entire text, not isolated fragments. "It is always possible to relate
the same sentence in different ways to this or that other sentence considered as
the cornerstone of the text. A specific kind of one-sidedness is implied in the act

of reading" (INT 78). This one-sidedness is another name for the perspectival character of a guess. Such a limited perspective is the condition for the possibility of understanding.

The third rule of validation involves attention to the other possible meanings that could affect the meaning of text that presents a range of possible interpretations. A guess is always putative, fallible, open to further revision and interpretation, and validated against the horizon of possible meanings by showing that one interpretation is more probable than another in light of what we already know. Validation is not verification but an argumentative practice similar to juridical procedures used in legal interpretation. It follows a "logic of subjective probability" like Popper's procedures for falsifiability.[24] One can argue for the relative superiority of a conflicting interpretation by showing how one interpretation is false or invalid, or that one interpretation is more probable than another. It is always possible to argue for one interpetation over another.

> If it is true that there is always more than one way of construing a text, it is not true that all interpretations are equal. The text presents a limited field of possible constructions. The logic of validation allows us to move between the two limits of dogmatism and skepticism. It is always possible to argue for or against an interpretation, to confront interpretations, to arbitrate between them and to seek agreement even if this agreement remains beyond our immediate reach. (INT 79)

The hermeneutics of texts applies to actions as well. Like textual interpretation, the interpretation of action is a dialectic of explanation and understanding because like texts, actions are readable, with a meaning that is distanced from the intentions of the actors, and subject to conflicting interpretations. In the same way that a text become detached from its author, an action is detached from its agent and takes on a meaning of its own, often in spite of the intentions of the agent. An action may develop consequences of its own as it unfolds into a course of events that exceeds, transcends, and overcomes the conditions of its production. The meaning of an action is then open to an indefinite number of interpretations by an indefinite number of possible "readers." Ricoeur believes that if human action can be read and interpreted like written works then the methods and practices of textual interpretation can function as a paradigm for the interpretation of action in general in the field of the social sciences. For example, there is the rule of hermeneutic holism to determine what is a relevant detail in relation to the whole; there is the rule of individuation to determine what is unique to the action; and there is the rule of plurivocity to determine good guesses among a range of possible interpretations. As the model of text interpretation shows, "understanding is entirely *mediated* by the whole of explanatory procedures that precede it and accompany it" (TA 167). In both texts and actions a guess represents an initial understanding that becomes enriched when validated through argumentation and reasoned appeals. The aim of validation is to produce an explanation that confirms an initial understanding. In turn, an explanation must be comprehended or appropriated back into understanding. Interpretation terminates in comprehension, which is another name for understanding that is informed and enriched by an explanation.

Narrative theory takes up and retains the dialectic of explanation and understanding but subordinates it to the configurational operations of creating and reading stories. The aim of explanations is still to further understanding but more in the sense of following and making sense of a narrative than as a methodological explanation dialectically related to hermeneutic understanding. An explanation in a narrative is a historic explanation relative to the emplotment that gives the entire history coherence and unity. It functions as a part of a whole geared toward helping the reader follow and understand the story. The revised model of the dialectic of historic explanation and narrative understanding is a continuation but improvement on the legacy Ricoeur inherited from Dilthey. More recently, Ricoeur has developed his claim that validating interpretations is like legal deliberation by proposing a new model of the hermeneutic circle as a dialectic of interpretation and argumentation. Like the dialectic of explanation and understanding (or its equivalent, guess and validation) interpretation and argumentation complete one another. Interpretation presupposes the anticipation of consensus of universally binding reasons, whereas argumentation presupposes an interpretative framework that delimits a context of relevant facts to be subject to justification.

Following Dworkin, Ricoeur says that the parallels between legal interpretation and literary interpretation are striking.[25] Dworkin's analysis centers on the "hard cases" of judicial practice where a judge must make a decision in the absence of a clear precedent. He identifies three theses that form the core of a positivist theory of law in order to show how the law is in fact irreducibly interpretative: (1) To the claim that in a hard case it is ultimately the judge who proclaims the law (thereby identifying its "pedigree" the way the intention of a legislator determines the nature of a law), Dworkin asserts that legal interpretation is like textual interpretation in which the meaning is never found in the intentions of the author. The meaning of a law is similarly not found not in the intentions of the judge or the will of the legislator. (2) To the claim that the

law governs unequivocal dispositions, he contrasts the open-ended character of
the law, which like a text is always open to plural readings. (3) To the claim that
the judge holds discretionary powers in the absence of the law, he argues that the
very notion of discretion suggests that the decision is somehow outside of or beyond the law. If a decision is beyond the law then it is arbitrary; if it is not then
it must retain a legislative claim by virtue of its relation to the law. The judge's
decision can only count as judicial in any meaningful sense of the term if it
draws on precedent. The problem for Dworkin is "how to justify the idea that
there is always a valid response, without falling into the arbitrary or into the
judge's claim to make himself a legislator?" (J 112). The answer is found in a
narrative model of literary interpretation.

The parallel disjunction in literary theory between the meaning of a text
and author's intentions in legal theory is between the meaning of a law and the
judicial discretion that legal positivism identifies as the source of the law. Literary theory dispenses with authorial intention in favor of reconstructing meanings in texts based on hermeneutic rules of holism. An interpretation of
particular passages should "fit" with an interpretation of the whole. The task is
to find an acceptable and defensible interpretation through the use of literary
evidence by evoking ideas of narrative coherence, intelligibility, acceptability,
and other interpretive practices that would make one reading more plausible
than another. The search for an interpretive fit in literature is guided by an anticipation of narrative coherence conjoined by an understanding of preceding
chapters. Similarly a legal interpretation is guided by the use of precedents and
past judgments conjoined with the "anticipated profile of the juridical enterprise
considered in terms of its historicity" (J 112). Legal interpretations search for a
fit based on the precedents of the past and the aim of the judicial enterprise as a
whole within a legal history that constitutes its interpretive framework.

Both literary and legal interpretations are rational, argumentative practices
that avoid the false dichotomy of the demonstrable and the arbitrary. Dworkin
unfortunately takes over this false dichotomy within legal positivism by assuming, when there is "no answer" to a hard case, that a judicial decision is either a
demonstrable application of a law or an arbitrary act by judge. Even though he
models judicial interpretation on textual interpretation to free the law from its
univocity and decisionism (or pedigree as he calls it), he fails to recognize the
implicit appeal interpretation makes to argumentation. He comes close when he
distinguishes between the law as an established system of "rules" and "principles" as an ethical-political normative force—between the spirit and the letter of
the law—rightfully noting that principles, not rules, resolve the hard cases, and
that principles must be interpreted if they are to apply to particular cases. We

must interpret a principle to show how it "counts in favor of" this or that solution, or how it "weighs" in this or that direction. But the notion of narrative coherence he offers is a rather weak criterion of a valid interpretation. Coherence in interpretation is necessary for legal judgment but not sufficient. One must offer compelling and relevant reasons for preferring one interpretation over another—especially if two interpretations are equally coherent. Ricoeur believes Dworkin's distinction between rules and principles prevents him from recognizing how a hermeneutic theory fits with a theory of argumentation. He fails to consider than the positivist conception of univocal, demonstrable rules is a caricature of universally binding argumentation.

On the other hand, theorists like Alexy and Habermas focus less on interpretation than juridical argumentation, considered as subordinate to a general theory of practical argumentation.[26] Juridical argumentation is a subset of a discourse geared toward the justification of the norms that govern the claims we make to correctness or rightness, through an exchange of arguments, in the sense of reasons aimed at mutual understanding and agreement. The claim to correctness is defined by a criterion of universality. A good argument for the correctness of an action is one that will be understood and accepted by all parties concerned. Ricoeur agrees with Habermas that the "thesis of a potential agreement at the level of an unlimited and unconstrained community" forms the horizon of universal consensus before which "we are to place the formal rules of every discussion claiming correctness" (J 117). Reaching agreement over normative claims presupposes both the anticipation of unlimited communication and a minimal set of rules of discourse, where the meanings of "discourse" and "argument" overlap. These rules govern the practice of discourse, giving everyone the right to participate, free from coercion or interruption; they govern the continuation of discourse, requiring that one offer reasons to explain propositions or for wanting to change the subject; and they govern what is at issue in discussion, requiring that everyone accept the validity of a norm if, as Habermas says, all affected can accept the consequences and side effects its general observance can be anticipated to have for the satisfaction of everyone's interests.

Practical argumentation is both formal and universal, substantial and particular. It is formal because it specifies the conditions under which participants reach agreement over potentially universally binding normative claims; it is substantial because a valid norm satisfies the shared expectation that the needs, interests, and desires of the participants in discussion will be met. Assuming people know their own interests, an acceptable norm embodies a general interest that is acceptable by everyone. Norms coordinate needs, interests, desires, and actions by constraining them and establishing legitimate expectations of their satisfaction.

Rational argumentation presupposes that participants are able to reflect on and interpret their own needs and interests before entering into discussion with other. As participants discuss them with each other, they learn which needs and interests are generalizable. Discourse involves taking the perspective of others to imagine what it would be like for others since valid norms must be acceptable to everyone, as a shared expectation that would resolve conflicts of interests. Argumentation is therefore inseparable from the interpretation of needs and interests. Participants must commit themselves to a universal perspective that anyone could adopt as they, at the same time, interpret their own needs, take an interest in each other's interests to discover which needs are generalizable in order to develop a shared understanding over what we may legitimately expect from one another. Need interpretations and rule-governed discussion go hand in hand.

> The notion of an ideal discourse situation offers a horizon of correctness for all discourse where the participants seek to convince each other through argument. The ideal is not just anticipated, it is already at work. But we must also emphasize that the formal can be inserted into the course of a discussion only if it is articulated on the basis of already public expressions of interests, hence of needs marked by prevailing interpretations concerning their legitimacy. (J 119)

Juridical argumentation is a species of practical argumentation subject to limits that are particular to legal deliberation. For example, it takes place in the particular institutional setting of courts, in the presence of lawyers; a trial limits who may speak, for how long, under specific constraints of procedural rules; the participants are not always there voluntarily; and the deliberation aims at producing a judgment, not agreement and consensus. The normative force of juridical discourse comes from the use of reasons that would motivate the participants to accept or reject the case. When a judge and jury rule on a case they implicitly adhere to the principles of normative discourse, aiming at correctness, by arguing rationally. Other than the specific constrainsts of legal discourse, its normative force is no different from that of practical discourse in general.

But like any discourse, legal argumentation is interpretive. The application of a norm or precedent to a particular case—a hallmark of legal argumentation—is a thoroughly interpretive act. One must first interpret the facts and then interpret the norm so that there is a "fit" in the way Dworkin means when he describes the application of a general rule to a particular situation. A complex process of mutual adjustment and revision between interpreted facts and norms is required to say that an act is criminal because it "falls under" such and such a precedent. An interpretation of facts takes the form of a story that recounts what happened by picking out, selecting, and highlighting some features and events over others to show how a connection of events places the case under a rule. To "relate" means not only to narrate and recount but also to connect and associate. What counts as a "case" is an interpretation of what happened; someone tells what happened by recounting events to construct a coherent story. In addition, the act of establishing a relation between a case and a law is also a narrative-interpretation that finds affinity between them, matching them in the mutual adjustment of interpreting facts and interpreting laws.

Interpretation, however, also employs a rule of universalization. We presuppose when we subsume facts to norms that any relevantly similar facts could also be subsumed to the norm. If a belongs to b and a equals c then c also belongs to b. But any, however minimal, principle of universalization that treats similar cases similarly presupposes a prior interpretation that would place a particular case under a general rule. What is it that makes two cases similar? Which similarities and differences are relevant? Even determining what counts as a fact is a highly interpretive act. There is no such thing as a brute fact that would count as evidence in a case. An action only becomes evidence when interpreted, that is, when configured into a narrative that confers meaning by describing and evaluating in a certain way.

> Universalization, then, only provides a check on the process of mutual adjustment between the interpreted norm and the interpreted fact. In this sense, interpretation is not external to argumentation. It constitutes its *organon*. (J 122)

Interpretation and argumentation overlap. Interpretation requires argumentation to redeem its validity claims to truth and normativity given the insuffiency in a model of narrative coherence. Argumentation requires interpretation to determine what counts as a fact and how a case is placed under a rule. Interpretation and argumentation are dialectically related in a way analogous to understanding and explanation. Just as we explain more to understand better, we argue more to interpret better. Argumentation constitutes the "logical framework" and interpretation the "inventive framework" (J 153).

Although Ricoeur's model of interpretation-argumentation concerns legal deliberation, it can be employed as a model of social understanding in general. Truth claims raised about human actions are interpretations, configured into narratives, open to rational argumentation. Truth on this model involves interpretation, narration, and argumentation. Unlike the hermeneutic philosophies of Heidegger and Gadamer, Ricoeur's theory of truth entails the argumentative vindication of claims under the presupposition of unconstrained communication. But unlike the universal pragmatics of Habermas, Ricoeur's theory of truth presupposes not only the prior interpretation of the subject of discussion within a broader, interpretive context but also the prior experiences participants bring to discussion. It includes the very descriptive, narrative, testimonial experiences that a consensus theory of truth forbids.[27] Apel argues that a transcendental-pragmatic theory of truth cannot help but take recourse into evidential experience.

> Evidence of perceptual judgment . . . belong to the very procedure of consensus-formation . . . to understand the evidence of perceptual judgments as good reasons for the reporter's accepting them and hence as criteria of possible truth to be discursively mediated with other criteria.[28]

Ricoeur and Apel have a similar conception of truth as both evidential and communicative.[29] Ricoeur's unique contribution to the problem of truth in the social sciences is the narrative dimension internal interpretation and argumentation essential for constructing a case history of the subject matter, determining what counts as evidence and how it is relevant, and for providing the *organon* for argumentation.

CHAPTER 3

SELFHOOD

Ricoeur's works can be described as a philosophical anthropology of human action. From his first major work, *Freedom and Nature*, where the subject is human freedom, to his last major work, *Oneself as Another*, where the subject is human acting and suffering, Ricoeur maintains an interest in the meaning of human agency. Although the philosophical methodology ranges considerably from his early to recent works, from a phenomenology of the will, to a semantics of actions, to a narrative-hermeneutics of the self, what remains constant is a conviction that to be human is to be embodied, free, rational, creative, moral, and finite. A philosophical anthropology thus connects his early philosophy of the will with his later reflections on selfhood, ethics, and politics. This is a connection, by the way, Ricoeur himself has made, as have many readers and commentators.[1] The importance of his notion of selfhood for critical theory, however, is less well known. The question is what kind of being is the self that it may be subject to ideological colonization yet capable of resistance. The subject of critical theory should be a social, political, and moral subject capable of reflection, communication, and collective action. This chapter highlights three themes in Ricoeur's philosophical anthropology. First, is the phenomenology of the "lived body" developed in *Freedom and Nature*. Second, are the analyses of speaking, acting, and narrating (in *Oneself as Another*) as activities constitutive of personal identity. Third, is the dialectic of self and other in its ontological and political forms. The notion of selfhood I wish to develop emphasizes embodiment, agency, conscience, and the inextricable relationship of self and other.

FREEDOM AND NATURE

In *Freedom and Nature*, Ricoeur employs the Husserlian method of eidetic analysis to the spheres of the will and voluntary action while avoiding "the famous and obscure transcendental reduction," which he considers "an obstacle to genuine understanding of the personal body" (FN 4). The goal is to describe the structures of the will to uncover our fundamental possibilities of existence through an eidetic, descriptive but not a transcendental version of phenomenology. For Husserl, willing and acting, or what in *Ideas I* he calls the "affective and volitive subjective processes," are no different than any other problem of phenomenological constitution.[2] One should be able to describe different acts of consciousness to show their different meanings, if their intentional correlates have different significations. Correlative to my wish, my regret, and my desire is what I wish for, what I regret, and what I desire. A noetic–noematic analysis shows that even the practical functions of consciousness can easily be described, identified, and reidentified as the same. Willing and acting are meaningful only when seen as representations that are constituted by and in consciousness like any other perceptual object. The task is to constitute phenomenological objects or the ideal contents capable of fulfilling different acts of consciousness appropriate to willful action—that is how we know the difference between a wish, a regret, and a desire, and how we can identify and reidentify them as the same or different phenomena.

The problem with Husserl's phenomenology of action, according to Ricoeur, is that he makes it seem as if my act of willing is something that I observe, not something I participate in. Granted my wish, regret, and desire have ideal contents that can be identified and reidentified as the same, yet each is also an action that engages me. I partake in my actions more than I observe myself acting. It is not that a phenomenology of action is impossible, or unfruitful. On the contrary, a description that articulates the various intermingled intentionalities to distinguish the various forms of consciousness is a valid form of intentional analysis. However, a phenomenology of action reveals the full extent to which consciousness is embodied and tied to involuntary bodily functions, not detached and disconnected as Husserlian reflection makes it seem. By describing both the subjective and objective "sides" of such intentions as willing, choosing, and desiring, Ricoeur finds that movement, action, and the involuntary contribute to the meaning of my conscious acts in a way that remains hidden from a phenomenology of perception. There is a fundamental reciprocity of voluntary decision, choice, and action with involuntary bodily functions that are the vehicle for the will. A close analysis of action "reveals an 'I can' at the heart of the 'I think.'"[3] Consciousness should not be defined by thought or reflection but by the ability to choose and decide. Consciousness is more practical than representational.

In *Freedom and Nature*, Ricoeur shows how the act of willing is both the realization of freedom and the reception of necessity. We understand ourselves based on our ability to say, "I will." In turn, willing presupposes the involuntary that enables and limits it. Willing has three moments, each inextricably related to involuntary bodily processes. The three parts are: (1) I decide, (2) I move my body, and (3) I consent. Each part has an object, or intentional correlate: (A) the decision or project, (B) the action or motion, and (C) the acquiescence or consent. Finally, each correlate is itself related to the different modes of the involuntary: (a) motives, needs, values, (b) skills, emotions, habits, and (c) character, unconscious, life. The voluntary and involuntary is a subtle dialectic of activity and passivity.

The first moment of the cycle of willing is a decision or project that is the intentional correlate of my will. Willing projects and decides the direction of an action to be done by me that is within my capabilities. To decide is to anticipate the future based on my capability or power to execute that action. A phenomenology of voluntary action shows that the realization of a decision is the fulfillment of a project or an intention-to-do something that is within my power. Ricoeur retains Husserl's conception of the fulfillment of intentionality but applies it to practical consciousness. The intentionality of a project is a thought, but only the execution of a decision fulfills the intentionality of the project. An action fulfills a decision somewhat like a perception fulfills an empty theoretical intention. "A projected willing is an incomplete willing: it is not put to the test and it is not verified. . . . The man who does not carry through did not truly will" (FN 201).

To will is to choose and to choose is to fix one's attention on something to be done by me. Attention is the act of focusing on and taking note of an aspect of experience within the flow of consciousness by accentuating, focusing, and bringing out that aspect with special clarity. To pay attention to something is to modify our mental processes in such a way that renders a certain aspect of it explicit—seizing, noticing, and heeding something. The visual characterization of attention is somewhat misleading since I can make any object of consciousness more or less explicit and clear if I pay attention to it. For example, I can pay attention to anything that is detectable, including a sight, sound, touch, smell, taste, mood, feeling, prejudice, tendency, omission, or absence. I can make any object of consciousness stand out from its background to become accentuated and more clear. Attention inaugurates voluntary action by focusing and narrowing the range of possible things I could do. Most of the time attention shifts in and out of focus involuntarily, although I have control of my attention when I decide and choose something.

In every moment of choice and decision, the will opens possibilities it is capable of fulfilling. But it may also create doubt and indecision. Hesitation is an attempt at choosing but it is an as yet unfulfilled intention. Hesitation marks the opening of possibility, attention marks the fixing of possibility, and choice marks the closing of possibility. The resolution of attention is the initiation of the project that occurs when I make up my mind and determine myself to do something that I am capable of. I project myself, involve myself, determine myself, and designate myself in the action to be done. All choice has this implicit history that could be explicated, although most choices happen in an instant.

The involuntary correlate of my decision or choice include motives, needs, and values. A motive is like an impulse, or a drive that inclines the will toward its project. In turn, every motive is a motive for a decision. It is a reason-for-acting that grounds, justifies, and legitimates an action. I decide *in order to* as well as *because of*. Needs, desires, and values are similar to motives in that they also incline us and compel us to act, but in a more precise sense they only "lend themselves" to motivation in the form of an impulse to acquire something lacking, or a desire for something. They incline the will toward some perceived good, or value, in the sense of something that would be good-for-me. The most basic source of motives, needs, desires, and "organic values" is the body. "The circular relation of motive to project demands that I recognize my body as body-for-my-willing, and my willing as project-based-(in part)-on my body. The body is *for* the will and the will is *by reason* of the body" (FN 85).

The second cycle of the will is action, which involves the body as the organ of movement. Decision entails action and becomes complete by it. To decide is to intend emptily; to act is to fulfill that intention. What is to be done by me is the "pragma," the intentional correlate of the will at the level of action. Acting is a "practical intentionality" oriented toward fulfilling a project. It is a power to produce and affect change in the world, and is, therefore, intentionally related to objects in the world. Practical intentionality is "the counterpart of the intuition which fulfills a theoretical intention, it is the action which fulfills the project" (FN 208).

The primary vehicle for my voluntary actions is my body. Included among the involuntary correlates of action are skills, emotions, and habits, all of which are used by the will in order to achieve its projects. Skills are the basic ability we have to control our bodies. They are like the instinctive actions that are acquired very early in life, like when a baby figures out how to move its body, how to touch things, and even how to see. Skills are not reflexes; they can be learned and shaped by the voluntary. They are what learning and habits are built on. "Skill is the source of all the bodily aptitudes which alone give substance to the will and allow freedom to inscribe itself into the world" (FN 244). Another related embodied intentional correlate to action are one's emotions. They too are organs of the will. An emotion is an involuntary dimension of action, meaningful only in relation to a will. The basic emotions are modes of our being, which include wonder, affective anticipation, joy, sorrow, desire, shock, and passion.

A habit, on the other hand, changes and modifies our intentions like an emotion but is acquired in a way that skills and emotions are not. A habit is a learned, developed, acquired pattern or set of skills that become an ingrained, spontaneous capacity. Sometimes I can acquire a habit deliberately by disciplining myself and practicing. Other times a habit can develop unnoticed over time, evolving without my attention. In each case a habit always has an origin. What was initially conscious and possibly deliberate gradually becomes habitual and invisible. In addition, knowledge, no less than action, can also be habitual. We speak of a "force of habit," to mean an involuntary tendency that compels us to think and act. It is like a second nature, not in the sense of a reflex or instinctual action but as a know-how, or a capacity to do something. It is a kind of spontaneous power that becomes assimilated into my activity, affecting and determining new activities. A habitual act is usually carried out inattentively; the spontaneity and familiarity of it makes it difficult to notice. "What once was analyzed, thought, and willed drifts bit by bit into the realm of that which I have never known or willed. . . . Thus we need not say that in habit *consciousness* is abolished: only *reflexive* knowing and willing are" (FN 285–286). Habits are usually the organ of a voluntary intention but can be made explicit as the object of a voluntary intention depending on how I focus my attention.

The final stage of willing terminates in consent. After I decide and act I must consent or acquiesce to my act of willing. Here willing confronts the absolutely involuntary, my character type, my unconscious, and my life as a biological organism that is born and dies. These form the very situation of my will. They must be accepted in order to act.[4] My character or temperament is what I am as something I cannot change. It determines how I act, perhaps the style of my action. Similarly, my unconscious marks off limits to conscious reflection. It remains hidden and often deceives me while it influences my actions. Finally, life itself is what incarnates my existence. I can realize my freedom precisely because I am incarnated in a body with a *telos* of its own, that was born without my assent and will die in spite of my wishes. The life that I inherited from my parents and ancestors constitutes the condition from which I can freely choose and act. Thus human freedom is found in the act of willing that unites decision, action, and consent. My incarnation both limits and enables me. "Human freedom is a dependent independence, a receptive initiative."[5]

Ricoeur's phenomenology of the will is remarkable for a number of reasons, two of which concern us here. First, is the way he retains the doctrine of intentionality even at the level of action, extending phenomenology "in the course of the blood stream."[6] It is not unlike his mediation of phenomenology and hermeneutics where he goes against the grain of some of the more popular interpretations of Heidegger and Gadamer by recovering the essentially phenomenological character of experience. It is fashionable today to read Heidegger as a kind of pragmatist whose interpretation of phenomenology displaces the epistemological problem onto a more primordial and practical relationship of being-in-the-world.[7] According to this reading, intentionality is derivative of a more fundamental kind of experience in which we are not consciously aware of ourselves as perceiving and experiencing. Instead we are always already engaged in the world without having to think about it. Intentionality, reflective thought, and, therefore, phenomenology occur only when something interrupts our habitual activities.

This reading of Heidegger almost makes it seem as if we do not perceive the world as we experience it; we only perceive the world when something interrupts habitual experience. It makes it seem as if the only kind of intentionality is a consciousness that is directed toward itself, aware of itself as perceiving. This reading mistakenly turns all intentional consciousness into explicit self-conscious experience when the doctrine of intentionality simply states that all consciousness is correlated with an object. The object can be anything, from an ideal, mathematical entity, to the nail that I am hammering. Consciousness and reflective consciousness have different intentional correlates. The difference between phenomenology and hermeneutics has little to do with reflective or unreflective experience. The important differences have to do with the displacement of meaning away from a self-founding act of consciousness onto language and writing, both of which have meaning apart from the intentions of the subject. The issue is centered on the constitution of meaning, not on the difference between practical activity and theoretical consciousness. Ricoeur's phenomenology of willing shows how thinking and acting are far from inimical but dialectically related. A habit retains its intentional correlate like any other mode of consciousness. It too is a kind of experience.

Second, is the importance of the imagination in action. Ricoeur shows how the imagination has a "projective function" that is a part of the very "dynamism of acting." "Without imagination," he says, "there is no action" (TA 177). Following the structure of voluntary action from *Freedom and Nature*, we find that imagination operates at the level of my projects—that is, my motivation and power to act. First, in my project or pragma, the thing to be done by me, I imagine and try out different possible courses of action. Both the imagination and my projects are oriented toward the future, opening possible ways of being.

I test, or "try out" options at this stage. At the level of motivation, the imagination is involved in figuring out all of the different possible elements that contribute to our motives and desires. Imagination creates a realm for comparison and evaluation of the various elements that act as motivating forces. It is what Ricoeur elsewhere calls the "realm of the as-if." This form of the imagination lets us explore options, conduct thought experiments, and figure out what would happen if I were to do something. The imagination contributes to moral judgments, helping me distinguish between good and bad motivations, and, hence good and bad reasons for acting. Finally, at the level of initiative as my power to act, the imagination mediates my self-estimation of what I am capable of. I can only determine what I could do by imaginative variations of what I can do. I impute my own power to act by depicting to myself imaginative variations of what I can do, what I could do, and what I could have done. Ricoeur explains that "I take possession of the immediate certainty of my power only through the imaginative variations that mediate this certainty" (TA 177). The imagination thus figures into the determination of my projects, my motives, and my capabilities, helping me understand what I am to do, why am I doing it, and what I can do.

The mediation of action by the imagination is important for two reasons. First, it links individual with social action by bridging the realms of discourse and action. The key is the tie between imagination and semantic innovation. As Ricoeur shows in his theories of metaphor and narrative, figurative uses of language have the ability to create new meanings in a way that literal uses of language cannot. Metaphors consist of unusual predications referring to a second order of meaning; narratives schematize experience into a new, coherent configuration. They are "imaginative practices" that cross over the realms of discourse and action. Second, the imagination either may be projected into individual action, or it may constitute the field of social action itself as the cultural imagination. If ideology and utopia are among the imaginative practices functioning as an interpretive grid, or imaginative schematism, organizing and codifying social action, then they also enter into individual and group actions, shaping and patterning who we are, what we are capable of doing, and how we understand. Ideology and utopia are embodied, operating at the level of motivation and desire—or what Foucault calls "bio-power" and Deleuze and Guattari call "micro-politics."[8] If Ricoeur first took phenomenology "into the bloodstream" he has now given us a vocabulary to take a critique of ideology into the bloodstream, as well.

For example, given the relationship between the imagination understood in terms of projects, motivation, and initiative, ideology must also figure into my voluntary actions, resulting in ideological actions. Each moment of voluntary action, including decisions, choices, attention, desires, needs, values, and habits are also mediated by ideology, as well as utopia and other configurations of the cultural imagination. Every aspect of meaningful action that can be identified and described may be affected by it. It could affect our senses, including sound, touch, smell, and taste. It could affect our attention, both in terms of what we notice and do not notice—or how we notice things. It could affect our decisions and choices as well, if the resolution of attention is the initiation of the project. We should also be able to speak of ideological motives, inclinations, moods, pleasures, and movement. If the cultural imagination indeed affects us at the level of our embodied voluntary action it could gradually become ingrained into an almost involuntary manner of being-in-the-world as body language. A rather productive dialogue could be opened at this point between Ricoeur's notion of ideological action and Marcuse's notion of false needs.[9] The advantage of Ricoeur's model of embodied imagination is that it shows how we can read the effects of ideology and utopia on several interrelated aspects of voluntary and involuntary action. My embodied being-in-the-world is the subject of both colonization and liberation.

SPEAKING AND ACTING

Just as Ricoeur's hermeneutic philosophy underwent a radical transformation from the 1950s to the 1980s, so did his conception of action and agency. In *Freedom and Nature* the meaning of the will is related only to the motives, goals, and volitional activity of a subject; in *Time and Narrative* the meaning of an action is related to a whole conceptual network or semantics of action. The most important difference between his early phenomenology of the will and his later semantics of action is that the will is defined in terms of an intention or project, which can be solitary, whereas an action is defined by its accomplishments and its intervention in public events and other public manifestations. "Action implies interaction and insertion in institutions and relations of cooperation and competition. In this sense, action expresses more than will."[10] Actions are textlike things that can be read and interpreted like written works, whereas agents are understood *in relation to* texts and other discursive formations and social practices that mediate the self. Or in the language of narrative theory, an action receives its intelligibility in relation to a narrative configuration, whereas agents are understood in terms of the mimetic activity of a narrative. The change over from early to late Ricoeur is in the increasing mediation of texts and narratives into the meaning of actions and agents.

But what remains constant throughout Ricoeur's career is his Kantian conviction that persons are ends in themselves, not mere means. It is necessary to distinguish between persons as agents from objects for the sake of moral and political deliberation. How else could we hold people accountable for their actions if we didn't have some notion of agency to which we attribute responsibility? Early in his career he evokes the distinction between voluntary and involuntary, later, in *Freud and Philosophy*, between motive and cause, and more recently between self-identity and sameness-identity. In each case, Ricoeur shows how we can simultaneously belong to two worlds, one of persons, one of objects, without either succumbing to an ontological dualism or reducing one to the other. Selfhood is a complicated matter. We are many things. We need at very least the Kantian distinction between what we are and are not if we are to appreciate not only the richness and depth of selfhood but also the complexity of human relationships.

In *Oneself as Another* Ricoeur approaches the self through four realms of philosophy corresponding to four questions: Who is speaking? (philosophy of language), Who is acting? (philosophy of action), Who is telling a story? (narrative theory), and Who is responsible? (moral philosophy). The many different ways of posing the question of selfhood suggest that there is no single, unitary conception of the self but multiple aspects of selfhood that are illuminated by posing different questions. One of the tasks of *Oneself as Another* is to shatter the illusion of the immediacy of the cogito that was meant to establish an ultimate foundation of knowledge. Another task is to shatter the illusion of the death of the subject and the subsequent deconstruction of the problem of any foundation of knowledge. The self is neither a Nietzschean-postmodern illusion, a Kantian limit, nor a Hegelian synthesis, but a narratively constituted "analogical unity" that is a socially responsible agent, capable of speaking, understanding, initiating, and suffering actions. Ricoeur shows how we can conceive of a self that is neither an ultimate foundation nor a fragmented illusion but a "capable person" who is able to speak, act, recount oneself, and act responsibly.

Three philosophical theses comprise the hermeneutics of the self in *Oneself as Another*: first is the primacy of reflection over the immediate positing of the subject; second is the distinction between two meanings of "identity," *idem*-identity as sameness, and *ipse*-identity as self-identity; third is the dialectic of self and the other-than-self within *ipse*-identity. I will very briefly sketch the argument of the first three questions—Who is speaking?, Who is acting?, and Who is telling a story?—in order to arrive at a fuller sense of the embodied self in Ricoeur's recent thought. We will return to the fourth question (Who is responsible?) in the following chapter.

Ricoeur starts *Oneself as Another* with a set of readings of analytic philosophy of language. In order to understand the self, he argues, we should understand the language we use to reflect on and talk about it. He starts with a semantic theory of language that offers the thinnest notion of what a person is to show that it is necessary in order to understand a more enriched conception of selfhood. According to Strawson's conception of "identification," to identify something is to designate to others one among many of the same type of which we speak and refer (OA 35). A person is simply an individual thing among other objects and bodies in the world we can distinguish and designate by means of identifying reference. The linguistic operator common to all languages that allows us to designate individuals is called "individualization." It picks out and designates particulars and individuals by means of individualizing operators like definite descriptions (the president of the country), proper names (Paul Ricoeur), and indicators such as "I," "you," "this," "that," "here," "there," and "now." To designate one and only one individual is the function of individualizing operators.

"Basic particulars" are the privileged particulars to which all entities that can be identified must refer. There are two kinds of basic particulars: persons and physical bodies. Because all basic particulars exist in a single spatiotemporal schema, the advantage of conceiving of persons in terms of identifying reference is that we can identify the self exclusively in terms of a public, shared reference. No hidden, nonpublic mental entities need to be posited in order to conceive of the self if selfhood is defined by means of identifying reference. Mental events are disqualified as candidates for basic particulars because they are private entities. Rather, consciousness and mental events are attributed to individuals but only as properties that are attributed to someone in the third person. Mental events are formed by psychic predicates ascribable to "someone," "each one," and "anyone else."

Ricoeur contends, however, that difficulties arise if we only conceive of a person as an objective body among other bodies situated in a single spatiotemporal schema. In what sense is the body mine? In what sense are my experiences my own? My experiences and my self are different from predicates attributed to someone. Experience has the quality of mineness. "My experiences" are not the same as "someone's experiences," and "your experiences" are not the same as "someone else's experiences." How can we ascribe a state of consciousness to oneself and to another if I *feel* the experiences I ascribe to myself but I *observe* the experiences I ascribe to someone else? The problem is that eliminating mental events as basic particulars conceals the question of the self as does the attempt to conceive of the self as only a thing that serves as a term in an identifying reference. A mental event is both a predicate ascribed to an entity and an irreducibly personal experience that can be designated from the perspective of the first person. It is impossible to designate an individual as a basic particular in terms of identifying reference alone without reference to the ability of speakers to designate themselves in dialogue. "The problem is to understand how the self can be at the same time a person of whom we speak and a subject who designates herself in the first person while addressing a second person" (OA 35).

Ricoeur retains three elements of the thin conception of the person that serves as the object of identifying reference: first, the notion of the person is determined by the predicates we ascribe; second, both physical and psychic predicates may be ascribed to the same thing; third, psychic predicates retain their sense when ascribed to different logical subjects. The advantage of such a conception of identifying reference is that anything that I can ascribe to myself I can also ascribe to anyone else. If a person is only a basic particular with predicates attributable to her then there are no meaningful differences between me and you. The problem is that a strictly referential analysis can only avoid the pronouns "I" and "you" for so long. We have to distinguish between ascribed predicates that are experienced and observed, as well as the difference between "me" and "you," "each one" and "anyone else." "We have to acquire the idea of reflexivity and otherness in order to pass from a weak sense of correlation between someone and someone else, to a strong correlation between belonging to the self, in the sense of mine, and belonging to another, in the sense of yours" (OA 39). Selfhood is better understood from the perspective of the speaker who designates him- or herself in speaking rather than as the basic particular that is the identifying reference of an individual entity.

Ricoeur next takes up the problem of the self from the perspective of the speech pragmatics of Austin and Searle. The shift away from semantics of the statement to a pragmatics of the utterance emphasizes the dialogical situation in which speakers address one another, and, at the same time, designate themselves reflexively. Speech act theory designates the speaking subject in the following way. When I utter a performative, I accomplish the very thing stated. I actually promise when I say, "I promise"; I actually bet when I say, "I bet." An utterance is a performative only when expressed by verbs in the first-person, singular, present indicative. To say "he promises" is a constative, not a performative. The speaker actually performs in performative speech acts; it is an action by which speakers do by saying that designates the self-reflexively as speakers do things with words. In addition, speech act theory also designates the second person, or the listener, to whom an utterance is addressed. Illocution is interlocution. For example, there is no logical difference between saying "I affirm that . . ." and "I affirm to you that . . ." The only difference is that the latter emphasizes the interlocutionary dimension of speech, which involves a reciprocity of intentions—I assume that you recognize my intention to promise, bet, order, or warn when I promise you, bet you, order you, or warn you. When dialogue partners understand what each other mean when they speak, they also understand the intentions of each other.

This reciprocity of intentions marks the contribution of speech act theory to the question of selfhood and its relation to others. Both self and other are imputed in the utterance of a speech act, which is uttered in the first person and addressed to another in the second person. Because a performative utterance is expressed by verbs in the first-person, singular, present indicative, the "I" is the privileged shifter that cannot be substituted for the referent of a statement in the third person. In other words, "I" does not equal "any person who in speaking designates himself." "I am happy" is not the same as "the person who designates himself in speaking is happy." The "I" of speech acts is not the same as the basic particular that is identified referentially. But if the approach of identifying reference privileges the third person, speech act theory not only privileges the first and second person but excludes the third person. It is here that pragmatics runs into a paradox. On one hand, "I" is a shifter, applying to anyone who in speaking designates himself; on the other hand, "I" is an anchor, in that it is not substitutable, but fixes the self-referential character of discourse.

To resolve the paradox Ricoeur suggests we unite the paths of identifying reference and the reflexivity of the utterance. For speech semantics, a person is a basic particular, to which physical and mental predicates are attributed; for speech pragmatics, the subject of an utterance is a speaker, addressing an interlocutor, in the first person. I am both the subject of utterance and the person referred to as a basic particular. To show how a person is at the same time the object of identifying reference and the subject of an utterance, Ricoeur draws on his analysis of the fictionalization of history from *Time and Narrative* in which the "dated now" appears through the narrative mediation of lived time and objective time. The deictic "now" connects phenomenological time with cosmological time by means of calendars, clocks, and watches that join together astronomical time that is tied to the rotation of the planet, with public, datable time. With a calendar comes the practice of assigning significant events with dates, thereby marking human time on cosmic time. The dated now is the complete sense of the deictic now; without a date, the deictic now is completely self-referential and fleeting. Similarly the deictic "here" and "there" function like dating in relation to a system of objective coordinates in terms of which I can situate myself. "Here," "there," and "now" are at the same time shifters with a meaning relative to the utterer, and objective, public locations and times related to shared, public criteria.

The performative utterance of "naming" connects the person as object of identifying reference and the subject as author of an utterance. Naming inscribes the meaning of the shifter "I" for a particular person. With a name I am the same person who designates himself reflexively as is the subject of attribution to which others can ascribe subjective and objective predicates. "I" and "David Kaplan" mean the same person. Ricoeur notes that a birth certificate literally inscribes a person temporally, spatially, and publicly in accordance with the conventional rules of naming. "A birth certificate contains a triple inscription; a proper name conforming to the rules of naming; a birthplace conforming to the rules of localization in public space, the whole inscribed in public records" (OA 54). The act of naming reconciles the object of reference with the subject of speech. I am, at the same time, a basic particular as a body that is not only the object of identifying reference and the subject of reflection. My embodied self is irreducibly my own but also an object in the world. Philosophy of language leads us back to the problem of Husserl's Fifth Cartesian Meditation.[11]

Philosophy of action reveals additional aspects of embodied existence that remain hidden to semantics and pragmatics. The answer to the question, who is acting, is a subject to whom actions may be ascribed. Approaching action in this way by asking *who* illuminates the internal connection between agents and actions. If we could not ascribe actions to agents it is doubtful there could be anything resembling a social order; there would be no sure way to tell who did what; there would be no sure way to tell people apart; we could not hold individuals responsible for their actions. Who we are as individuals is tied to what we do, and how we do it. In addition, if we could not ascribe actions to agents in the sense of attribution or imputation, there would be no way to hold people accountable to assign both praise and blame. Without a notion of responsibility in both the moral and nonmoral senses there would be no way to determine who should be rewarded, punished, and treated as they deserve; there would be no rules, no laws, and no morality, to name just some among many problems.

Ricoeur's argument connecting actions and agents is typically dialectical. He reads analytic philosophy of action to show that it is impossible to define a human action apart from an agent. The argument for an agentless semantics of action assumes that the answer to *why* an action was done is also the answer to *what* an action is.[12] In order to determine what counts as an action, one seeks in the explanation for the action the criterion for what an action is. The answer to the question *why* is a reason, or intention, defined in opposition to causal events.[13] But Ricoeur contends that the distinction between a motive and a cause is far from obligatory, as is the requirement that all explanations must be causal. The fact that the question "why did you do that?" can also be asked as "what caused you to do that?" does not mean that the only acceptable answer is a causal explanation. One could answer that it was an impulsive action or a drive, an enduring character or personality trait, or a circumstance that affected me but not necessarily everyone else. To describe action adequately we also need a teleological explanation that recovers the full meaning of causality, including the final cause, or reason for an object or event. A teleological explanation is an explanation that shows how an action or event is required in order to bring about a given end. It can also account for the temporal and anticipatory character of an intention better than the adverbial definition. An intention is also an intention-to as a decision directed toward some object, to be done by me, that is within my power.

The preoccupation with the pair of questions *what-why* conceals the question *who*. And because such questions belong to an interrelated conceptual network of meaning, the answer to the question *who* is implicit in the pair *what-why*. An ontology of impersonal events is incapable of thematizing the relation between an action and its agent so long as it ignores the ordinary language question *who*. Ricoeur argues that the failure of an agentless semantics of action is to distinguish between ascribing an action and imputing an action. To ascribe an action to an agent is to attribute reasons or causes; to impute an action to someone is to hold a person responsible for it as a person, not as a mere thing in an ontology of impersonal events. Both ascription and imputation are necessary but not sufficient conditions for understanding meaningful action. Both are valid because people belong to two realms simultaneously; we are objects in the world like any other object but also subjects for whom the objects in the world have meaning. In *Freedom and Nature*, Ricoeur explains this dualism in terms of voluntary and involuntary action; in *Freud and Philosophy* he explains that desire crosses over the universes of discourse of subjective motives and objective causes as both a force that impels me and a reason for acting. "Being human belongs both to the domain of causation and to that of motivation, hence to explanation and understanding" (TA 135).

Following G. Von Wright, Ricoeur adopts a "quasi-causal" model of action as intervention that "joins together teleological segments amenable to practical reasoning with systematic segments amenable to causal explanation" (OA 110). To intervene is to initiate a course of action that effects changes in the world in relation to a system, composed of an initial state put into motion by an agent.[14] Intervention implies both my capacity to be able to do something and a course of events into which my action takes place so that something else happens in the world. An agent's power to act gives rise to the problem of initiative and raises the question to what extent can we ascribe a beginning of an action to an agent, and to what extent can we impute responsibility. The problem is one of linking an agent's power to act with a world in which such actions have an effect. Ricoeur now calls a philosophy of action a "phenomenology of the 'I can'" and an "ontology of one's own body." "That is, of *a* body which is also *my* body and which, by its double allegiance to the order of physical bodies and to that of persons, therefore lies at the point of articulation of the power to act which is ours and of the course of things which belongs to the world order" (OA 111). Selfhood is to be understood in terms of embodied agency, inserted into a world of events, capable of initiating and suffering actions imputable to me and to others. The concept of initiative implies agent's ability, powers, and capacities; my body as the vehicle for my being and doing; my intervention in the world of events; and my moral capacities in which I continue to act, persevere, and keep my promises. With the concept of initiative, Ricoeur retains what is valid in an agentless semantics of action and ontology of impersonal events, along with Strawson's notion of ascription, reinterpreted as imputation, in order to show how selfhood consists of embodied capacities to inaugurate events imputable to me that I am responsible for, and hence responsible to others. To be a person is to be a moral agent as well.

NARRATIVE IDENTITY AND SELFHOOD

A person is, of course, more than an embodied subject, capable of initiating and suffering actions, imputable to me and others. An agent is a human being with a history, a social life, and a personal identity that changes over time. However, identity, as Ricoeur astutely notes, has two meanings: *idem*-identity, or sameness, and *ipse*-identity, or selfhood. Sameness consists of numerical identity, qualitative identity, and some form of permanence in time, or uninterrupted continuity that allows us to identify and reidentify a person as the same over time. Selfhood consists of a form of permanence in time or self-constancy in the face of desires, beliefs, and adversity. Selfhood is a dialectic of two characteristics, "character" and "keeping one's word."

"Character" refers to the descriptive criteria that permit the identification and reidentification of an individual as the same. It is like a form of *idem*-identity but represents the aspect of the same within selfhood. A character is made up of the lasting dispositions, habits, and traits by which a person is recognized, including fingerprints, DNA, birthmarks, and other physical attributes. These traits may also be acquired identifications like values, models, and ideals in terms of which one identifies oneself and is identified by others. Unlike the concept of character, which answers both who and what, the concept of keeping one's word, in the sense of remaining faithful to one's promises and commitments, suggests a kind of self-constancy that answers only the question who. To keep a promise is less to remain the same person through time than it is to remain steadfast and trustworthy in spite of the passage of time and other conflicts and contingencies that may occur. When I keep my promises I "hold firm" even if my desires, inclinations, or opinions change. If we are to be accountable for our actions, we must be able to be identified as the same person who maintains an integrity of character over time.

A theory of narrative identity, first introduced in *Time and Narrative*, reconciles the two aspects of selfhood. The thesis is that we understand a person's identity as we would a character in a fictional or historical narrative. The self is a narrative identity constituted by means of emplotment, which configures and synthesizes diverse and multiple elements into a unified whole. "The identity of the character is comprehensible through the transfer to the character of the operation of emplotment, first applied to the action recounted; characters, we will say, are themselves plots" (OA 143). Just as the story of a life unfolds like a narrative, the identity of a character also unfold in a narrative. Because narrative theory articulates our temporal and historic constitution of the world, and because the self has a history, changes over time and yet maintains a constancy of selfhood by keeping promises, a personal identity can only be understood as a narrative identity.

> A life as a whole when then embraced in a single glance, appears to us as the field of a constructive activity, borrowed from narrative understanding, by which we attempt to discover and not simply to impose from outside *the narrative identity which constitutes us*.[15]

And yet, the narrative function constructs an imperfect mediation, constantly changing as we change. A narrative identity is never a fixed substance or structure but rather is a "dialectic of order and disorder," issuing from the "concordance of the story . . . and the disconcordance imposed by encountered events."[16]

Telling a story can answer the questions of who, what, why, and how because story telling permits us to describe and attribute predicates from either the first-, second-, or third-person perspectives. In a narrative, more than anywhere else, we can see the connection between actions and an agents. Narratives not only confer initiative on characters, they also describe and determine what counts as a beginning, middle, and end of an action. Narratives ascribe actions by identifying the causes of action and by attributing both origin and responsibility to someone. In this way narrative theory retains the great achievements of an agentless semantics of action and an ontology of impersonal events each as constitutive of *idem*-identity within a broader narrative configuration. A narrative identity is constituted by whatever permits the identification and reidentification of a character as the same, which includes both public events and experiences that belong uniquely to someone. A narrative identity is a dialectic of personal experience and impersonal circumstance, or *ipse*-identity and *idem*-identity, selfhood and sameness.

Nowhere is the nature of the self more thoroughly examined than in literary fiction, which performs imaginative variations of our being-in-the-world. Literature is a "vast laboratory for thought experiments in which the resources of variation encompassed by narrative identity are put to the test of narration" (OA 148). The reason we can identify with fictitious—and historic—characters is that they are set in contexts and situations that resemble our own. What is invariant in life and literature is "our corporeal condition experienced as the existential mediation between the self and the world" (OA 150). In particular, embodied existence is the structure of being-in-the-world that is imitated by fiction through a preunderstanding of action in its structural, symbolic, and temporal dimensions—that is, mimesis$_1$. Fiction is familiar to us because it imitates the corporeality of our embodied being-in-the-world.

That is what makes the science fiction examples of Parfit so vexing.[17] It is precisely because he treats identity as sameness, not selfhood, substituting the brain for a "cerebral trace" in an ontology of impersonal events for the self. Parfit asks, If my brain could be replicated and all of my memory transplanted into another person, is it conceivable that I could be two people at the same time? Would the other person be the same as me? Or if I were cloned and then died, would I survive in my clone? Such science fiction dilemmas arise only if we treat identity simply as sameness. They neglect the existential invariants of corporeality and worldliness, or what Ricoeur elsewhere calls "belonging," as the existential condition for the possibility for any discourse or action. Belonging is precisely what is ignored by imaginative variations of sameness, cloning, and brain duplication. The identity of a character resembles the life history of a person because both entail a more fundamental relation of belonging before becoming articulated in a narrative.

In addition to attributing actions, narrative discourse also attributes moral obligations to agents, who have the power to act and who are capable of being acted on. A narrative identity establishes the enduring notion of a subject, as well as the ethical and moral dimensions of a subject "to whom an action, whether good or not, whether performed out of duty or not, can be imputed" (OA 18). The subject of moral imputation is a unity of *idem*- and *ipse*-identity, that is, a character who has the capacity to keep promises. The importance of the notion of self-constancy is that it denotes a consistency of character such that others can count on that person, who, in turn, is accountable for others.

> The term "responsibility" unites both meanings: "counting on" and "being accountable for." It unites them, adding to them the idea of a response to the question, "Where are you?" asked by another who needs me. This response is the following: "Here I am!" a response that is a statement of self-constancy. (OA 165)

The ethical implications for personal or narrative identity is that an agent must maintain some kind of continuity of time in order to be accountable for one's actions. Identity is constitutive of accountability; narrative is constitutive of identity. Ricoeur reminds us that sometimes not acting is still acting and therefore interacting. To let something be done by someone else is a kind of action; to forget, to neglect, and to omit are actions; to endure and to suffer are also actions. Every action has its agents and its patients.[18]

Narration also mediates between description and prescription by providing "supports" and "anticipations" to ethical questioning. The hypothetical realm of the "as-if" opened up by stories provides a stage for thought experiments, which allow us to test moral judgments in imaginary cases. "The thought experiments we conduct in the great laboratory of the imaginary are also explorations in the real of good and evil. Transvaluing, even devaluing, is still evaluating. Moral judgment has not been abolished; it is rather itself subjected to the imaginative variations proper to fiction" (OA 164). Narration thus forms not only our moral ideals but also the stories we tell of ourselves and each other that help us determine if we have achieved it.

At the start of the *Oneself as Another*, Ricoeur announces that the concept of "attestation" would be the "password" for the entire work, linking a hermeneutics of the self with moral philosophy.[19] When I attest to something, I not only believe that but I believe in something. It is more of a statement of confidence and conviction than knowledge and certainty. If verification is reserved for the realm of objects, then attestation is reserved for the realm of selfhood. I can say *what* I am with certainty but I can only attest to *who* I am with conviction. A hermeneutics of the self is based on "credence without any guarantee, but also a trust greater than any suspicion" (OA 23). The difference between a true and false testimony has to do with credibility and reliability. Ultimately, when I testify to something, I commit myself and impute myself. I exist in my words when I ask that you believe in me. "Attestation is fundamentally attestation of self" (OA 22). Ricoeur has to maintain a distinction between testimony and verification if he is to maintain a distinction between persons and objects, sameness and selfhood, and, above all, ascription and imputation. Attestation is crucial for moral and political judgments, where rationality requires we offer reasons in support of our convictions in the absence of the kind of verification available to the natural sciences. Attestation is credence, reliability, and trust.

In the concluding chapter of *Oneself as Another*, he fleshes out the ontological implications of a hermeneutics of the self evidenced by the concept of attestation, arguing that otherness is not external to selfhood but internal to and constitutive of it. The "variety of experiences of passivity" attests to the inseparability of otherness and selfhood. First, is the passivity experienced of one's own body that mediates our understanding and action in the world. Second, is the passivity experienced with another in the relation of intersubjectivity. Third, is the passivity experienced in the relation of the self to itself, or conscience.

> By placing conscience in third place in relation to the passivity-otherness of one's own body and to that of other people, we are underscoring the extraordinary complexity and the relational density of the meta-category of otherness. In return, conscience projects after the fact its force of attestation on all the experiences of passivity placed before it, inasmuch as conscience is also, through and through, attestation. (OA 318–319)

The first form of experienced passivity is the otherness of one's own body. The key is Husserl's distinction between the "body" and "flesh," where my flesh refers to my lived, embodied experience, and my body to the object others can experience. The paradox for Husserl is how the flesh can be at the same time my ubiquitous perspective from which I experience the world but also a body among bodies. The flesh curiously mediates between the self and the world. Ricoeur's solution is to unite the dual experience of passivity and exteriority of the flesh with the notion of the "connector."

> The problem we called the reinscription of phenomenological time in cosmological time in *Time and Narrative* finds a series of equivalences here: just as it was necessary to invent the calendar to correlate the lived now with the anonymous instant and to draw up the geographic map to correlate the charnel here with an indifferent place, it is necessary, as Husserl himself states, to *make* the *flesh part*

of the world (*mondaneiser*) if it is to appear as a body among bodies. (OA 326)

Ricoeur says that Husserl cannot answer how my flesh can also be a body because he "thought of the other than me only as another me, and never of the self as another" (OA 326). Once we begin to recognize oneself as another then we can make sense of the enigmatic experience of the passivity of the body. It is in the suffering of others, exceeding far beyond that of physical pain, that we seeing how impossible it is to speak of a person acting without considering a person suffering.

The second form of experienced passivity is the experience of the otherness of other people. If the other for Husserl is the same as me, the other for Levinas is the other than me.[20] In fact, for Levinas the other is so radically other that I cannot even represent its appearance to myself nor can it enter into a relationship with me. To do so would be to assimilate the other into oneself and thereby reduce the other to the same. For Levinas the ontology of the same signifies totality, and hence the other is not truly other but is ultimately the same. When the face of the other appears before me, it is not as a mere spectacle, or image for me. Instead the face is an epiphany that speaks and commands me to be responsible. The voice of the other comes from the outside and constitutes me as responsible, that is, capable of responding. "In this way, the word of the other comes to be placed at the origin of my acts. Self-imputation . . . is now inscribed within an asymmetrical dialogic structure whose origin lies outside me" (OA 336). The other is absolutely exterior to the self, which is separated and closed in on itself. For this reason the other must break into my separation and appear as a revelation that commands and summons me from the outside.

Ricoeur contends, however, that the voice of the other can only command me to responsibility if it presupposes that I am capable of hearing and recognizing it.[21] The self must be receptive to the other if it is to hear the commandment addressed to it. Furthermore, the self must be able to discern and recognize the legitimacy of the commandment of the other, who may be either a master who commands justice, or a master who commands a slave. The master who commands me presupposes that I will recognize his voice as superior and just. To be heard and understood, the voice and commandment of the other must become my conviction. The reciprocity of dialogue is attested to by the reversibility of personal pronouns that also suggest a reversibility of roles in dialogue as well. Dialogue institutes a relationship between oneself and other in which the roles of speaker and hearer, or, for

Levinas, "separate ego" and "teaching other," are reversible and interchange-able. The act of assigning responsibility in the second person presupposes both the ability to designate oneself in the first person and the ability to attribute to the third person who is capable of saying "I." Ethics demands our ability to think of ourselves as others and others like me. Levinas makes it seem as if we must choose between the same or the other, interiority or exteriority, totality or infinity. Ricoeur, however, suggests that the experience of the same and the other complement one another. "Was not this intersecting dialectic of oneself and the other than self anticipated in the analysis of the promise? If another were not counting on me, would I be capable of keeping my word, of main-taining myself?" (OA 341).

The third form of passivity is the experience of conscience. The dialectic between selfhood and otherness is a fragile balance between attestation of the self and the injunction of the other. On the one hand, conscience is evidence of identity as *ipse*-identity. I am who I am because of my capacity to endure through time, to remain constant and reliable so that others may count on me, especially my capacity to keep my promises to another. Conscience is the attes-tation of self. On the other hand, conscience is evidence of the otherness of my self. It is an inner voice that commands me because it is superior to me. "Lis-tening to the voice of conscience would signify being-enjoined by the other. In this way, the rightful place of the notion of *debt* would be acknowledged" (OA 351). If the voice of the other is the voice of other people, then I am also in-debted to previous generations as well as other individuals. The origin of con-science, however, is completely enigmatic. "The conscience, as an interior voice, could be that of my ancestors, that of my deepest being as Heidegger claims, or the word of a living God."[22] Or it could even come from "some empty place."[23] This is a question that philosophy cannot answer. Conscience is another name for the otherness that haunts selfhood.

Although we may not know exactly what the other in me is, we do know that the self is so thoroughly imbued by its other that we cannot even think of one without the other—but we can think of oneself as another without reduc-ing the other to the same. The idea of conscience helps us make sense of the idea that we are indebted to our predecessors, and obligated to our successors. We are always connected in a continuity of generations, linking us to the past and the future. So long as our identities are constituted by stories, our lives are intertwined with the stories of others; I am a part of the story of my parents, my sister, my friends, my enemies, and other random interlopers.

My identity is tied up in larger group identities, as well. Like a personal identity, our collective, political, and social identities are partly chosen, partly inherited, constituted by the stories we tell about it. "The identity of a group, culture, people, or nation, is not that of an immutable substance, nor that of a fixed structure, but that, rather of a recounted story."[24] However, like any imaginative configuration, the stories groups tell about themselves are always susceptible to ideological colonization. This is especially true of political identities, whose very establishment and perpetuation requires that its members are convinced of the truth and rightness of their story. To be effective, these narratives have to shape how the members understand themselves as a part of the group.[25] Political narratives are always ideological and utopian, distorting as they integrate a society while legitimating power and authority. Ricoeur is particularly interested by stories of founding events that establish and sustain communities.

> Ideology is a function of the distance that separates the social memory from an inaugural event that must nevertheless be repeated. Its role is not only to diffuse the conviction beyond the circle of founding fathers, so as to make it the creed of the entire group, but also to perpetuate the initial energy beyond the period of effervescence. It is into this gap, characteristic of all situations *après coup*, that the images and interpretation intervene. A founding act can be revived and reactualized only in an interpretation that models it retroactively, through a representation of itself. (TA 249)

Perhaps no social group, he goes on to say, could exist without this kind of memory of its own inaugural events. Nations have their revolutions or independence days, religions their stories of origins, social movements their conflicts and victories, disenfranchised peoples their persecutions, expulsions, and other less felicitous founding events. Along with collective memory and ritualized events of retelling are also images, icons, symbols, and ceremonies commemorating events of the past. The representation of these founding events functions as both an interpretation of the real and a closure of the possible interpretations of the past events. We understand ourselves through the memory and images of our founding events, which, in turn, reinforces the interpretation that we already have about ourselves.

The danger of the stories groups tell about themselves is that they often become frozen oversimplifications, expressed in slogans and caricature, serving only the interests of power and authority. Ideology functions through this kind of collective memory, as well as through ritualization, stereotypy, and rhetoric, all of which prevent us from interpreting and recalling things differently. Even though all narratives are interpretations open to endless reinterpretation, the stories that constitute our identity function ideologically when they become sedimented into doctrine.

> What really prevents cultures from allowing themselves to be recounted differently is the influence exercised over the collective memory by what we term the "founding event," the repeated commemoration and celebration of which tend to freeze the history of each cultural group into an identity which is not only immutable but also deliberately and systematically incommunicable.[26]

Until we are able to recount events differently and allow plural readings of the past—without forgetting the past—nations, groups, and peoples who have been in conflict may never overcome their differences, and perhaps even reconcile and forgive.

Ricoeur proposes three models to help conceive of new institutions through the "political imagination" that would bring together nations, peoples, and groups, without failing to respect the differences among us. The proposed models may be seen as contributing to "the crucial ongoing debate between the right to universality and the demand of historical difference."[27] First, we need what he calls a "translation ethos," or an "ethics of linguistic hospitality" to reach out to people who speak other languages and to prevent all of us from withdrawing and retreating into our own linguistic traditions. Translation between and among any language is always possible thanks to "the principle of universal translatability," which is another name for the communication apriori inherent in discourse. Speakers oriented communicatively presuppose that what they say could be understand by another, even if it need be translated into another language. Unless one asserts something racist about different capacities and natures tied to different languages, if there is one human race it is because we can translate meanings from one language to another. Ricoeur proposes both bilingual education and "cultural bilingualists" capable of translating traditions, beliefs, and convictions from one culture to another.

Next is the model of the "exchange of memories." To translate is to take account of and recognize perspectives of others, including the stories they tell about themselves and tell about us. Understanding the stories of others opens the way for an exchange of memories that, in turn, helps us interpret and recount ourselves differently. It is similar to what Nussbaum calls "literary imagination," in which we learn to identify with others as we identify with characters in stories.[28] Understanding the stories of others helps us understand what events are like from their perspective. When we consider the founding events of our national or group history from the perspective of others, we open the door for a reinterpretation of our past.

> In this exchange of memories it is a matter not only of subjecting the founding events of both cultures to a crossed reading, but of helping one another to set free that part of life and of renewal which is found captive in rigid, embalmed and dead traditions.[29]

Reading history differently may help to liberate the unfulfilled potential of the past, including promises that were never kept, options and alternatives never taken, and debts and betrayals that were long since buried. An exchange of memories is tied not only to translation but to a critique of ideological formations within our traditions that prevent plural readings of the past. We must free ourselves from frozen social relations, through free, unconstrained communication and creative interpretations to revive the unfulfilled promises of the past, to recognize the suffering caused and endured, and the pay back the debts we owe to our ancestors and outsiders.

Next is the "model of forgiveness." Through an exchange of memories may come forgiveness, which is a specific act of reinterpreting the past concerned with understanding the suffering of others in the past and present. When a dominant group requests forgiveness, it is an admission that it has inflicted suffering on others and that it does not deserve to be forgiven. It is to beg for mercy. From the perspective of the suffering group, forgiveness is a gift of generosity in an attempt to heal itself and its offender for its unforgivable acts. The power of forgiveness

> consists in shattering the law of the irreversibility of time by changing the past, not as a record of all that has happened but in terms of its meaning for us today. It does this by lifting the burden of guilt which paralyzes the relations between individuals who are acting out and suffering their own history. It does not abolish the debt insofar as we are and remain the inheritors of the past, but it lifts and the pain of the debt.[30]

Forgiveness is a deliberate personal and political choice to put aside anger and resentment and to decide not to punish an offender over an injustice. To forgive is not to condone or justify an action; it does not mean that one gives up or gives in, nor does it require than one deny or forget an experience. Instead it is a way of coping with injustice without violence, hatred, or retribution. Individuals and groups have to learn to forgive—as well as apologize—if reconciliation is desired and appropriate. The alternative perpetuates rather than terminates anger and acrimony and provides no opportunity for apology, restitution, and restored social bonds. The key is figuring out when to forgive. That takes patience, compassion, generosity, and understanding, as well as the willingness and ability to share the stories and memories of others. "Forgiveness is the best way of shattering the debt, and thus of lifting the impediments to the practice of justice and recognition."[31]

The implications of Ricoeur's phenomenology of the self are significant for a moral philosophy and, consequently, for a critical social theory, as well. Selfhood is embodied, mediated by narrative, dialogical, and suffused with otherness. The self and other are dialectically related in a way that never reduces the other to the same but treats oneself as another. Ricoeur's notion of selfhood plays a crucial role in his theory of practical wisdom, which I read as a version of communicative ethics. Moral dialogue presupposes the ability to take the perspective of the other, learn from one another, communicate and convince each other, and to reach understanding over generalizable interests. Anytime we use the *ought* word, we assume that it means the same thing for everyone, we can offer reasons for it, it is valid for everyone, and that our reasons should persuade people to act. As I will argue in the next chapter, Ricoeur's notion of selfhood not only contains the intersubjective, interlocutionary character communicative ethics requires but it is also capable of expanding moral discourse beyond "ought" questions onto a broader horizon of evaluative questions. It also serves to provide a thicker, subtler, embodied notion of self-identity unavailable to Habermas. Social cooperation can then be interpreted more broadly to include the very substantive, historical, particular goods of our shared lives that Habermas excludes from moral discourse.

CHAPTER 4

PRACTICAL WISDOM

The fourth set of studies in *Oneself as Another* (following the studies on speaking, acting, and narrating) asks the question "who is the subject of moral imputation?" They form what Ricoeur ironically calls his "little ethics," an ambitious attempt to mediate between an Aristotlian, teleological conception of the ethical aim and a Kantian, deontological conception of the moral norm. The nonsynthetic third term is a version of practical wisdom designed to help us act appropriately and justly when confronted by the tragic dimension of action. The design of this set of studies follows two axes. The "horizontal" axis of moral philosophy refers to the dialogical constitution of the self in relation to others socially and politically, as friends and as citizens; the "vertical" axis refers to the predicates we attribute to agents and acts, such as "good" or "obligatory." The "password" for entire set of studies on the self is "attestation." It characterizes the middle ground between absolute certainty and complete suspicion and represents the kind of confidence I can have in my convictions when acting in a climate of conflict and uncertainty. Attestation is "the assurance of being oneself acting and suffering" (OA 22). The pair attestation/conviction is, however, thoroughly rational and argumentative. I can offer good reasons for my testimony and for the rightness of my convictions. It is here that Ricoeur's theory of practical wisdom intersects with Habermasian discourse ethics. I argue that Ricoeur's little ethics retains the advantages of discourse ethics while contextualizing it within a broader conception of the self and its relation to historical communities and shared notions of the good life. Ricoeur's little ethics mediates the theoretical dispute between not only Aristotle and Kant but also that of political liberals and communitarians, as well.

ETHICAL AIM AND MORAL NORM

Ricoeur proposes three theses with respect to ethics and morality, where "ethics" refers to the teleological aim of living a good life characteristic of the Aristotelian tradition, and "morality" refers to the obligation to respect universal norms characteristic of the Kantian, deontological tradition: (1) The primacy of ethics over morality; (2) the necessity that the ethical aim be mediated by the moral norm; and (3) the recourse morality must take in ethics to resolve conflicts and aporias. Ethics encompasses morality—but while it is subordinate to ethics morality is a necessary, deontological moment of the actualization of ethics. Between the Kantian and Aristotelian traditions Ricoeur proposes to establish "a relation involving at once subordination and complementarity, which the final recourse of morality to ethics will ultimately come to reinforce" (OA 170). The final recourse to ethics (informed by morality) is a form of practical wisdom geared toward the appropriate application of universal norms in particular situations—especially tragic situations produced by conflicting obligations. Practical wisdom is the art of mediating the particular requirement of the ethical aim and the universal requirement of the moral norm geared toward acting appropriately and justly in order to achieve happiness with others in a good and just society.

The relationship between a hermeneutics of selfhood and the ethical and moral dimensions of action hinges on the use of the predicates *good* and *obligatory*, both of which find counterparts at the level of self-designation. *Self-esteem* corresponds to the ethical aim, "self-respect" to the moral norm. Following the pattern of the relationship between ethics and moral, Ricoeur proposes,

> (1) That self-esteem is more fundamental than self-respect, (2) that self-respect is the aspect under which self-esteem appears in the domain of norms, and (3) that the aporias of duty create situations in which self-esteem appears not only as the source but as the recourse for respect, when no sure norm offers a guide for the exercise hic et nunc of respect. (OA 171)

Self-esteem and self-respect together form the most advanced stages of the growth of moral selfhood. Yet as with the analyses of language, action, and identity, the moral dimensions of selfhood is impossible without reference to the other. In order to show the various ways one's self is as another, Ricoeur traces the notion of the self with respect to itself, to others, and to anonymous third parties (which occurs on both on the ethical and moral planes). "The *autonomy* of the self will appear then to be tightly bound up with *solicitude* for one's neighbor and with *justice* for each individual" (OA 18).

Ricoeur defines "ethical intention" as "aiming at the 'good life' with and for others, in just institutions" (OA 172). The first component of the ethical aim recalls the Aristotelian notion of *eudaimonia* or living well. As Aristotle explains in Book I of the *Ethics*, every action and decision aims at a good; goods correspond to ends, or what something is good for.[1] For a more contemporary version of the ethical aim, and one that does not commit us to an Aristotelian hierarchy of goods culminating in a highest good, Ricoeur turns to MacIntyre's notion of a "practice"—a complex, socially established, cooperative human activity aiming at a good internal to it.[2] Internal goods are good-in-themselves, not good-for something else, and can only be recognized by participating in a practice. What counts as a practice depends on the "constitutive rules" and relevant standards of excellence, both of which are tied to the traditions and communities that confer meanings on action. A virtue is a quality or habit we acquire that enables us to achieve those goods internal to practices. Goods can only be achieved by subordinating ourselves to the standards of excellence set by the best practitioners, the experts, the masters, and the virtuosi. They set the goals we try to live up to.

What MacIntyre calls "the narrative unity of a life" is a configuration of our various "life plans," including the practices that make up one's occupation, recreation, family, goals, and projects for the future, forming the basis for the good life. The idea of the good life is itself an ideal and standard of excellence that functions as a limit idea of how I should live and how we should live together. Determining whether my particular actions and decisions approximate the good life is the work of hermeneutics. A circle exists between my aim to live the good life and my particular choices, not unlike the way a text is understood as a relation of parts and wholes. The standards of excellence provide the basis for my self-esteem.

> By the same token, our concept of the self is greatly enriched by this relation between interpretation of the text of action and self-interpretation. On the ethical plane, self-interpretation becomes self-esteem. In return, self-esteem follows the fate of interpretation. (OA 179)

In other words, my interpretations and choices about how I should live my life and attain my ideals involve an understanding of who I am and who I want to become. I am capable of evaluating my actions, assessing my goals, and determining if they are good, just as I am capable of evaluating, assessing, and determining if I am good. My self-esteem and my aim at the good life is, however, something I can only attest to, not demonstrate through a causal chain of reasoning.[3]

The second moment of ethical intentionality is solicitude, or the desire to live "with and for others." Solicitude is related to our desire to live the good life through the "dialogic dimension" of self-esteem, which links self and another so much so that they "cannot be experienced or reflected upon without the other" (OA 180). "Self," Ricoeur reminds us, is not the same as "myself." Everyone can say "self." Each person interprets and explains himself in relation to other selves, as well as to shared, standards of excellence, and ideals of the good life. Self-esteem is a self-interpretation mediated by an other and internally related to solicitude for others. Ricoeur turns to Aristotle's analysis of friendship in the *Ethics* to show how the self is dialogically constituted, and why we need each other to live the good life.[4] According to Aristotle, friendship is a mutual, reciprocal relationship that is the highest good toward which life and action, and therefore happiness and pleasure, are oriented. Given that people desire what they lack, we need the friendship of others to provide us what we lack in ourselves and prevents us from living the good life. I need the friendship of another just as another needs my friendship. Aristotle goes so far as to say that a friend is like "another self," comparable to a man's relationship with himself. Friendship is based on self-love. We care for a friend for all of the same reasons that we care for ourselves. Ricoeur retains from Aristotle an ethics of reciprocity, sharing, and living together. Friendship adds reciprocity to self-esteem. "As for the corollary of reciprocity, namely equality, it places friendship on the path of justice, where the life together shared by a few people gives way to the distribution of shares in a plurality on the scale of a historical, political community" (OA 188). The reciprocity of friendship is a nascent form of social justice.

In contrast to the Aristotelian symmetry of reciprocity and friendship is the Levinasian asymmetry of the injunction of the face of the other. The other, according to Levinas, summons me to responsibility—appearing as my master, forbidding murder and commanding justice. The other is exterior to, separate from, and unequal to me. Ricoeur takes interest in Levinas in order to show how various representations of ethical life have primacy over moral obligation. With Levinas we can discover an ethical sense that precedes the level of obligation and which we can invoke in difficult matters of conscience. Ricoeur proposes we construe the Levinasian injunction to responsibility in terms of solicitude, or "benevolent spontaneity." On the basis of this benevolent spontaneity, "receiving is on an equal footing with the summons to responsibility, in the guise of the self's recognition of the superiority of the authority enjoining it to act in accordance with justice" (OA 190). Unlike the equality of friendship, in which giving and receiving are balanced, benevolent spontaneity compensates for asymmetry of the other who commands me "through the reverse movement of recognition" (OA 190).

Solicitude is a spectrum, with friendship at the middle, the summons to responsibility at one end, and the injunction to sympathize at the other. The inverse of the commandment of the master to obey is the benevolent act of sympathy for others who suffer. Sympathy is also an asymmetrical relationship, in which the other who suffers is incapable of acting and giving but instead can only receive. The injunction here is to have compassion, understanding, and to try to experience the world from the perspective of someone else. The initiative comes from my generosity, not the commanding other. The ethical aim of solicitude is to spontaneously feel and act benevolently toward others whether I am summoned to responsibility, moved by compassion, or guided by the sense of equality shared with my friends.

The third component of Ricoeur's definition of ethical intention is mediation by "just institutions." Aiming at the good life with and for others extends beyond interpersonal relationships and face-to-face encounters connected to our institutions and anonymous relations with others. By "institution" Ricoeur means the various structures of living together and belonging to a particular community united by the bonds of common mores. Institutions regulate the "plurality," in Arendt's sense of the term, of anonymous third parties that constitute the social bond.[5] Institutions are rule-governed interactions and practices with their own standards of excellence that embody a corporate dimension of the good life. Just institutions feature an aspect of equality that is not found in solicitude. Consequently, we need more than solicitude to live well together. According to Ricoeur, "the individual becomes human only under the condition of certain institutions" (OA 254).

The kind of justice found in institutions at the level of the ethical aim is a "sense of justice" that precedes and grounds justice at the level of the moral norm. The sense of justice points in two directions: toward the good as part of the institutional mediation of our desire to live well together, and toward the legal as a system of laws, rights, and constraints. Our sense of justice is first felt as a sense of injustice, a basic feeling that I have been wronged. The word *plaintiff*, Ricoeur notes, contains the root of the word *complain*.

> "Unjust!" "What injustice!" we cry. . . . The sense of injustice is not simply more poignant but more perspicacious than the sense of justice, for justice more often is lacking and injustice prevails. And

people have a clearer vision of what is missing in human relations
than of the right way to organize them. (OA 198)

The virtue of justice, according to Aristotle, is concerned precisely with cor-
recting wrongs and fairly distributing material goods and other advantages.[6] Justice seeks to restore balance as a mean that apportions what is fair and
appropriate. Distribution, taken broadly to include the features of all institutions
that govern the equal apportionment of benefits and burdens of shared social life,
is the key to the transition Ricoeur wishes to make between the sense of justice
and equality present in the ethical aim, and the liberal notion of justice that legitimizes authority and constraint. Institutions are governed by distributive justice in the sense of "proportional equality," regulating what is fair to each one as
anonymous members of society. A distributive interpretation of institutions "assures the cohesion between the three components—individual, interpersonal,
and society—of our concept of ethical aim" (OA 201). It establishes a notion of
equality relevant to institutions that parallels what solicitude means to interpersonal relations. The senses of justice and solicitude are dialectically related. "The
sense of justice presupposes it, to the extent that it holds persons to be irre-
placeable. Justice in turn adds to solicitude, to the extent that the field of application is all of humanity" (OA 202).

The tripartite structure of the ethical aim is paralleled in the morality of
duty by the three formulations of the Categorical Imperative. The teleological
aim toward the good life corresponds to the principle of universality, in which
agents achieve freedom under self-imposed law; solicitude corresponds to the for-
mula of the "end in itself," in which we are bound to respect others as ends and
not as mere means; living in just institutions corresponds to the obligation to pursue the "kingdom of ends," in which we must act on maxims that would generate a community of free and equal members, each of whom would further the
aims of others while realizing his own intentions. But Ricoeur claims that more
than a parallelism exists between ethics and morality. The ethical aim must "pass
the test" of the moral norm, implied by the principle of equality. This will occur
on the level of the "rule of justice," not the sense of justice proper to the good
life. A formal principle of justice is necessary to ensure that the application of
equality extends to everyone. Yet the formal, deontological conception of justice
is never free from reference to the good. Ultimately, justice is a good to be desired—but it is a deontological notion of justice (broader and more comprehensive than the Aristotelian notion of just distribution) that is required to live the
good life. The good is prior to the right but requires the right in order to achieve
a full sense of the good life, which is a just life, with others, in just institutions.

The transition from the aim of the good life to moral obligation is achieved via Kant's conception of the "unconditionally good will," announced at the start of the *Groundwork of the Metaphysics of Morals*.[7] What is good is good without qualification, and what is good without qualification is a goodwill. Both Aristotle and Kant share a conception of the will that chooses the good under certain rational constraints. The difference between the Kantian and Aristotelian conception of the goodwill is that the will "takes the place in Kantian morality that rational desire occupied in Aristotelian ethics: desire is recognized through its aim, will through its relation to law" (OA 206). The unconditionally goodwill for Kant is self-legislating and acts out of duty. The morality of obligation is tied to the universality of the will, characterized by constraint, which imposes limitations on the will. A free individual acts under a self-imposed law, according to which each person freely submits to self-discipline under the same rules one would prescribe for others. We must submit a maxim to the "rule of universalization" in order to test the claim to universality that is the requirement of the truly goodwill. Kant's morality of obligation can be seen as the "progressive strategy of placing at a distance, of purifying, of excluding, at the end of which the will that is good without qualification will equal the self-legislating will, in accordance with the supreme principle of autonomy" (OA 207). The rational, autonomous will must be free from desires, hypothetical imperatives, and heteronomy.

Ricoeur calls attention to the element of receptivity and passivity found "at the heart" of autonomy. If the goodwill cannot free itself from desires, hypotheticals, and heteronomy then Kant's goal of an autonomous, unconditionally goodwill is severely compromised. Of course, Kant himself recognized this difficulty, and even made it more problematic given what he says is our "propensity" for evil. Radical evil is part of our nature and can never be eliminated. The will is equally predisposed to choose what is evil as what is rational, a perversion of the moral order that reverses the priority of duty over inclination. If a propensity for evil haunts our every choices, the will is never unconditionally good in itself. That is why it is necessary that we submit our desires and inclinations—to live the good life—to the test of the moral norm. The specter of evil or, in contemporary language, of violence and domination inherent in our desires and choices makes it imperative that there be a test for the good life. Modifying Kant, Ricoeur suggests the test be that one "act solely in accordance with the maxim by which you can wish at the same time that what *ought not to be*, namely evil, will *indeed not exist*" (OA 218).

The relationship between the ethical aim and moral norm is more clearly seen in the second formulation of the Categorical Imperative. To show the connection between solitude and the moral norm, Ricoeur interprets the Kantian imperative to treat others with respect as a stronger, formalized version of "The Golden Rule." Solicitude corresponds to the dialogical character of morality. Respect is to autonomy (on the moral plane) as solicitude is to the aim of the good life (on the ethical plane.)

> Just as solicitude is not an external addition to self-esteem, so the respect owed to persons does not constitute a heterogeneous moral principle in relation to the autonomy of the self but develops its implicit dialogic structure on the plane of obligation, of rules. (OA 218)

The Golden Rule characterizes the norm of reciprocity at the level of moral obligation, stating that you should treat others as you would have them treat you, or to refrain from doing to others what you would not like them to do to you. We are commanded to love our neighbor as we love ourselves. The Categorical Imperative is, of course, even stronger than that, requiring that we treat others with respect even if we do not want to be treated that way in return. The second formulation of the Categorical Imperative preserves the intersubjective dimension inherent in solicitude by commanding that I respect myself, others, and humanity as a whole. It aims to establish reciprocity where it is lacking. "It is what, ultimately, arms our indignation, that is, our rejection of *indignities* inflicted on others" (OA 221).

Autonomy, respect, and the "rule of justice" on the level of morality correspond to the good life, solicitude, and the "sense of justice" on the level of ethics. The ideas of a fair share and just distribution, mediated by institutions, are found in both the sense and rule of justice. Both can be characterized as a combination of "mutual indebtedness" and "disinterested interest." Yet the sense of justice emphasizes justice as solicitude, while the rule of justice emphasizes justice in the sense of the "legal" not the "good." A formalization of the sense of justice is a "procedural" conception of justice geared toward legitimating political authority, and establishing an underlying notion that would govern the just distribution of the benefits and burdens of shared social life. The deontological tradition joins the contractualist tradition to establish justice in institutions.

At this point in *Oneself as Another*, Ricoeur turns to Rawls for a conception of procedural justice that consciously and deliberately avoids recourse to any conception of the good life.[8] We will return to his argument in more detail in the following chapter. Ricoeur's thesis is that any procedural conception of justice is merely a formalization of the sense of justice that it presupposes. Like Kant, Rawls's contractarianism makes it impossible to adopt rules to the advantage of some at the expense of others; it also prohibits forms of treatment that no one would want for themselves. But the argument from a hypothetical "original position" presupposes the very historic, particular notions of the good that it explicitly forbids from entering into consideration.[9] It is impossible even for Rawls to divorce a deontological viewpoint from the teleological perspective it is founded on and presupposes. This is what Ricoeur means when he says that ethics encompasses morality—yet morality must be understood in the sense of both formalism and solicitude.

MORAL NORM AND PRACTICAL WISDOM

The third thesis Ricoeur defends in *Oneself as Another* is that morality must have recourse to ethics in the form of practical wisdom to resolve the conflicts that often arise at the level of morality. Why does morality cause conflicts? Because universal norms cannot do justice to the complexity of human life. Sometimes there is no single right thing to do. What we learn from Greek tragedies, like *Antigone*, is that sometimes our obligations conflict, and finding the right course of action is a delicate and difficult task.[10] What do we do when, like Antigone and Creon, we find ourselves with conflicting obligations? "Tragic wisdom" instructs us by suggesting a course of action. Tragedy guides ethics by refusing to offer us easy solutions; it highlights the difficulties of our moral dilemmas, and shows us that sometimes the best we can do is respond to tragic actions in a way that is consistent with our deepest convictions.

Practical wisdom neither rejects morality, nor synthesizes ethics and morality into a third term, like the Hegelian notion of ethical life or *Sittlichkeit*.[11] Ricoeur is deeply suspicious of the "seductive concept" of *Sittlichkeit* that would reconcile abstract morality with concrete ethical practices in political institutions. He often speaks of the "Hegelian temptation" and asks "should we renounce Hegel?" (TN3 193). Ultimately the answer is yes—and no. Yes, we should reject any Hegelian pretense to absolute knowledge and complete mediation; no, we should not reject the attempt to locate a rational, moral, collective agency that would establish the legitimacy of political institutions. The choice between Kantian objectivism and Aristotelian contextualism is false, as is the choice between moral absolutism and moral relativism. If we reject a totalizing third term that reconciles the ethical aim tested by the moral norm, "conviction remains the only available way out" (OA 240). My convictions are a response to tragic situations and other conflicts arising out from the level of morality.

They represent a practical mediation of the universalist and contextualist claims, aiming at the good life, with and for others, in just institutions.

> My wager is that the dialectic of ethics and morality . . . develops and resolves itself in moral judgment in situation . . . in the conflicts to which morality gives rise, only a recourse to the ethical ground against which morality stands out can give rise to the wisdom of judgment in situation. From tragic *phronein* to practical *phronesis*: this will be the maxim that can shelter moral conviction from the ruinous alternatives of univocity or arbitrariness. (OA 249)

In practical wisdom deontology and teleology, universality and historicity achieve a delicate balance.[12]

Sittlichkeit should be avoided, Ricoeur says, not only because it requires us to make metaphysical commitments to an untenable ontology of *Geist* but also because of the phenomenon of twentieth-century totalitarianism and the horrifying atrocities carried out by governments in the name of the popular spirit it claims to embody. We should renounce Hegel if only to renounce a legacy of state violence that is often driven by a perverted the notion of *Sittlichkeit*. The only virtue in the spirit of a historical community is that the moral consciousness it embodies is usually found in small groups of decent individuals in which "the spirit takes refuge, once it has fled the now-criminal institutions" (OA 256). Granted, the conflict between moral consciousness and the spirit of a people is not always so disastrous. But there is good reason to be wary, if not fearful, of anything resembling political totalitarianism.

But Ricoeur does not dismiss Hegel entirely. He retains the idea that political institutions are the realization of historic communities while emphasizing that institutions are places of conflict and contestation that bear little resemblance to a unified totality. Political practice in general gives rise to a unique form of tragic action, so we must "shift Hegelian *Sittlichkeit* in the direction of Aristotelian *phronesis*" (OA 258). At issue is the crucial distinction (particularly for a democracy) between legitimate political authority, or power-in-common, and illegitimate political domination, or power over. Any legitimate political order is conferred with the authority to use force over its members to achieve its end. The task of democracy is to make sure that power in the good sense controls power in the bad sense. What Ricoeur has elsewhere called the "political paradox" refers to the tenuous, fragile nature of all political institutions in that they are never free from power, conflict, or domination. It is the task of practical wisdom to respond to conflicts generated by the application of the moral norm. Ricoeur shows how conflicts arise at the level of institutions, then at the level of respect, and ultimately pave the way for a reinterpretation of the cornerstone of Kantian morality, the autonomy of persons.

We find three levels of conflicts in political institutions. At the first level, these are the conflicts found in deliberations over the priority of goods to be distributed. In a pluralistic society, policy over public goods and the ordering of goods is always contestable. The numerous conflicting claims that confront one another attests to "an initial degree of indetermination in the public space of discussion" (OA 258). The art of practical wisdom is to find a way to make fair decisions, following acceptable procedures, that would allow us to make decisions when we cannot reach consensus. In the absence of clear principles of justice determining a priority of goods, the recognition that the public is divided, political discussion contested, and the goods themselves determined historically and culturally, adds to the understanding that the best we can do is to deliberate well.

The same is true at the second level, where the conflicts are over the proper role, means, and ends of government. There may be no single end of government; the realization of one set of values may conflict with the realization of others. Given our contingent, historical situation even a principled decision, such as the choice of a democratic constitution, is ultimately based on the convictions of political actors and their sense of the virtue of their political institutions.

At the third level, the conflicts in institutions are over the very legitimacy of their existence. Yet in offering reasons for our preference for democracy over totalitarianism, we draw on several of our inherited traditions (e.g., the Enlightenment and various religions) that are constitutive of our desire to live together. Public debate based on "the memory and the intersection in the public space of the appearance of the traditions that make room for tolerance and pluralism, not out of concessions to external pressures, but out of inner conviction" is what ultimately answers the legitimation crisis (OA 261). The sense of justice again offers guidance when the rule of justice does not.

The second area of conflict arises in the application of the second formulation of the Categorical Imperative. For example, Kant's case of keeping promises is meant to show how we are obligated to obey the moral law, and failure to keep my promise would require that I exempt myself from the universality of the moral law. To break a promise is like lying, something that is strictly forbidden—at least as a goal that I should strive to attain. Following Marcel, Ricoeur notes that keeping promises is not just an issue of maintaining rational, hence moral, consistency. There is a dialogic structure to a promise. A promise is always made to someone else. I not only perform a speech act in promising but I am also obligated to keep my promise to that person. It is what Ricoeur calls "the principle of fidelity," and what Marcel calls "disposability or availability." I am obligated to maintain a constancy of character for the sake of another, to whom I am responsible. My commitment is itself a response to the other, to whom I am determined to remain faithful. When I make a promise to you, you can rightfully expect me to remain faithful to my word, because I have made it clear that you can count on me. Promise keeping connects the moral character of self-constancy with the principle of reciprocity found in solicitude.

Since fidelity consists in responding to the expectation of the other who is counting on me, I should use this expectation to guide my decisions about how to apply the rule to keep one's promises. Practical wisdom should help us through tragic cases where neither keeping nor breaking promises, or lying and telling the truth, is clearly the right thing to do. Unlike Kant, who is less troubled by the specter of conflicting duties and inquiring murderers than he should be, Ricoeur proposes two no less difficult cases to test the resources of practical wisdom to respond to conflicts of the Categorical Imperative. The first is the case of telling the truth to the dying; the second is the question of abortion. Thus we have problems of the "beginning of life" and the "end of life."

The issue of lying to the dying is the conflict between two extremes: telling the truth out of respect for the moral law without regard for a person's capacity to hear the truth, and lying knowingly in order to spare someone unnecessary suffering. The practical wisdom here is to respond to the particulars of each case showing both respect and compassion for the dying. In some cases happiness and suffering may not be incompatible; I may lie to someone I believe is too weak to hear the truth, or I may tell the truth in order to provide an opportunity for communication, understanding, and closure as death approaches. Practical wisdom is tailored to find the appropriate action for each situation.

The same is true in the case of abortion. If the moral standing of a fetus depends on when life begins, then determining if an embryo is a person or a thing also determines if *it* can be treated a mere means to end, or if *he* or *she* has a human dignity we are obligated to respect. At one extreme is the argument that genetic heredity, present at conception, constitutes a human being; at the other is the argument that only fully developed, rational beings have moral standing. Ricoeur suggests we find a middle ground between person and thing, using biological criteria to determine thresholds and stages of development that would articulate our duties and the fetus' rights. We need a "progressive ontology" that recognizes that an embryo is a being in development, whose capacities will be actualized over time. Corresponding to the stages and thresholds of a potential human being is a progression of qualitatively different rights and duties: the right not to suffer and the duty to prevent suffering, the right to protection and the obligation to offer it, and the right to respect and duty to give it. These rights and duties change once a fetus and a mother begin to exchange something like preverbal signs to one another.

Practical wisdom in these and other seemingly intractable situations has three features: (1) It always upholds the moral norm, although it may be applied differently according to the particulars of the situation; (2) it is a search for an Aristotelian mean, less in the sense of a compromise than an attempt to find common ground; (3) so as not to appear arbitrary, it should seek the advice of others, especially competent, wise, experienced people. A person of practical wisdom confers with others in order to arrive at an informed, just, and appropriate action. When the moral norm produces conflicts, we refer back to solicitude for others for guidance, but it is "a 'critical' solicitude that has passed through the double test of the moral conditions of respect and the conflict generated by the latter. This *critical solicitude* is the form that practical wisdom takes in the region of interpersonal relations" (OA 273).

The importance of showing the conflicts generated by the moral norm in institutions and interpersonal relations is to challenge the monological character of the Kantian notion of autonomy. If the self is inseparable from other selves and institutions, we have to abandon a "self-sufficient autonomy" for a conception of autonomy that is dependent on various figures of otherness. The distinction between autonomy and heteronomy begins to disappear if autonomy means only that we are self-governing independently, free from control or influence of others, and heteronomy means that we are subject to another's rules or laws, imposed from the outside. Ricoeur has shown how the self is mediated by others and the other than self, including rules, precepts, standards, and institutions, while, at the same time, insisting on preserving a form of autonomy affected by the other.

> Autonomy therefore appears to be dependent on heteronomy, but in another sense of "other": the other of freedom in the figure of the law, which freedom nevertheless gives itself; the other of feeling in the figure of respect; the other of evil in the figure of the penchant toward evil. (OA 275)

This "threefold otherness within the self" opens the way for a dialogic or communicative notion of autonomy that is tied to justice in institutions, reciprocity with others, and ultimately, to the good life it presupposes and takes recourse in when it generate conflicts.

Ricoeur gives a qualified endorsement to the ethics of communication found in Habermas's and Apel's reinterpretation of the deontological tradition. "The demand for universality," Ricoeur says "finds its most adequate expression in the morality of communication" (OA 281). Ricoeur agrees that communicative ethics overcomes the subject-centered, monological limits of Kant, and provides a framework for resolving conflicts and reaching consensus regarding moral imperatives. Communicative ethics preserves both the universal validity and impartiality of moral judgments, as well as the essential reciprocity and historicity of human understanding. Above all, it retains the central Kantian notion of autonomy but reinterpreted as "communicative autonomy," which is the ability of speakers to express themselves freely to others.

> The force of the morality of communication lies fundamentally in the fact that it has merged the three Kantian imperatives into a single problematic: the principle of autonomy following the category of unity, the principle of respect following the category of multiplicity, and the principle of the kingdom of end following the category of totality. In other words, the self is founded in a single stroke in its dimension of universality and in its dialogic dimension, interpersonal as well as institutional. (OA 281)

Communicative ethics turns the Kantian categorical imperative into what Apel calls a principle of "universalized reciprocity" that requires that norms be justified by an agreement on the needs and interests of everyone concerned.[13] Autonomy is thus inseparable from the influence of others, which is precisely what Kant calls "heteronomy." To be autonomous, as the term is understood by Habermas and Apel, is to be able to communicate and act successfully with others within the context of our desire to live well together mediated by the institutions that shape us. Communicative ethics presupposes and preserves the "threefold otherness within the self" that constitutes moral selfhood.

Ricoeur is in full agreement with Habermas over the basic principles of communicative ethics—that the very process of justifying normative claims presupposes that speakers have a shared understanding of what norms and reasons are and what they expect of us. When people discuss norms they assume that they are binding for everyone, and that the reasons they offer about them are also binding and valid for everyone. "Ought" means the same thing for everyone; the reasons I offer for or against an "ought" claim should apply to everyone as well.

Valid norms are discursively redeemable, impartial, universal, and rationally justi-fiable. Ricoeur accepts the Habermasian argument, and, therefore, the validity basis inherent in discourse. But his acceptance is qualified. He is concerned that the emphasis on the justification of normative claims "tends to conceal" the con-flicts that occur in their application. This is particularly so in their application in tragic situations where we must take recourse to practical wisdom. If we are only concerned with the "regressive path" of justification, we might overlook the po-tential conflicts along the "progressive path" of actualization of norms. Ricoeur's theory of practical wisdom, which I read as a version of discourse ethics, attempts to examine the progressive path of the actualization of norms in practical, con-flictual situations. In so doing, practical wisdom not only has a better response to tragic situations, but also takes account of the legitimate concerns of advocates of contextualist, communitarian ethics, like MacIntyre and Taylor.

PRACTICAL WISDOM AND DISCOURSE ETHICS

It may appear ironic to maintain that a moral philosophy that begins and ends with Aristotle is ultimately a version of discourse ethics, but that is the reading I wish to advance. Ricoeur's ethics has unabashedly universalist ambitions. He is in full agreement with Habermas and Apel that the transcendental-pragmatic presuppositions of discourse entail a moral principle of universalization. The task is to steer a middle course between the strong formalist versions of the impar-tiality implied by moral universalism and the contextual, historical character of actual moral judgments in situations. The key to this task is to be clear on the difference between discourses of justification and discourses of application. The reason there is an apparently irresolvable dispute between universalists and com-munitarians is because universalists tend to overlook the actual conflicts that arise in the application of moral norms, while the communitarians "simply exalt, through overcompensation" these conflicts and thus adhere to a problem-atic, potentially relativistic, moral historicism. Ricoeur's version of discourse ethics preserves the requirement of impartiality associated with a universal point of view yet is responsive to the substantive bonds that form the ethical life of particular communities.

> There would be no room for a tragedy of action unless the univer-salist and the contextualist claim had to be maintained each in a place yet to be determined, and unless the practical mediation capa-ble of surmounting the antinomy were entrusted to the practical wisdom of moral judgment in situation. (OA 274)

Practical wisdom is the art of acting appropriately when conflicts arise over communicatively justified principles.

The argument for a communicative ethics is based on the commitments speakers make whenever they discuss morality. The argument is that anyone who participates in communication implicitly assents to the universal norms of communication. These norms consist in the pragmatic presupposition speakers make when engaged in discourse, which is a kind of communication geared toward reaching understanding with each other regarding a validity claim. In other words, whenever a speaker questions someone about the rightness, appropriateness, truth, or sincerity of something said or done, one presupposes a mutual understanding of what constitutes valid normative expectations. I would not say "that's good" or "that's wrong" to someone without assuming they knew what a normative claim is—that is, something that shapes our expectations of what is and is not permitted, and something we can offer reasons for with the assumption that others will recognize the force of our words and be motivated to change their behavior or expectations.

According to Habermas, the principle of universalism is derived from the universally binding pragmatic presuppositions of this kind of argumentative speech. Every valid norm must fulfill the following condition: "*All* affected can accept the consequences and the side effects its *general* observance can be anticipated to have for the satisfaction of *everyone's* interests."[14] Closely related to the principle of universalization is the principle of discourse ethics: "Only those norms can claim to be valid that meet (or could meet) with the approval of all affected in their capacity *as participants in practical discourse*."[15] To deny the validity of universalism one implicitly adheres to the universal validity of the norms of rationality necessary to raise and test the validity claims inherent in speech. "Every argumentation, regardless of the context in which it occurs, rests on pragmatic presuppositions from whose propositional content the principle of universalism (U) can be derived."[16] The justification of discourse ethics is based on the argument from "performative contradiction" whereby a speaker who disagrees with universalism relies on the very discursive practice he supposedly wishes to challenge. The performance of communication contradicts the content of communication. Given the impossibility of contesting universalism without presupposing it, the transcendental-pragmatic rules of argumentation has apriori, universal validity.

Through such communication participants overcome their initially subjective viewpoints by trying to see things from the perspective of others. Unlike Kant, who insists that reason and inclination remain separated, on the model of communicative rationality participants must take into account the needs and interests of the other in order to achieve a consensus on "generalizable interests" and "generalizable needs" that are shared by all. Although needs and interests are subjective, they can be generalized and shared through communication and argumentation. The activity of raising and testing validity claims that achieves a consensus about a generalizable will, under conditions that approximate the ideal speech situation, express the common will. Therefore, will formation, which is inseparable from the interpretation of interests and needs, emerges as a result of communication.[17] Participants decide together which needs and interests are acceptable and generalizable by raising and testing subjective validity claims in terms of accepted norms of social interaction. A norm that represents idiosyncratic needs and interests cannot be universalizable. The universal validity of an ethical norm must derive only from universal or generalizable needs and interests. Reciprocal role-taking involved in communication results in understanding, taken broadly in the sense of mutual comprehension and empathy, as well as knowledge and agreement.

Ricoeur, however, is skeptical of the use of the argument from performative contradiction as a foundation. It is precisely by renouncing the idea of ultimate foundations "that we are invited to follow the inverse path from that of justification" (OA 282). Ricoeur does not offer an argument against taking recourse to performative contradiction; he simply suggests that instead of following the regressive path of justification we follow the progressive path of the application of moral norms in actual situations. It is important to distinguish between discourses of justification and those of application so as not to confuse skeptical arguments about the possibility of a universal, impartial moral perspective with arguments about conflicting obligations and choices made in particular, cultural contexts. It is equally important not to dismiss the real conflicts people encounter as mere problems of application and not as genuinely difficult, if not intractable, moral situations.

Ricoeur recognizes that discourse ethics is premised on finding a fair resolution to conflicts in the absence an overarching and commonly recognized vantage point. The only recourse available is to discourse itself, the aim of which is to respect the claims of individuals in order to reach understanding and restore the bonds of social cooperation. What he objects to is not the practice of finding the best argument to resolve conflicts and restore social bonds but "the reconstruction under the title of a strategy of *purification*, taken from Kant, that makes impossible the contextual mediation without which the ethics of communication loses its actual hold on reality" (OA 286). Where Kant purifies reason by separating it from inclination, Habermas purifies communicative action distinguishing it from convention and tradition. Echoing his debate with

Gadamer, Habermas again affirms the importance of conventions and traditions in forming the cultural and historical basis of understanding. Habermas maintains, however, that they lack the universality necessary for critical evaluation. Discourse ethics thus does nothing to move us beyond the stalemate between universalism and contextualism.

Ricoeur suggests that we integrate the requirement of universalization attached to an ethics of argumentation with the historical and contextual concept of conviction to show that the condition for the requirement of universalization is a cultural and historical context of application. Argumentation is not the antagonist of conviction and tradition. Rather argumentation is the practice that leads to a potentially universal practical judgment in a particular situation.

> What has to be questioned is the antagonism between argumentation and convention, substituting for it a subtle dialectic between *argumentation* and *conviction*, which has no theoretical outcome but only the practical outcome of the arbitration of moral judgment in situation. (OA 287)

The dialectic of argumentation and conviction is carried out at the level of actualization not justification. But even at the level of actualization argumentation is only one language game among many related to our ethical choices and moral judgments. Narratives, humor, irony, life histories, descriptions, explanations, and other uses of language help us to understand ethical action, and to perform thought experiments that inform moral judgment.

> These language games constitute as many communicative practices in which humans learn what is meant by wanting to live together, on a level prior to any argumentative formulation. To be sure, argumentation is not a language game like others, precisely by reason of its requirement of universalization. But this requirement becomes operative only if it assumes the mediation of other language games that participate in the formation of options that are the stakes of the debates. (OA 288)

Argumentation is a particular, sometimes formalized, practice in which participants clarify their convictions in order to resolve conflicts and reach understanding. Argumentation never stands above our convictions or conventions, but instead is the "critical agency operating *at the heart* of convictions" (OA 288). The task is to transform our conviction through argumentation into "considered convictions" in the Rawlsian sense of a "reflective equilibrium," which is a balance between what we agree on rationally and what our heartfelt beliefs are. Whatever we agree on should square with our convictions about who we are, what kind of people we should be, and what kind of society we want to live in—in short, our shared notions of the good life. In turn, our convictions should be considered, that is, open to deliberation, argumentation, and revision.

For Ricoeur the task is to find a reflective equilibrium between an ethics of argumentation and our considered convictions. The only way to find out which of our convictions are truly universalizable is to submit them to actual—not hypothetical—argumentation, understood in a broad sense of using the multiple resources of language to reach understanding. Considered convictions contain "potential or inchoate universals" that can be raised above ordinary conventions through argumentative practice. This idea of inchoate universals, according to Ricoeur, "best accounts for the reflective equilibrium that we are seeking between universality and historicity" (OA 289).

We find an example of this dialectic between argumentation and conviction in discussions about the universalizability of human rights. Although the notion of human rights originated in Europe and have been adopted and ratified by almost every nation in the form of the United Nations Declaration of Human Rights (1948), many countries still do not recognize them. How are we to view this development? Is it an example of illegitimate Eurocentrism to demand that others obey a foreign morality? Or is it the case that all nations are bound to respect human rights because these rights are indeed universal? Rather than viewing the difference in the recognition of human rights as a conflict between universal moral norms and particular historical conventions, Ricoeur suggests we submit the claim to universality to argumentation at the level of particular convictions embodied in practices and forms of life. If others are to recognize the potential universality of human rights, then we must recognize that the conventions and convictions of others contain potential universals, as well. The art of practical wisdom involves testing conflicting convictions in an ethics of argumentation and, inversely, testing universalizable principles of discourse against particular convictions.

Habermas, on the other hand, clearly distinguishes between argumentation and conventions. The process of discursive will-formation, whereby participants attempt reach understanding over generalizable needs and interests, applies only to the normative validity of action, not to culturally specific value preferences. Cultural values are "at best *candidates* for embodiment in norms that are designed to express a general interest."[18] We must, therefore, distinguish between "moral questions" and "evaluative questions." Only moral questions are based on generalizable interests; evaluative questions are based merely on cultural and historical values and conventions.[19] They only become universally binding through discursive will-formation that determines if such values describe and regulate generalizable needs. Particular needs and interests are closely tied to the forms of life that give meaning to particular cultures and traditions. As such they must be considered as "nongeneralizable interests" that can play no role in moral judgment. Discourse ethics is only concerned with what is equally good for everyone, in other words, questions of justice. Habermas recognizes the importance of evaluative "ethical-existential" questions that "are of a far more pressing concern for us," and "may well be of greater concern to us than question of justice."[20] Unfortunately, these questions cannot be answered in a way that takes fair account of everyone's interests and needs. They must be answered within particular cultures and contexts.

Ricoeur's version of discourse ethics similarly attempts to identify universalizable norms. He agrees with Habermas that the impartiality of moral norms implies their universalizability, hence they must have a wider scope than evaluative questions. Moral imperatives, by definition, are valid for everyone; ethical-evaluative imperatives are valid only with respect to those affected within a particular cultural horizon. Ricoeur agrees with contextualists and communitarians that moral norms only have meaning, value, and significance because of the communal-historical context in which they are applied. In other words, we have rights because of communities, not before or in spite of it. But he also maintains that the priority of the good does not undermine the universality of the right, which is required for a particular community to live well together in just institutions. Justice is present in the good life as the sense of justice, while the rule of justice presupposes and is founded on the ethical aim of the good life. The right is present in the good just as the good is present in the right. This what Ricoeur means when he refers to "inchoate" and "potential" universality. The universal exists only in context as an inchoate universal. Every cultural practice contains a potentially universalizable norm. The task for an ethics of argumentation is to see if these "candidates for embodiment in norms" as Habermas says, are truly generalizable. Ricoeur and Habermas agree that moral and evaluative questions are different, and that universality is grounded in, derives from, and yet transcends particular cultural.

Where they disagree is in their account of how one actualizes potential universality. Ricoeur argues that our cultural and historical conventions are not antagonistic to rational argumentation, but instead complement rational argumentation in a dialectical relationship. Argumentative discourse is inseparable from the indefinite number of ways we use language to communicate. Habermas makes it seem as if raising and testing validity claims is a language game un-like any other. This is what Ricoeur calls his "strategy of purification." It is the attempt to purify argumentation from the multiple forms of life, language games, conventions, and convictions that form the context and horizon of com-munication. As Ricoeur says, argumentation is not the antagonist to conviction, but the activity that brings to light its potential universality.

Of course, a charitable reading of Habermas shows that he too recognizes the fluidity between ordinary communication and argumentative discourse. Just because he makes the distinction does not mean that there is a different language used specifically designed to raise and test validity claims. Argumentative dis-course is ordinary language concerning truth claims of statements and rightness claims of normativity. Reaching communicative understanding is nothing other than dialogue among participants, who take an interest in each other's perspec-tives. It would be impossible to communicate with others if we were to free ourselves from our conventions and convictions. Habermas explains that "argu-mentation is not a decision procedure resulting in *collective decisions* but a prob-lem-solving procedure that generates *convictions*."[21] Clearly argumentation is not antagonistic to convictions; it is simply a practice that generates and clarifies the bonds of social cooperation. Perhaps Ricoeur and Habermas are even closer than Ricoeur would have us believe.

There is, however, a difference between the two in the way they conceive of the relationship between justification and application. Habermas argues we must distinguish between discourses of justification and discourses of applica-tion. The right thing to do in a given situation "calls for a two-stage process of argument consisting of justification followed by application of norms."[22] It is not enough to know how to justify a moral norm; one has to know how to apply it as well. If the principle of universalization governs justification, the "principle of appropriateness" governs application. The two principles together determine impartiality. Like Ricoeur, Habermas argues that both discourses are needed to resolve conflicting norms, for in such cases participants must nevertheless decide what to do in a particular situation. The norm that is not chosen is not invalid, but simply ranked in a "coherent normative order" determined by the princi-ple of appropriateness.

> From the standpoint of coherence, the relations within this order shift with each new case that leads to the selection of the "single appropriate norm." Thus, it is the system of rules as a whole that ideally permits just one correct solution for every situation of appli-cation. Conversely, it is the particular situation whose appropriate

interpretation first confers the determinate shape of a coherent order on the unordered mass of valid norms.[23]

Applying moral norms thus depends on how we interpret a moral situation. Such an interpretation should be guided by a principle of appropriateness that governs how a valid norms is to be applied in this particular situation in a way that squares with the sensibilities of the actors and the cultural context.

In many ways, Ricoeur would agree with Habermas's characterization of the difference between discourses of justification and discourses of application, as well as the importance of a principle of appropriateness to resolve conflicts of valid norms. But where Habermas finds a coherent normative order, Ricoeur finds tragic situations. Although each describes what is involved in the art of making decisions in difficult situations, Ricoeur is concerned with the particularly intractable cases, where the "heartfelt conviction" made "within a climate of conflict and incertitude" is the best we can do given "the tragic dimension of our actions" (J xii). In such cases, it is one's conviction that she has done the apparently better thing given the circumstances. "Wisdom in judging consists in elaborating fragile compromises where it is a matter less of deciding between good and evil, between black and white, that between gray and gray, or, in the highly tragic case, between bad and worse" (J 153). The real tests people face in making moral choices are not over conflicting interpretations of goods or norms. The test lies in tragic cases where we hope our actions are not only just but wise—that is, they follow the way the *phronimos* would act. Habermas's characterization of the choices we make and the convictions we affirm—that is, as a matter of ranking obligations in a coherent normative order—fails to recognize both the tragic dimension of human action and the importance of conscience as the inner voice of our heartfelt convictions.

Perhaps the most important difference between the discourse ethics of Ricoeur and Habermas has to do with the purpose and place it occupies within the thought of each philosopher. For Habermas it is an elaboration of his earlier studies on communicative action and, in particular, his idea of an ideal speech situation as a counterfactually anticipated regulative ideal of discourse. The principle of universalization he develops is an updated version of a universal, idealized account of an impartial moral point of view. For Ricoeur, on the other hand, what I call his version of discourse ethics is part of broader, hermeneutical reflection on the self. He employs an ethics of argumentation appropriated from Habermas as a part of a theory of practical wisdom used to test conflicting convictions. But there is much more to Ricoeur's "little ethics" than discourse ethics. It is a reflection on "critical *phronesis*," in which our desire to live the good life is mediated by others and just institutions, and which satisfies the demand for justice and responds to tragic actions. It is at the very least a version of discourse ethics; it may also be a framework for the ethical evaluation of the very goods and ends of shared social life that Habermas recognizes but is reticent to discuss.[24]

Above all, Ricoeur's discourse ethics is only one part of a hermeneutics of the self. It reveals the character of the self to whom the predicates "good" and "obligatory" may be imputed. We learn who someone is when we consider actions that are chosen because they are good, conform to the dictates of duty, and are deemed the wisest in tragic situations. Corresponding to "good" and "obligatory" actions is a person's self-esteem and self-respect, both of which are tied to solicitude for one's neighbor and justice for each individual. The answer to the question "to whom is an action imputable?" is an autonomous self who is accountable for his actions and responsible to others. The notion of responsibility recalls Ricoeur's earlier discussion of narrative identity, in which the very meaning of one's identity is determined by one's ability to keep promises and remain constant over time. To be held accountable an agent must maintain some kind of continuity of time.

Responsibility, furthermore, implies three different temporal relationships to another. From the perspective of the future, responsibility implies that someone is accountable for the consequences of her actions. Although the connection between an action and its consequences is often unforeseeable and even accidental, we hold people responsible for those consequences both for the sake of praise and blame. The danger, according to Hans Jonas, of some of our technologies is that the power we have to change the future of the entire habitable environment changes the conventional notion of what it means to attribute responsibility.[25] With our powers comes corresponding responsibilities to future generations and to protect the environment, which is the condition for possible life itself. The ecological problems we face are caused by policy decisions based on accountability only to present and not to future interests. Furthermore, Ricoeur argues that not only do we owe a debt to the future but we are indebted to the past in that we inherit a condition we take to be ours. We hold ourselves responsible to the past when we recognize our indebtedness to that which has made us what we are. Finally, is one's responsibility to the present, which takes the form of a promise to remain steadfast over time. "But this responsibility in the present assumes that the responsibility of the consequence to come and that of a past with respect to which the self recognizes its debt are integrated in this pointlike present and in a sense recapitulated in it" (OA 295). The recapitulation of responsibility is another name for the various figures of recognition found in solicitude for others, reciprocity of respect, and conscience, whereby one recognizes oneself as another.

With responsibility and its tenuous relationship to the present, we are lead back to the theme of attestation, the password for Ricoeur's studies on the self. It represents the highest degree of certainty one can offer to another. For example, when I assure you that you can count on me, or when I promise you I will act responsibly, all I can offer is my word, my assurance, and my commitment. All you can do is believe in me and trust me. Attestation highlights the various ways that the self and other are necessarily related. In the last chapter we noted the various figures of passivity that constitute the self, including the experience of our own body, the relation of intersubjectivity, and, finally, of conscience. Ricoeur states that conscience *is* attestation. It is the inner voice that both belongs to me and to others, commiting each of us to one another. Yet conscience signifies not only our mode of being human but also those convictions that bind us together and resolve our disagreements.

> Wisdom in judging and the pronouncement of wise judgment must always involve more than one person. Then conscience truly merits the name conviction . . . after having traversed the rigor, intransigence, and impartiality of abstract ethics, and having confronted the tragic dimension of action. (J 155)

Attestation of self is another name for conviction, and thus joins the triad of ethics-morality-conviction that forms the basis of Ricoeur's little ethics. Attestation is undoubtedly fundamental for Ricoeur's moral philosophy but so is argumentation.[26] I prefer to highlight the discursive, communicative aspect of Ricoeur's discourse ethics to emphasize that self-attestion and convictions are not only *heartfelt* but also *considered*.

CHAPTER 5

POLITICS

Ricoeur's main contribution to political philosophy is his notion of the "political paradox." On the one hand, political authority is legitimate if it comes from the rational consent of the governed; on the other hand, political practice is often coercive, even violent, which is something, in principle, to which individuals cannot consent. The paradox of authority is permanent. If would be a mistake to attempt to eliminate it by making it seem as if state authority was complete and always justifiable—the mistake of authoritarianism—or rejecting the notion of political authority altogether—the mistake of libertarianism. Rather we should think of the political realm as a quasi-independent sphere of control that overlaps with the spheres of ethics and economics. This will preserve, Ricoeur argues, the best of the liberal, communitarian, and Marxist traditions of political thought. The state should be a state of laws that protects our rights and ensures our liberties; it should foster the well-being of social life in particular communities; and, finally, it should eliminate economic exploitation and alienation. The political sphere is a fragile balance of authority and domination, law and community, reason and tradition. Ricoeur's proposal that democracy is the political system that best responds to the political paradox may at first seem banal and predictable. But it is a unique version of democracy precisely because it mediates traditionally opposed political traditions. It is based on a theory of practical wisdom designed to mediate conflicts based on considered convictions, good arguments, and the desire to live well with and for others in just institutions. Ricoeur's model of democratic political practice fulfills the promise of critical theory.

ETHICS AND POLITICS

In his 1983 essay "Ethics and Politics," Ricoeur advances the thesis that politics must first be defined in relation to the economic and social realms before being contrasted to ethics (TA 325–337). He follows Arendt and Weil in contrasting political rationality (governing customs, mores, and actions of historical communities) to socioeconomic rationality (governing the spheres of material reproduction, the organization of labor, production, consumption, and control over nature).[1] Following Weil, Ricoeur defines the economic realm as an "abstract social mechanism" autonomous from the state. Although related to ethics and politics, economics is governed by a logic of calculation and efficiency that is becoming increasingly autonomous with the globalization of the market. Socioeconomic rationality, up to a point, is not a bad thing. It has always been "the great educator" of individuals to exercise at least a minimal form of rationality. "The man of technology, of economic calculation, of social mechanisms, is the first man who lives universally and who understands himself by means of this universal rationality" (TA 327). The expansion of a potentially universal socioeconomic order is key to the rise of the modern state. The political and economic realms function together for the rational organization economic life, or "the struggle of man against nature" in which a rationality of calculation and efficiency "tends to become the new form of the sacred" (TA 327). Although distinct, the economic and political realms overlap—for better or worse—in the modern state.

But to conflate the political and economic realms would be a mistake. According to Ricoeur, the mistake made by Marx and subsequent Marxists is to consider the realms of politics as reflections of an economic order they function to legitimate. Because Marxism fails to recognize the quasi-autonomy of the political, it fails to recognize pathologies specific to politics. It overestimates the role of modes of production and surplus value in the evolution of society. Consequently, all social pathologies are seen as derivative of economic alienation. If all social evils originate from economic evil then any political order that eliminates exploitative labor relations and the accumulation of surplus value is seen as legitimate. The key to Marxism is understanding the dynamics of capital as a social relation, the overcoming of which is the aim of ideology critique and class struggle.

Ricoeur believes that the danger of Marxism's reduction of the political to the economic is that it has undertheorized problems specific to political power. Although Marxists correctly recognized that much of nineteenth-century political liberalism functioned as an ideological justification of economic liberalism, the mistake they have since made is to throw the baby out with the bathwater by rejecting political liberalism based on its false identification with economic liberalism. Neither Marx nor Marxists are, of course, responsible for the various forms of totalitarian political experiments this century has seen. But the lacuna in Marxist thought is to have sometimes justified political terror so long as a state proposed to eliminate alienating modes of production and capitalist appropriation of surplus value. Ricoeur attributes this error to the strict identification of political and economic liberalism. The "catastrophic confusion" between political and economic liberalism not only blinds us to specifically political problems of state power but also to the technologically mediated character of advanced industrial economies.

Again following Weil, Ricoeur explains that "the dissatisfaction of modern man" comes from conflicts we experience from being simultaneously economic and political beings. As economic beings we are subject to a rationality of calculating efficiency geared toward the production of surplus value. We are alienated from production and from each other. Work is no longer the educator and liberator it was for Hegel and Marx; rather work makes our lives devoid of meaning. As a result, we retreat from work into our private lives or seek meaning in the traditions of our historical communities, which economic globalism unfortunately disrupts and destroys. The contradiction individuals and nations find themselves in is that the very technological order in which they must participate to survive at the same time undermines and erodes the ethicopolitical core of historical communities. We find ourselves trapped in between two competing rational orders: the new rationality of technocapitalism and the old rationality of our shared cultural and political life. More and more people flee from both into a private—and increasingly privatized—world. To resolve, or at least to understand this contradiction, Ricoeur suggests a terminological distinction between "the rational" and "the reasonable." The rational, economic order is the source of our dissatisfaction. We need to recover another kind of rational order—a more reasonable order—that would satisfy our desire to live well together in communities. The reasonable is the realm of political action.

Ricoeur defines the political realm by the central role the state holds in the life of historical communities. "The state," he explains paraphrasing Weil, "is the organization of a historical community; organized into a state, the community is capable of making decisions" (TA 330). Ricoeur stresses historical communities to emphasize that political theory needs to be concerned with more than normative issues. It must also consider the concrete particulars of historical communities. The state is inseparable from the particular norms, mores, customs, and practices that constitute the narrative and symbolic identity of a community or collection of communities. We cannot understand the state in terms of moral principles. Nor can we understand its organization on a purely formal level. The organization of the state is governed by "reasonable action" in the form of institutions, agencies, government departments of public concern, governing bodies, and practices that hold a community together. This organization into a whole makes human action reasonable for that particular community. Thus, the issue for political philosophy is citizenship. What are the conditions for citizenship? What are the state's responsibilities to ensure it? What constitutes a citizen's rights and freedoms?

If the state is an organization capable of making decision, the question then is how the state organizes the community—how it makes its decisions, and for what reason or end. Ricoeur rejects the idea that the state is mere artifice as Hobbes held it to be, or that it is only the result of violence geared toward control of its citizens. Rather he believes what defines the state is its ability to make decisions that help a historical community endure, survive, and create its own history while protected from internal and external threats. The central issue is survival of the historical community. There are two ways political philosophy analyzes the survival of a community. One is to emphasize "form," in the tradition of rationalist philosophers, including Arendt and Weil, which leads to a consideration of republicanism and the role of the constitutional and legal character of the state. The other emphasizes "force," in the Marxist tradition and critics of totalitarianism, which leads to a consideration of the political paradox of the role of power and violence in establishing and perpetuating the state.

Ricoeur starts with an analysis of the form of a state as a state of laws aiming to establish the conditions of equality and equal protection for all citizens. When approached from the perspective of form, the emphasis is on the policies that embody the law, the role of bureaucracy in administering it, and the parliamentary or representative system that creates and controls laws. The state as a state of laws constitutes the realm of reasonable action, the goal of which is to reconcile the two rationalities: the rational, technoeconomic, and the reasonable, social-historic. "The state is then the synthesis of the rational and the historical, of the efficient and the just" (TA 331). Its virtue is "prudence" in the Greek and medieval sense of temperance and moderation; in this case the state exhibits prudence by mediating between the demands of rational efficiency and reasonable needs of the historic community. The state thus functions as an educator, developing the capacities in its citizens to cope with competing demands through schools, media, and cultural institutions. However, the idea of "a state that would only be an educator is a limit idea, a regulative idea to which no empirical description yet corresponds" (TA 331). There has never been such a state, nor could there ever be one, although the idea of it is an important ideal that represents the reasonable core of the state as form.

Turning to the state as force, Ricoeur credits Weber with the insight that the state can also be defined in terms of its monopoly on legitimate violence.[2] But he disagrees with Weber on the definition of "legitimate violence." The state has the authority of legitimate uses of violence in the sense of political force or power—for example, through a criminal justice system. But Ricoeur contends that it would be a mistake to define the state solely in terms of violence and political power although it is true that states usually are established by acts of violence and often use it to advantage and privilege class or group interests at the expense of equal treatment of all citizens. Nevertheless, to define the state in terms of violence alone would be to neglect the great achievement of modern liberal political philosophy and the rights and freedoms that have been established in constitutional governments since the eighteenth century. Ricoeur believes that to "denounce a state as bourgeois is, in reality, to say two things and not just one: it is a *class* state but it is also a *citizen* state" (TA 332). That the state is a state of law for at least some of its members is no small achievement; the task is to ensure that equal protection under the law applies to everyone, not the privileged few. Liberal political life is, however, "unavoidably marked" by a struggle over political power, control, and domination. This confrontation between form and force, law and violence, constitutes the political paradox.

The state of law is further marked by economic violence, which takes the form of the conflict between the particular interests of different political communities and the global interests of "technoeconomic" structures. Part of the function of the state is to preserve its identity in the face of an increasingly global economy that consistently privileges technoeconomic imperatives of profit and efficiency over the needs and interests of particular communities and regions. No worldwide state of law exists unless one finds promise in the potential of the United Nations and its limited political powers. Ricoeur, however, questions the desirability of such a state. If the political paradox of form and force, law and violence is indeed unavoidable, then the capacity for violence of a supranational state could threaten the existence of every historic community. Given the technological capacities we have to destroy the planet with nuclear weapons, poison it gradually with toxins and pollution, or degrade it permanently through industrialization and agribusiness there is good reason to be wary of a supranational authority conferred the use of legitimate violence.

Ricoeur echoes Hans Jonas, arguing that the very survival of the environment and our species must become the most important political consideration of independent states. We need to exercise and extend the virtue of prudence to global governance. If prudence is the name he gives to the art of balancing technoeconomic rationality and "the reasonable" within the state, then "generalized nonviolence" would be the name for the art of governing among states—not unlike Kant's notion of perpetual peace among a federation of nations. The world state would "become the means of survival of the states as nonviolent educators" (TA 333). The goal of a world state is even more utopian than the idea of the state as educator, but it is by no means unreasonable. The welfare of the planet would then be determined by agreements among states in a fragile balance of form and force, nonviolence and violence, guided by what is reasonable (not rational) to ensure the well-being of us all.

Ricoeur emphasizes the intersection of ethics and politics in order to guard against the cynicism and complacency that arises from and depends on the separation of the two. When we view politics as nothing but strategic alliances, expediency, favoritism, and political realism, we fail to recognize its ethical dimension and we become more likely to tolerate unacceptable state violence. In other words, it is better to confuse ethics and politics than to separate them even though they only overlap. But where they do overlap is decisive for the state of law as an institutionalized ethical relationship. Politics extends the range of ethics to include considerations of the rights and freedoms of neutral third parties. The ethics of politics "consists in nothing other than the creation of spaces of freedom" (TA 334). The state of law regulates the freedom of individuals by ensuring their equal protection, access, and opportunity. As such it is an ethical agency that establishes legal equality.

Closely related to legal equality is democracy, which Ricoeur defines in ethical terms with respect to conflict and power. With respect to conflict, a democratic state is one that maintains procedures not so much to eliminate conflicts but to allow them to be openly discussed and negotiated. A state of law is a state based on free discussion. With respect to power, a democratic state is one that guarantees its citizens the right to participate in decision making. It is the form of government that limits the separation between the rulers from the ruled. Ricoeur follows Montesquieu, however, in asserting the necessity that state power be divided within itself in order to allow for the greatest popular participation in decision making. For example, the separation of powers among the legislative, executive, and judicial functions better approximates the utopian ideal of democratic participation than that of a unified public achieved through a rational, consensus-bringing activity in the tradition of Rousseau, Kant, and Hegel. The ethical character of the state is thus a matter of both the prudence exercised by governments and the participation of the citizens in democratic processes geared to negotiating conflicts and distributing power.

But the sphere of ethics and politics only overlap, they are not coextensive. The ethical basis of a political community is comprised only of the values about which there is a consensus; it necessarily leaves out the justifications and motivations for the sources of these values, which are often plural, divisive, and conflicting. Advanced Western democracies, for example, are the result of numerous Western traditions, not counting the various non-Western traditions found in its citizens who emigrated from Asia, Africa, and Latin America. It would be impossible for citizens to reach a consensus unless each bracketed the particular, tradition-based motivations that justify common values. Consequently, the values of a society have an abstract character "severed from their roots" in the multiple traditions and sources of motivation and justification. The values of a society take on an ideological character when they become empty stereotypes used for the sake of political rhetoric. Political consensus is, therefore, only the thinnest kind of ethical relationship among citizens. The state is a fragile construction based on a political consensus of values posing as a genuine ethical agreement. Sometimes a political consensus is indeed based on an ethical agreement. But more often than not there is a gap and the putative values of the state are little more than ideology.

The gap between ethics and politics recalls Weber's distinction in "Politics as a Vocation" between an "ethics of conviction" and an "ethics of responsibility."[3] The former represents the ethics of traditional moral values as practiced by communities and individuals; the latter represents the exercise of force, power, and sometimes violence. An ethics of conviction is based on what is preferable, whereas an ethics of responsibility is based on what can be achieved. According to Weber, the well-being of a society depends on political leaders who are able to balance these two ethics, maintaining them in a lively tension. On the one hand, the ethic of responsibility without the ethic of conviction would confuse means and ends, and ultimately degenerate into Machiavellism. On the other hand, the ethic of conviction without the ethic of responsibility would "sink to all the illusions of moralism and clericalism. The ethics of conviction can only operate indirectly by the constant pressure which it exerts on the ethics of responsibility and power" (PS 288). What this means for citizens is that we should have a dual allegiance to both ethics; we should be motivated by our convictions but join with others at the level of political force and action.

Political power is both rational and irrational. The rationality of the state (in the sense of "reasonable," not the technical sense of economic rationality) is embodied in a constitution. This is important for at least three reasons: (1) This rationality establishes a geographical unity of the state's legal apparatus; (2) it ensures the continuity of a society for a time-span greater than that of a single generation; and (3) it allows for intergenerational integration that links past heritage and traditions to future projects and possibilities for the historical community.

But the state is also irrational by virtue of the trace of the violence that remains from the founding acts that established it. The violence that establishes political power itself belongs to a heritage Ricoeur confesses he finds puzzling. Political power always seems to rely on the "tradition of authority" even more than the "authority of tradition" to legitimate itself. The tradition of authority is origin-less. No one really knows where it comes from. Yet the trace of violence left by the founders always haunts the authority of the state.

All states are born out of some form of violence. Although Ricoeur agrees with Arendt that it is necessary to distinguishing legitimate "power in common" from illegitimate "power over" (violence and domination) he agrees with Weber that political institutions are in fact often characterized by domination. Even though there is indeed an ethical element to political insti-tutions that originates from our ability to act in concert together, legitimate political power cannot be explained solely in terms of our power in common. Political institutions are different from other institutions. They are "sovereign" with respect to the power they possess. Although political power is moderated by a constitution, which aims to eliminate the heritage of violent founding act, ironically it restores and enables this irrationality by granting the state de-cision-making authority and the ability to use force legitimately. This recourse to violence is precisely Weber's definition of the state. Even legitimate, consti-tutional democracies must occasionally use force to enact its decisions. Ri-coeur suggests that to think philosophically about political power is to recognize that even advanced forms of rationality include an "archaic form" of irrationality in the tradition of authority it perpetuates. This form of violence and irrationality "imposes on the citizen a duty of vigilance—vigilance with respect to the outbreaks of violence that are inscribed in the very structure of the political" (CC 98).

In *Oneself as Another* Ricoeur showed how that political institutions me-diate both the ethical aim and moral norm. At the level of the ethical aim, po-litical institutions mediate the individual, interpersonal, and societal aspects of justice in the concept of equality. At the level of the moral norm they are the point of intersection of justice in a contractarian theory of the state and the law. Political institutions thus point in two directions: toward the good and toward the legal. They embody principles of justice and equality geared toward both the historical communities from which they originate and toward a state of law that guarantees human rights. He describes the dual character of political institutions as having a "horizontal plane" and a "vertical plane." The horizontal plane is what Arendt calls "power" in the sense of the power-in-common that issues from a community's desire to live well together. The vertical plane is what

Weber refers to as the use of violence that the governing can legitimately use over the governed. The enigmatic character of political power comes from the contradictory demands of political institutions. On the one hand, we feel that political power should be a form of self-government emanating directly from our desire to live well together. One the other hand, by subsuming the vertical to the horizontal plane we would have to give up the benefits of political power that assures geographical stability, links generations, and reconciles traditions and projects. These positive functions of government can only be worked out in a compromise between the hierarchical relations of power-over and the consensual relations of power-in-common.

> The democratic project would then be defined as the set of measures that are taken so that the rational prevails over the irrational, but at the same time so that the horizontal tie of wishing to live together in general prevails over the irreducible, hierarchical relation of command and authority. (CC 98)

If the political is defined in terms of a conflict between form and force, power and domination, democracy is defined in terms of the institutions and practices that allow for conflicts to be negotiated in accordance with fair rules of arbitration. In *Oneself as Another* Ricoeur identifies three kinds of conflicts internal to democratic political institutions: conflicts over the priority of goods to be distributed, the ends of good government, and the legitimation of democracy itself. He concurs with Claude Lefort that democracy is a system designed to cope with the paradoxes of political power. A democratic society accepts its contradictions and institutionalizes its internal conflicts.[4] But he disagrees with Lefort's claim that the historical, "unknowable, unpredictable, and indeterminable" character of democracy means that it has no foundation whatsoever.[5] The choice is not between a model of political power based on absolute foundations or no foundations. For Ricoeur, democracy

> is always founded on the anteriority of itself in relation to itself. Can this be called a foundation? If so, it would be in the sense in which one speaks of founding events. But these presumed founding events do not escape the enigma of the receding origin, or, to put it better, of the dialectic of the immemorial origin and the dated beginning. (CC 101)

The anteriority of the state refers to the enigmatic character of political authority which is always-already there as a moral-political agency. The ultimate foundation of democracy is as enigmatic as the relationship between autonomy and political authority in the contractarian tradition: individuals are only self-legislating under the moral law.

Yet the enigmatic origins of political authority should not prevent us from offering good reasons prefering democracy over all other political systems. We can offer a number of good reasons ranging from claims to universality, historic contingency, shared traditions, and personal convictions (this would transpire in what Rawls calls an "overlapping consensus"). Central to democratic political theory is the idea that citizens have the ability to make and revise decisions together under fair conditions. There need not be a single foundation or overarching consensus in order for there to be an institutionalized authority geared toward collective decision-making. There need only be the ability of citizens to reflect on their institutions and practices to determine if they are fair and do not unfairly privilege some at the expense of others. Justice as fairness, Rawls says, is a device for political representation; it is not a metaphysical, or comprehensive, moral doctrine. Instead it refers to the way that citizens compare their considered convictions against the principles of justice in their society to establish a reflective equilibrium that both tests and grounds justice. "Liberal democracy," Ricoeur says summarizing Rawls, "is meant precisely for citizens who are in virtual disagreement over what is essential. It undertakes to limit the extent of public disagreement" (J 72).

The idea of overlapping consensus intersects with a number of democratic traditions, among them not only the Enlightenment project of Habermas and the liberal tradition but also the Jewish, Christian, Muslim, Roman, Greek, and other premodern traditions that have shaped Europe and the West. Our various traditions need to be tested in a reflective equilibrium or Habermasian action oriented toward mutual understanding. Yet our democratic political heritage is unique among traditions. Unlike Walzer, who would make that the political sphere one among many spheres of justice, Ricoeur maintains the tie of citizenship is presupposed before we belong to any society and thus unifies the political realm in a way that is different from other spheres of justice. Membership in a political body is superior to our membership in any of the other many spheres that define our roles, advantages, obligations, and responsibilities. Ricoeur describes the tie of citizenship as an "encompassing-encompassed" relationship. Even when we are not engaged in specifically political activities "the state continues to encompass all the spheres of belonging with respect to which we pay allegiance" (CC 103). It is encompassed, however, by the illusion of being merely one sphere among many. The danger we face today is less from political totalitarianism than from the disappearance or invisibility of our political membership, which makes it seem as if the political dimension of our lives no longer matters. Unlike other spheres of justice, political power extends over others spheres—sometimes legitimately, sometimes illegitimately. It also is uniquely self-limiting, for example by a separation of powers or other constitutional restraints. The encompassing nature of political power leads back to the political paradox—political force with a tenuous claim to legitimacy.

CRITIQUE AND CONVICTION

The legitimacy of political power is further complicated by ideology and utopia, the two poles of the cultural imagination that always constitute and distort social life. The very communal bond, or "political space" as Arendt calls it, is constituted by a symbolic structure shaped by the cultural imagination. Ideology and utopia, as we have seen, function by coordinating understanding and social integration as an interpretive schema that distorts, dissimulates, integrates, but most important, legitimates power, authority, and domination. Both are ultimately about power. Ideology attempts to legitimate power, while utopia attempts to replace power with something else. Ricoeur's readings of Marx, Althusser, Weber, Geertz, and Habermas are crucial to understand what he calls "the fragility of politics." Political fragility stems from the fragility of political language, which always contains ideological and utopian elements. Political language is a form of rhetoric in the sense of both rational demonstration and sophistical argument.[6] We have already seen how Ricoeur's version of critical hermeneutics and practical wisdom copes with false consciousness and distorted communication. We should turn our attention now to ideology and utopia in the context of the fragility of politics to better understand what our response to it should be as philosophers and citizens.

Ricoeur begins his studies of ideology and utopia with readings of Marx's early works. The main contribution of Marx to Ricoeur's theory of ideology is the notion of ideology as distortion, or inversion, that conceals and mystifies reality by representing the real as an illusion and the illusion as real. In the *Economic and Philosophical Manuscripts*, Marx tells us that the real, material basis of human existence is the creative and productive life of social beings.[7] But because of capitalist ownership and control of the means of production, labor is alienated, or estranged from itself, and objectified into an object outside of itself. Wages are a consequence of alienated labor, which is the cause of private property. "To be submitted to the power of another is the contrary of the creation of oneself. Estrangement is fundamentally the reversal, the inversion, of the human capacity for the creative process of objectification" (IU 44). Alienation is a condition whereby human labor becomes externalized and inverted into something alien and transcendent that dominates the life of working people. We are alienated not only from the object of labor but also the act of labor, our human nature, and other people. The political economy conceals the domination within the creative process of labor. Ideology is a consequence of the alienation of the essential activity of human labor into private property and capital.

In *The German Ideology* Marx shifts his characterization of ideological inversion away from productive human activity toward the material conditions in which we all live and work.[8] It is movement away from the Feuerbachian conception of species being toward the more historical and materialistic conception of "the real individual" that is related to anonymous forces like modes and forces of production, classes, and so on. He retains the notion of productive human activity but now emphasizes the material conditions we produce and, in turn, depend on for our existence. The actual life-processes of humans under historical conditions form the basis of reality. Anything that is not a part of the material basis of existence in considered to be ideology, including consciousness and all representations of life. Marx calls ideology a "camera obscura" that inverts the image and reality. Ideology is a reversal of the relationship between individuals and the historical conditions of their existence. It is a historical formation providing a worldview that supports and justifies capitalist class relations.

One thing that Marx never explains is how dominant material relationships become reflected in ruling ideas. Marx says that ideas that serve particular interests are made to appear as the only valid and rational ones, hence what is essentially particular and contingent is made to appear universal and necessary. Yet the nature of the relationship between the ideological distortions and the real economic base remains to be explained. Some Marxists like Althusser have interpreted the relationship causally between the economic base and the superstructure of ideas from which it derives.[9] Base determines superstructure; the economy determines ideas. Ideology is an "apparatus" that functions to preserve state domination and control over ideas and institutions, including religion, family, educational systems, in short, culture in general. For Althusser everything that is not a part of the economic infrastructure (which can be explained completely in terms of objective structures like forces of production, relations of production, and division of labor) is ideological.[10]

The most important idea Ricoeur retains from Althusser is his interpretation of the Freudian concept of "overdetermination," which replaces the Hegelian concept of contradiction or negation as the explanatory concept for the nexus of interrelations between base and superstructure. The ideological superstructure is seen as resulting from a combination of heterogeneous forces including historical events, circumstances, accidents, and other factors. The economic base is still the fundamental determinant in a society but the ideological superstructure is not simply the result of causal forces or the development of an inner necessity of the base. In fact, the base itself is informed by the superstructure through a combination of forces and levels within a society. Although Althusser retains a causal framework to explain overdetermination, Ricoeur believes that the concept of overdetermination does more than just mitigate the strong causal relationship of base and superstructure found in orthodox Marxism and dialectical materialism. Once we recognize that the superstructure may be informed by something other than the base then the framework of base and superstructure loses both its explanatory power and conceptual necessity. The model of base and superstructure falls apart as soon as we recognize that we need some kind of intermediary concepts to explain how and why people believe in and assent to ideological distortions. Ricoeur believes that both Althusser and Marx correctly recognize that dominant interests are represented in dominant ideas and that the task of a critique of ideology is to unmask the power structures underlying ideas, exposing them as ideology. But it is hard to make sense of how people are motivated by ideology in terms of the causal, deterministic framework of base and superstructure, especially in light of the overdetermination of meaning. How exactly are ideas caused by an economic base? How does that framework explain conflicting interpretations that arise from the same economic base? Why do some people accept ideological doctrines and beliefs while others reject them?

Ricoeur suggests that we cannot understand the notion of overdetermination apart from a theory of meaning and the reasons we offer why we should accept the ideological claims of authority as legitimate. So he turns from Althusser's causal framework to Weber's motivational framework to account for the psychological factors involved that would explain what motivates members of society to accept the claims to legitimacy by the ruling authority.[11] The appropriate model for understanding class or state domination is motivational because any system of authority must establish the grounds or basis for belief in its claim to legitimacy. We must be motivated to believe and assent to the claim of legitimacy of power and authority. An important aspect of the motivational model is the concept of "order" that is related to authority and domination but also has the meaning of "organization." Social order is related to legitimacy and legitimacy is related to motives. Order requires belief from the participants in its legitimacy so that they orient themselves appropriately to the actions of others.

Legitimacy becomes a problem, however, as soon as there are rulers who enforce rules and the ruled who must accept the rules. The requirements of a system of order are that we obey, follow the rules, and be motivated to accept the legitimacy of the order and its enforcement of powers. Although Weber has no theory of ideology, the place for it in his thought, according to Ricoeur, would occur "in the gap between a system of authority's claim to legitimacy and our response in terms of belief" (IU 183). Ideology adds a "surplus-value" to our belief in a system of authority; its function is "to fill the credibility gap in all systems of authority" (IU 183). The function of ideology is to legitimate a system of authority when a credibility gap exists between the claim to authority of the rulers and the belief in the claim by the ruled. The credibility of an order depends not only on the power of the rulers but also on the willingness of the ruled to recognize that authority. The claim to legitimacy involves a claim of order that shapes and patterns a group, a claim of a ruling group with authority over a ruled group, and, finally a claim of the validity of the use of power to implement order. Ricoeur argues that any system of authority claims more than people are motivated to believe and, therefore, there is always a "supplement of belief" provided by an ideological system. So long as there are rulers and ruled there is ideology.

But the key notion for Ricoeur's conception of ideology is Geertz's idea of symbolic action. Before an action can be distorted or legitimated it must first be symbolic so that it can "express" a system of ideas. Symbolic action is a part of the background of experience that shapes the conditions for possible knowledge—or what in *Time and Narrative* Ricoeur calls mimesis$_1$. Following Geertz, Ricoeur defines ideology as among the symbolic systems that constitute the social bond and form our various collective identities. The most basic function of ideology is that of "mediating and integrating human action at its public level" (TA 316). Ideology is like a blueprint for social organization. But because it creates and preserves order it is always conservative. It patterns, organizes, orders, and ensures the stable functioning of a community as it distorts, legitimates, and integrates. If the positive function of ideology is to constitute and preserve identity, the negative function is to resist the transformation of an order that has frozen social relations in such a way that sustains domination. "It preserves, it conserves, in the sense of making firm the human order that could be shattered by natural or historical forces, by external or internal disturbances. All the pathology of ideology proceeds from this 'conservative' role of ideology" (TA 318). This conception of ideology as integration does not eliminate the problems of distortion and legitimation. It only displaces the problem to a more fundamental level of symbolic action. Ideology, then, is more than a distortion of communication, or false consciousness; it is a way in which individuals and groups are integrated and identified at the level of action.

Ricoeur highlights three aspects of Geertz's conception of ideology as integration: (1) The Marxist distinction between base and superstructure disappears if all action is already symbolically mediated. A symbolic system of action belongs to both base and superstructure, as well as to the very constitution of all levels of human action. As a result, we cannot understand domination exclusively in terms of economic domination resulting from class relations. There are other forms of domination that cannot be explained by class structure. (2) The link between ideology and language implies that ideology not only distorts communication, but in fact constitutes it. Habermas recognizes this fact as well, but he conceives of ideology only as systematic distortion, not systematic integration. (3) The problem of integration gives rise to ideology only when there are competing conceptions of integration. If there were no disagreement, there would be no reason for an ideology to exist to facilitate social integration. A dominant ideology emerges from disagreement and conflicting ideologies. The resulting ideology functions, above all, to consolidate and integrate a society; the distorting and legitimating functions are derivative. This is not to say that this nonpejorative conception of ideology means is ultimately a value neutral concept and that there are no reasons to prefer one ideology over another or to resist it altogether. As Geertz points out, ideology is always about power.

Ricoeur's unique take on ideology, as we said before, contrasts it with utopia, its opposing pole of the cultural imagination. Utopia balances the conservative, integrating power of ideology by calling authority into question to show that a society need not be integrated in the way that it is. If ideology functions to preserve frozen social relations, utopia opens the possibility for things to be otherwise. If ideology is the surplus-value added to the lack of belief in authority, then utopia is what reveals and contests this surplus-value, exposing the credibility gap of a system of authority. If ideology legitimates power and authority, utopia replaces power with something else. Like ideology, utopia operates on the level of distortion, legitimation, and integration. At the level of distortion, utopia is a form of escapism, or an implausible, far-fetched notion. At the level of legitimation, utopia is an alternate form of power and authority that seeks to challenge and shatter the existing social order. At the level of integration, utopia is an exploration of possible individual and group identities.

What makes political discourse fragile is the inescapability of ideology and utopia. One is identified and criticized in the name of the other. The destructiveness of conservative ideology is countered by the constructiveness of utopian possibilities; the destructiveness of utopian escapism is countered by the positive, integrating function of ideology. Ricoeur goes so far as to say that "we only take possession of the creative power of the imagination through a relation to such figures of false consciousness as ideology and utopia" (IU 324). In other words, we cannot avoid ideology and utopia in political discourse. The best we can do is to proceed with caution.

But he also says that the circle of ideology and utopia does not have to be a vicious circle; it can be a spiral. We can move forward and cope with the pathologies of ideology and utopia by exercising practical reason, judging what is best to do in a particular situation. In the absence of a perspective that transcends the cultural imagination all we can do is interpret, judge, and act in the most appropriate and just way we can. Ricoeur echoes his mediation of the Habermas-Gadamer debate when he says that "instead of a pseudo-Hegelian claim to have a total view, the question is one of practical wisdom; we have the security of judgment because we appreciate what can be done in a situation" (IU 314). There is no substitute for the work of critical hermeneutics—the recollection of tradition and the anticipation of freedom. It is a task that is ongoing and never complete. It is important to remember that the interests in communication and liberation are inseparable. Ricoeur warns that "the moment these two interests become radically separate, hermeneutics and critique will themselves be no more than . . . ideologies!" (TA 307).

But even practical reason may be subject to ideological and utopian distortions that "slip in" during deliberation of appropriate ends of action. They belong to the interpretive code in terms of which we think and act. Again and again, Ricoeur warns of the "Hegelian temptation" for precisely this reason: our belonging to a tradition in the sense of *Sittlichkeit* is itself constituted by the cultural imagination and, hence, inseparable from the ideological function that distorts, legitimates, and integrates social action. Practical reason must also serve a critical function so that we do not follow Hegel's model of the state that completely reconciles and integrates individuals with society, history, and Absolute Spirit. Even if there were such a thing, it would not be desirable. Instead it is important that a theory of practical reason be able to distinguish between legitimate and illegitimate social integration.

> The critical function of practical reason is here to unmask the hidden mechanisms of distortion through which the legitimate objectification of the communal bond becomes an intolerable alienation. I consider legitimate objectifications here the set of principles, rules, and symbolic mediations that found the identity of a human community. By alienation, I am referring to the systematic distortions

that prevent the individual from harmonizing the autonomy of her will with the demands coming from these symbolic mediations. It is here . . . that what has been termed "ideology critique" is to be incorporated into practical reason as its critical moment. (TA 206)

Like Marx, Ricoeur contrasts legitimate objectifications with illegitimate alienation. However, unlike Marx, the epistemological and normative bases for critique are never completely free from ideology. A critique of society is an act of practical wisdom ultimately based on our considered convictions, good arguments, and desire to live well with and for others in just institutions. The task of identifying the systematic distortions that prevent an individual from "harmonizing the autonomy of her will" is a far more fragile endeavor than Marx would have us believe.

The fragility of a critique of society stems from the rhetorical fragility of political language, situated in a "vulnerable zone" between rational argumentation and sophistry. Ricoeur distinguishes among three successive levels of the rhetorical function of political language, corresponding to three kinds of conflicts found in democratic institutions.[12] First, is the relationship between consensus and conflict in political deliberation. The hallmark of a democracy is that it contains mechanisms and institutions that allow for public discussion and debate so that we may negotiate our conflicts. To eliminate all conflicts in a pluralistic society is neither possible nor desirable. As Mill argues, a healthy democracy requires that differences of opinion be discussed freely and openly.[13] Negotiating conflicts publicly, however, presupposes rules that make negotiations possible. Conflict presupposes consensus over agreed-on rules of discourse that make political conflicts possible. Political language "is a language that is conflictual and consensual at the same time."[14] That is why it is also so vulnerable. Neither the place of political discussion, the participants, nor the conclusions are ever fully decidable.

The second level of political rhetoric is over the ends of good government, centered on such key terms as "security," "prosperity," "freedom," "justice," and "equality." These terms are all highly ambiguous, open to interpretation, and subject to ideological appropriation. Yet they are essential for political deliberation over the ends of good government. Ricoeur suggests that we should neither reject such terms altogether nor attempt to fix their meanings once and for all. Instead we should recognize that each term is characterized by a plurality of senses given the plurality of ends of good government. In other words, the question may be theoretically undecidable because there may be no single goal of government. It would then be impossible for a government to meet satisfy every end at the same time. Political action is often tragic. In politics, as in ethics, practical wisdom is the art of coping with tragic situations when we are forced to make decisions in difficult circumstances. Ricoeur implores us "not to flee the field of political confrontation, but to enter it with a sense of measure that leads to great respect for the extreme fragility of the 'good life' a life for which 'good' government serves as the most proximate figure open to us as political animals."[15]

The third and most problematic level of political discourse has to do with conflicts over what counts as the good life—or pursuit of happiness in more American and less Aristotelian terms. Ricoeur calls this level of the "horizon of values within which the formulation of the project of good government rejoins our representation of the good life."[16] The issue here is the ambivalence many people feel about contemporary life in advanced industrial societies. The same material possessions we love and values we embrace are also the things we hate and reject. The same consumerism, industrialism, and individualism we cherish is also the cause of widespread feelings of anonymity, disaffection, loss of community and sense of belonging, and lack of purpose. On the one hand, people appreciate the conveniences of a consumer society; on the other hand, people recognize its perverse effects on social life, their children, and our collective future. The ambivalence of modernity stems from its silence about the ends of life. As a result, people have to find meaning and a sense of identify in some place other than civic life. It is what Habermas calls a "legitimation crisis" that originates in a sense of doubt people feel about their allegiance to their society. Our ambivalence about the good life affects our conception about government itself. How can it enable us to pursue happiness and promote the general welfare if we have mixed feelings about what these goals should consist in? Ricoeur explains that "from such conflict, such a plurality of ends, and such a fundamental ambivalence come the fragility of political language."[17] This fragility makes it impossible to eliminate the use of political language as rhetorical sophistry.

The task of political philosophy, according to Ricoeur, is to clarify the conditions of modernity affecting human beings and their identity. It can expose how our society systematically undermines its own legitimacy. After that political philosophy can help diagnose advanced industrial societies by measuring and comparing them to ideals of the past. The least we can do is to recover the Enlightenment ideals of "justice," "equality," and "freedom" on which our society is partially based. We need to go back even further than our Enlightenment traditions and recover our premodern heritage that extends to the teachings of the early Christians, and Ancient Israelites. Ricoeur does not disagree with Habermas's claim that the Enlightenment project has not yet been achieved but believes we need to do more than recover the ideals of the Enlightenment in order to "find appropriate correctives for those perverse effects that, today, disfigure the undeniable gains of our modern age."[18] We need to take a longer look at our history and relearn the lessons from the countless beginnings, failures, revolutions, and successes of the past.

> There is nothing better to offer, in reply to the legitimation crisis . . . than the memory and intersection in the public space of the appearance of the traditions that make room for tolerance and pluralism, not out of concession to external pressures, but out of inner conviction. . . . It is by calling to mind all the beginnings and all the rebeginnings, and all the traditions that have been sedimented upon them, that "good counsel" can take up the challenge of the legitimation crisis. (OA 261)

By "good counsel" Ricoeur means the practical wisdom required of individuals as citizens to be able to negotiate our conflicts together so that we may live well together in just institutions. It is practical wisdom exercised at the level of political discourse. Although we can never be sure when our political discourse is perverted by ideology or rhetorical language in the bad sense, Ricoeur is confident that we can use political rhetoric in the good sense to complete the Enlightenment project and recover the forgotten memories and unfulfilled promises of the past.

Ricoeur singles out the "political educator" whose responsibility is to motivate people to become responsible citizens and thus cause a "chain reaction" through a "kind of intellectual midwifery" (IU 298). Political educators are not limited to academics, politicians, or teachers, but are found throughout society in unions, parties, and cultural and religions groups. They should addresses themselves both to the interests of freedom and to the creative renewal of cultural traditions through three spheres of society: industries, institutions, and values. At the level of industry, the political educator should help show the ethical significance of every choice appearing to be purely economic and further the struggle to establish a democratic economy. The goal is to democratize the economy by allowing for the greatest possible participation in discussion and decision. At the level of institutions, the political educator should foster discussion of the often competing demands of moral rightness and political efficacy. The goal is to balance the requirement that power be legitimate with the need that political institutions remain efficacious. The utopian goal is to achieve a balance between our dual affiliations to our moral convictions, but to join with others at the level of the political and, thus, enable the needs of the group while protecting the autonomy of individuals. Finally, at the level of values, the political educator should endeavor to mediate the inevitable pull toward consumer society by a recovery of the past by the living traditions that help resist the effects of a global market economy. The need to balance technical universalism and cultural particularity applies both to exploiting and exploited nations. According to Ricoeur, the expansion of global capitalism results in "anonymity," "dehumanization," "barbaric forms of urbanism," and "totalitarian peril." "All the struggles of decolonization and liberation are marked by the double necessity of entering into the global technical society and being rooted in the cultural past" (PS 292). The task for critical pedagogy is to help work toward democratizing society at the levels of industry, institutions, and values by balancing the demands of an industrialized, technological society with the preservation of individual and group identity and cultural heritage.

POLITICS AND THE LAW

As in politics, the domain of the law is a fragile balance between argumentation and rhetoric. The law is related yet distinct from either the moral or political domains. As a form of justice, law overlaps with morality (in the Kantian sense) but it also involves conformity to external, not internal, laws and it is concerned with the legitimacy of the coercive powers to enforce them. The law also overlaps with politics as a constitutional state but it also outstrips the state as the very thing that confers political legitimacy. Political power creates the law but also must appeal to it for legitimacy. The law, however, is far from pure. It is free from neither rhetoric, ideology, nor political power. Conventions and convictions are also inseparable from rational argumentation and just institutions. Instead, legal decision are a form of practical wisdom understood as a fragile balance of argumentation, interpretation, and conviction. The law is best seen as the formal rules, procedures, and practice of practical wisdom geared toward prudence and equitable judgments in situations of conflict and uncertainty.

In a rather original turn, Ricoeur defines the law in relation to conscience. Instead of seeing the law as universal, constraining, and objective, and conscience as circumstantial, variable, and subjective, he pairs the two to show how they work together in the act of judging wisely. There are three levels where law and conscience relate corresponding to the three moments of practical wisdom. First, is the level of our desire to live well together. At this fundamental level we find ourselves making crude distinctions between good and evil, right and wrong, permissible and forbidden, and other moral attributes and character traits we define in terms of binary oppositions. It is what Taylor calls the "strong evaluations" humans make because our lives our not morally neutral.[19] We form hierarchies of evaluations or "hypergoods" in order to help orient ourselves toward fulfilling lives. At this level, law and conscience correspond to the pairing of selfhood and the idea of the good. The answer to the question who am I finds an answer in terms of the strong evaluations to which we define and orient ourselves. What Taylor calls "moral space" is the way we find ourselves and define ourselves in moral terms. Conscience at this level is this orientation of oneself in moral space. The law at this level is secondary to determining how I wish to live my life in relation to strong evaluations. The polarity between law and conscience, Ricoeur says, "can be summed up in terms of the pair 'strong evaluations-strong adherence'" (CC 118).

Second, is the level of univeralizable norms. The law is now defined in terms of morality in the usual sense of constraint and obligation. Ricoeur's strategy is to show how legality leads back to morality and how morality leads to conscience. At this level morality and the law have three things in common: interdiction, universality, and human plurality. (1) Morality and the law set limits and prohibitions to actions that help establish the bonds of social life. (2) They both claim universality by presupposing that their prescriptions are valid for everyone. (3) Both order human plurality in relation to the norm in what Kant called the state of "unsociable sociality" that makes the bond between humans so fragile (J 150). In other words, both morality and law are required to mediate and order otherwise conflicting and competing individuals.

There are, however, important differences between morality and law with respect to interdiction, universality, and human plurality. If we follow Ricoeur's argument from legality to morality and morality to conscience, each of these three features—interdiction, universality, and human plurality—is completed and fulfilled in moral conscience as a counterpart to the law. At each stage we find a movement of internalization of the norm (i.e., from an external legality to an internal morality) to be complete in conscience as an inner voice of justice. First, what distinguishes legality from morality is the role of interdiction. For the law it is external obedience; for morality it is, as Kant says, respect for the moral law from love of duty. Second, legality and morality make different claims to universality (i.e., external legislator or the autonomy of a self-legislating will). Third, the norm as a principle of order of human plurality for the law is to constrain individuals and competing wills, whereas for morality norms emerged communicatively as the dialogical aspect of the second formulation of the categorical imperative. With the notion of mutual respect we can see how social legality is internalized into morality and even further into conscience. At this stage, conscience is an inner voice of respect for the moral law. The voice of conscience retains each of the three aspects of the law: it is the voice of constraint, universality, and impartiality.

The reason Ricoeur does not stop at this point is because the implied model of moral selfhood is too thin. It fails to recognize individuals in their "unsubstitutable singularity." Human beings are more than mere tokens. Instead we are determined by the strong adhesions we have to evaluations within a moral space aiming at the good life. At this level the notions of law, morality, and even conscience cannot do justice to the complexity of moral judgments in situations. Following the movement in Ricoeur's little ethics, he then takes up the relationship between law and conscience at the level of practical wisdom.

Making legal judgments in particular situations is more difficult than simply applying a norm to a case. It is a complex process involving interpretation and judgment. On the side of the particular case, the problem is to interpret it in such a way that links relevant events into an intelligible whole. Of course, in a hearing both sides present interpretations of what happened, making it difficult to determine which version is more plausible. On the side of the norm, it is not always clear how the case should be construed in terms of legality, or under which legal norm the case should be construed. A judgment in a situation comes at the crossroads of two interconnected interpretations. We have to figure out what happened, what the law says, and how it should be applied to the case. The legal judgment determines what the law is. As for conscience it is

> nothing other than the inner, heartfelt conviction that inhabits the soul of the judge or the jury, equitably pronouncing the judgment. In this regard, we can say that the equity of a judgment is the objective face for which this inner conviction constitutes the subjective guarantor. The tie between inner conviction and the speech act consisting in stating the law in a particular circumstance removes the judgment in situation pure arbitrariness. (J 153)

Those charged with making legal judgments must balance the law and conscience in order to determine what the right decision is in what are often tragic circumstances. Wisdom in judging consists of "fragile compromises" not only between good and bad, but often bad and bad if not bad and worse. Conscience then becomes conviction when it adheres to impartial norms while confronting the tragic dimension of action.

As with ethics, the law is related to politics but irreducible to it. Politics and the law strike a fragile and paradoxical balance between force and form, or domination and rule of law. The balance is fragile because the horizontal dimension of political power, emanating from our desire to live together, produces a vertical dimension that differentiates between governing and governed. The state of law as sovereign power is a paradoxical form of self-government. In a democracy, one's elected officers are both representatives of citizens and agents of power over citizens. Democratic governments are based ultimately on a bond of trust between governing and governed. A just society aims to distribute power evenly and equitably among its citizens who share power in common; an unjust society distributes power unevenly.

Ricoeur describes the relationship between law, morality, and politics in terms of three concentric circles: conflicts, exchanges, and distributions. As citizens, we experience the law first as conflict resolution in criminal law, then as contracts and torts in civil law, and last as a political system that apportions the benefits and burdens of shared social life in a state of law. The first encounter citizens have with the law is in criminal law as a search for justice instead of vengeance. Justice is a third party that intervenes in between crime and punishment. This third party constituting the criminal justice system implies a state, without which there would be no laws, as well as a corpus of written laws, legal institutions, judges, juries, lawyers, and law enforcement. In addition, justice interposes in between crime and punishment in the form of legal argumentation that changes the relationship between individuals from victim and aggressor to plaintiff and defendant. The change in legal status is a result of the mediation by a judicial authority and formalized rules of deliberation and decision in the context of a trial. Legal argumentation is a particular form of rhetoric where procedural rules organize the deliberation over conflicting interpretations and arguments. The kind of reasoning used aims to establish probability not certainty. But, although it is a form of rhetoric, judicial rationality constitutes an intermediary rationality in between moral rationality and the rationality of the state that is always tied to violence. Judicial reasoning presupposes a break between discourse and violence. "The trial is, in this regard, the privileged place for an ordered and ritualized discussion" (CC 118).

The second circle of law citizens encounter is wider than and irreducible to criminal law. The obligation of civil law is designed to repair damages, which is not the same as the obligation to punish an offender. The domain of this second circle is that of contracts, for social life consists not only of conflicts but also of the promises and commitments we make to one another. Conflicts arise here precisely when individuals fail to keep their promises and break their word. In civil law "we find ourselves in the vast domain of the mutual obligations which bind us together" (CC 119). Contracts display a fundamental ethical core of human relations. The bonds of trust and promising are built into our use of language; we have to believe that people mean what they say. Language is a "fiduciary institution." Embodied in contracts we find "one of the most basic convictions and probably the one most irreducible to any change of mores: one must keep one's word. *Pacta sunt servanda*, agreements must be kept" (CC 119). This fiduciary relationship extends beyond contracts and obligations between individuals to relations and treaties between nations.

After criminal and civil law we enter an even broader circle of juridical relations in which citizens come to understand that society as a whole is a system of distribution of roles, goods, benefits, and burdens. What is distributed are shares of market goods, property, opportunity, security, health, education, and citizenship (among many multiple marketable and nonmarketable goods). But the most difficult thing to distribute are positions of power and authority. It is not clear that the same criteria should be used to distribute a marketable good (e.g., property) as a position of authority (e.g., the role of a teacher). Just distributions of this kind of the most difficult. Power and authority often cannot be divided equally. Although we should continue efforts to bring about a more just system of distribution, the utopian dream of equality is misguided. A society capable of enforcing such an egalitarian dream would have to be extremely powerful, even violent. It could not be a free society. Instead, the search for justice involves a dialectic of freedom and equality.

Each circle of law implies a different conception of responsibility. It is sometimes difficult, however, to hold individuals and groups legally responsible when there are more than a few protagonists. When there are only a few actors involved in a criminal or civil case it is not difficult, in principle, to attribute responsibility to persons and hold them accountable. But it becomes increasingly difficult to attribute legal responsibility when there are several actors, several plaintiffs, several different actions and decisions as well as other contingencies such as unforeseeable or hidden consequences. In such cases it is less than clear who is responsible. Even more difficult are action taken by institutions. Not only are there several different actors, action, and consequences, but often there is not a hierarchy in place in the sense of there being superiors who can hold an institution accountable. For an institution to be "accountable" for its actions it has to give an accounting to one who asks. "Responsibility" and "accountability" mean the same thing. In the internal goings-on of a organizational hierarchy an authority is usually held accountable for the actions of one's subordinates. The responsibility of an organization or institution to the public is more difficult to establish. The public can rightfully expect that there be an authority who will take responsibility for the actions of the entire organization including one's subordinates. How such positions of responsibility are distributed are among the difficulties implied by a system of distributive justice. All positions of authority are also positions of responsibility. The difference between criminal responsibility and political responsibility is that the former rests on an individual whereas the latter rests on the state as "the ensemble of institutions that made possible, and sometimes authorized . . . criminal actions to take place. This sort of state has a duty to make reparation" (CC 122).

The role of the state in criminal law, according to Ricoeur, follows a related sequence consisting of sanction, rehabilitation, and pardon. Following a trial, the sequence starts with a conviction, followed by a sentencing geared toward restoration and reparation rather than punishment, and is concluded with a pardon or act of forgiveness that completes the restoration of the individual and ends the sequence of criminal justice. The trial is crucial in that it allows the public to clearly distinguishes between justice and vengeance. It establishes a "just distance" between the crime that brings public and private calls for vindication and the punishment inflicted by the state in the name of the law. A criminal trial is a "third party" that establishes a gap between violence and justice by providing a state sanctioned, rule governed hearing where the plaintiff and defendant may confront one another armed only with arguments. State power and judicial power are conjoined in that the state writes the laws that define crimes while the judicial system interprets the laws and is empowered to decide the relation between crime and punishment. The purpose of a criminal trial is to arrive at a verdict that is a performative speech act that states the law bring the case to a close. The verdict

> brings an end to uncertainty; it assigns the parties in the trial places that determine the just distance between vengeance and justice; finally, and perhaps above all, it recognizes as actors those person who are accused of the offense and who stand to suffer the penalty. In this very effect lies the most significant reply given by justice to vengeance. It sums up the suspending of vengeance. (J 136)

The verdict begins the sequence of sanction, rehabilitation, and pardon. Starting with sanction, Ricoeur follows Kant and Hegel in the idea that sanction restores the law. The sanction is that which owed to the law, and because of that, owed to the victim. The law expresses the moral conventions of the political body and assures order; thus any violation of the law also upsets the order. The first function of punishment is to re-establish order. At the same time, punishment recognizes the victim as someone who has been wronged. It helps to restore the victim's honor and self-esteem and even contributes to the "work of mourning" in which the "wounded soul is reconciled with itself" by "prolonging the public recognition of the offense" (J 137). One must recognize that one has been wronged before beginning the process of mourning and eventually coping with the loss or offense. For this reason sanction is also owed to public opinion as the vehicle for vengeance but also for justice. Sanction is addressed to the public's indignation by providing a catharsis in response to its thirst for vengeance. Finally, Ricoeur again echoes Kant and Hegel in affirming that sanction is owed to the offender, who is in the process respected as a rational and autonomous human being. Sanction recognizes the offender as a responsible being who deserves to be punished because he or she is reasonable and free to act. If the sanction is not recognized by the offender as reasonable then it has not reached the offender as a reasonable person. When the sanction fails to be recognized by the offender in the course of the trial then the state must continue the sequence and rehabilitate or pardon an offender.

Imprisonment as a form of punishment takes the idea of just distance too far. By excluding prisoners from society we impose an "excess of distance" that includes such additional penalties as loss of public and private esteem, loss of legal rights, and the lasting effects of a criminal record. The aim of rehabilitation is to restore a condemned person to full citizenship and thereby reduce the excess of distance to a just distance. There are two forms of legal rehabilitation. First, there is the automatic rehabilitation that any condemned person undergoes after having served a sentence. This form of rehabilitation restores all of the lost rights, privileges, and capacities so as to give a prisoner an opportunity to enjoy full citizenship again. Second, there is the rehabilitation in the form of reeducation and resocialization that prisoners experience while incarcerated. It, too, aims to reestablish citizenship and "to end the physical and symbolic exclusion that finds its fullest expression in imprisonment" (J 141). The very idea of a life sentence constitutes a "flagrant negation" of the very idea of rehabilitation because it completely negates the reestablishment of a just distance between the offender and the rest of society. Instead of resocializing prisoners, excessively lengthy sentences desocialize them.[20]

The third part of the sequence following rehabilitation is pardon. Ricoeur is quick to distinguish between pardon and amnesty. Despite their apparent similarity, they are antithetical. Amnesty, on the one hand, is a political act that not only releases a person from punishment but also forbids others from referring to the actions as criminal. Amnesty asks us to forget what happened. Sometimes national reconciliation requires we forget the offenses of the past but at the heavy price of wiping away all traces of public indignation. Pardon, on the other hand, requires that we remember and recognize the offender and offense so that everyone involved can cope with injustice without violence, hatred, or vengeance. Pardon is not on the same legal plane as sanction and rehabilitation. To pardon is to forgive, and forgiveness is never owed to anyone. Only the victim can forgive; the offender has no right to expect it. It is more like a gift or act of charity than an act of justice. Pardon follows "the logic of superabundance" as opposed to the "logic of equivalence" found in justice. The aim of pardon never to forget an action but to overlook the debt owed to us by others. "Pardon is a kind of healing of memory, the end of mourning. Delivered from the weight of debt, memory is freed for great projects. Pardon gives memory a future" (J 144). The importance of pardon in a judicial system is to complete the sequence of restorative justice and to eliminate the remnants of vengeance that haunt retributive justice.

Restorative justice may be operative at the level of political responsibility as well. Although it is difficult to make sense of a "collective crime," if by a criminal act we impute responsibility to individuals, we can nevertheless speak of a "collective offense." The counterpart to an individual offense and judicial responsibility is the notion of a collective offense against a group and the political responsibility to make reparations. Institutions, groups of peoples, and even nations can be held responsible to others. In Chapter 3 we spoke of Ricoeur's three models for a new ethos for Europe that involved translation, exchange of memories, and forgiveness. This model is more relevant for political responsibility than the model of sanction, rehabilitation, and pardon. But notions of responsibility share the idea of reinterpreting the past, remembering things differently—either individually or collectively—to forget past debts in order to heal, move forward, and perhaps reconcile. Political forgiveness also goes beyond justice and approaches the order of charity and gift-giving. To ask for forgiveness is to recognize that a crime may be unforgivable, the wrong irreparable, and the debt infinite. But, as with a life-sentence or death penalty, forgiveness is the best way to "shatter the debt," remember events that permit more hopeful futures, and to lift the impediments to justice and recognition. Of course, there is a time for both the unforgivable and forgiveness. There is no recipe for determining when to forgive. What is certain, however, is that to overcome conflicts individual and groups must learn to remember events differently if we are going to approach anything even resembling perpetual peace.

CHAPTER 6

CRITICAL THEORY

For a social theory to be considered a critical theory it must not only analyze and explain social phenomenon but also criticize and judge domination and oppression informed by a theory of liberation. Critical theory overlaps considerably with traditional or mainstream social and political theory. It will often employ conventional research methodologies and rely on liberal political presuppositions of the importance of rights, liberty, individuality, and equality. But critical theory outstrips and surpasses traditional theory by broadening the categories of social justice, happiness, and freedom to include the phenomena of oppression and domination traditional theory either overlooks or is structurally incapable of addressing. Critical theory often speaks the language of mainstream social and political thought supplemented by a conceptual vocabulary necessary to address changing social conditions and new forms of injustice and oppression. Part of this vocabulary includes traditional Marxist concepts of alienation, exploitation, and ideology; part comes from poststructuralist political philosophy, which speaks of marginality, difference, otherness, and heterogeneity; part comes from feminist philosophy, which includes concepts of gender, sexual and sexist domination, chauvinism, and patriarchy; part comes from critical race theory, which speaks of racism, colonialism, ethnocentrism, and Eurocentrism; and finally, part of the vocabulary of critical theory also includes the language of liberalism, with its emphasis of freedom, equality, and rights.

A new kind of critical theory is taking shape that is less concerned with allegiances to any particular philosophical tradition than with examining and criticizing power, authority, gender, race, culture, ethnicity, the political economy, the environment, and other issues having to do with social justice. Critical theory challenges power and authority everywhere it resides, especially in public policy, mass media, the law, multinational corporations, and global economic and political organizations. It is interdisciplinary, empirical, normative, practical, and emancipatory. It is practiced not only by academics but journalists, social scientists, public advocates, grassroots organizers and activists, and others connected with social movements. The advantage the new critical theory has over traditional critical theory is its ability to cross over into mainstream discourses and steer the conversation regarding social and economic justice to the far left. This is the direction in which I want to move Ricoeur's critical theory—away from slippery terrain of intraphilosophical debates to the rough ground of political concerns. I will focus on the politics of identity and recognition, technology, and economic globalization, to show how his works add depth, complexity, and sometimes practical solutions to these problems.

IDENTITY AND RECOGNITION

One of the main contributions of poststructuralist philosophy has been to challenge the metaphysics of a self-founding subject as an enduring essence that underlies modern social ontologies. The problem with self-founding subjectivity is that it forms the basis for a model of collective subjectivity as the subject of political action that denies difference, particularity, and heterogeneity among its members. When Adorno says that "the whole is false," he means the *Aufhebung* of individuals into the totalizing concept of society fails to do justice to difference, especially the difference of those individuals and groups that resist assimilation.[1] One of Iris Young's contributions to the postmodern challenge to identity logic is to show how the reduction of difference to sameness underlies the liberal moral ideal of impartiality, which in turn serves the ideological function of reproducing relations of domination and repression.[2] The ideal of impartiality legitimates hierarchical decision-making, privileging some individuals and groups over others. The political counterpart to the moral ideal of impartiality is the political ideal of a civic public. It too contributes to group oppression by creating a myth of a common good that forces individuals to abandon their particular group affiliations if they wish to participate in political life. Young says that the task for a critical social theory is to argue for a conception of justice that challenges institutionalized domination and oppression while affirming a heterogeneous public and group differences.

On Young's reading, the moral ideal of impartiality is the search for a universal, abstract, moral point of view, detached from our particular, historical situation, personal perspective, embodied feelings, inclinations, and group affiliations. The abstract view from nowhere denies difference in three ways: (1) It denies the particularity of situations by forcing a moral agent to adopt a universal point of view following universal principles that must apply to all who are in a relevantly similar situation; (2) the impartial point of view requires that we abstract from our particular, different, embodied feelings and desires in order to take the perspective that any rational agent could adopt; and (3) the detached, dispassionate, universal ideal is monological, reducing the plurality of particular perspectives into a unified, or single, collective subjectivity. The same logic of identity of impartial moral reasoning provides the justification for a political theory geared toward establishing a democratic ideal of a homogenous civic public.[3]

However, such an ideal of a universal citizen, unified civil society, or unified nation is more than just an impossible fiction. It also serves an ideological function by justifying the idea of the impartial decision-maker who ostensibly administers justice in a fair and impartial manner, but in fact perpetuates the oppression and disadvantage of some groups and the privilege of others. Such bureaucratic, hierarchical authority excludes particularity, personal feelings, and subjective desires either to a domestic private sphere or to the margins of society by silencing or ignoring groups whose needs and interests fail to conform to the universal, impartial ideal. Above all, the ostensibly neutral, impartial, universal moral standpoint is, in fact, a nonneutral, partial, and particular standpoint. Any individual or group whose experience differs from the universal standpoint is viewed as deviant and inferior, or merely that of a member of a "special interest group." The result is that people must either adopt the identity of the mainstream—assimilate to a white-Anglo-heterosexual-male identity—or be disadvantaged by their different identities. The ideal of impartiality and a unified civic public is a false universal that fails to represent group differences.

By focusing on group oppression, the politics of difference distinguishes itself from the liberalism's emphasis on individualism. Social groups constitute the identities of their members based on shared experiences, common history, practices, and forms of life. Groups are social constructions that reflect social relations among groups. We are all "outsiders" and "insiders" of the various groups to which we belong and which make up who we are individually and collectively. Young is concerned with what she calls the "five faces of oppression," which include exploitation, marginalization, powerlessness, cultural imperialism, and violence committed by groups against each other.[4] The politics of difference affirms justice and the rule of law, while recognizing group differences and promoting diversity and multiculturalism. As opposed to the supposedly neutral ideal of assimilation that would obliterate our different identities, collapsing them into a homogenous public in a way that perpetuates the five faces of oppression, the politics of difference promotes justice and emancipation by promoting value of the distinctiveness of oppressed groups. "Radical democratic pluralism acknowledges and affirms the public and political significance of social group differences as a means of ensuring the participation and inclusion of everyone in social and political institutions."[5] Respecting group differences instead of overcoming them is the key to overcoming political exclusion, segregation, and domination.

Taylor takes a somewhat different approach to show how the liberal democratic tradition is at odds with the politics of difference and recognition.[6] The thesis underlying the demand for recognition is that our identity is partly shaped by the recognition of significant others, and that nonrecognition or misrecognition can significantly harm, demean, and oppress individuals and groups by consigning people to false or distorted characterizations that present real obstacles to social justice. Recognition is something we owe to others not merely as a courtesy but because it is a necessary human need. According to Taylor, the need of oppressed groups for recognition by has historic roots in modernity. The collapse of feudal social hierarchies of "honor," where a minority was identifiable by its title, gave way to modern notions of inherent human dignity that everyone shares in. Whereas before only some people were "Lord" and "Lady," now anyone is "Mr.," "Mrs.," or "Ms." The concept of equal recognition of human dignity is the only one compatible with a democratic society. The importance of recognition was intensified but complicated by Romantic thinkers, who introduced an inward turn that further individualized personal identity with ideas of "authenticity," "being true to oneself," and conscience as an "inner voice within." Each person —and culture—is so unique and original that the prospect of conforming to external constraints is a moral issue because it endangers the very thing that makes us human. Both Rousseau and Kant have versions of a morality that demands fidelity to oneself to attain a unity of purpose with others.

Modernity thus created two competing modes of politics: one geared toward respecting the universal rights of each citizen, another geared toward respecting the distinctiveness of individuals and cultures. The politics of universalization emphasizes the equal dignity, rights, and entitlements of all citizens, whereas the politics of difference requires that we recognize the uniqueness of individuals and groups as distinct from everyone else. Both modes of politics have a universalist basis requiring equal respect for *everyone*. However, what is to be respected in everyone is not the same. The politics of difference asks that we acknowledge "something that is not universally shared," or what "is universally present . . . through recognizing what is peculiar to each."[7] In other words, it asks that we (universally) recognize specificity, not universality. The liberal notion of respect can mean both the respect owed to the unique identities of individuals in a difference-blind way, as well as the respect for the particular practices, traditions, and cultural forms of life valued by various social groups. Walzer calls these two universalistic perspectives of liberalism, "Liberalism 1" and "Liberalism 2," respectively. Liberalism 1 requires political neutrality among diverse groups; Liberalism 2 requires that public institutions further the values and protect the identities of particular cultural communities.[8]

The difference between the two can be seen in the way they fight against discrimination. The politics of universal dignity fights discrimination by being blind to the ways people are different; the politics of recognition redefines nondiscrimination as requiring differential treatment to protect the distinctiveness of individuals and groups. One will champion "reverse-discrimination" as a remedy for past injustices that deny equal opportunity and prevent us from achieving a difference-blind society of equals; the other will champion "preferential treatment" in order to preserve distinctive cultural identities for their own sake. Like Young, Taylor warns that the supposedly neutral set of difference-blind principles in fact are reflections of a hegemonic culture masquerading as universal. The politics of universal dignity then violates its own principle of respect by suppressing, marginalizing, or demanding conformity of minority cultures.

Given the tension in liberalism between universalism and cultural distinctiveness, public institutions cannot refuse to respond to the demands for recognition by its citizens when cultural survival is at stake—or even when cultural enhancement or flourishing is at stake. As societies become increasingly multicultural, the demand for recognition will have to outweigh "the rigidities of political liberalism" if the rights of cultural communities are to be supported. The politics of recognition simply asks that we respect the experiences, works, and identities of those belonging to other cultures, and that we should comport ourselves under a "presumption of equal worth" before passing judgment of any kind. It is arrogant to rule out the possibility a priori that we could not learn something about "the good, the holy, the admirable" from people from different cultures. Like Gadamer, Taylor says we should be willing "to be open to comparative cultural study of the kind that must displace our horizons in the resulting fusions."[9]

Ricoeur prefers to address the issue of multiculturalism in terms of recognition rather than identity. The problem with many discourses on identity is that they give rise to problematic notions of sameness, essentialism, and homogenizing assimilation in a way that the idea of recognition does not. "The demand of

identity," Ricoeur says, "always involves something violent with respect to others. On the contrary, the search for recognition implies reciprocity" (CC 60).
The idea of recognition always involves an encounter with otherness in a way
that is less apparent in the idea of identity. Even if this characterization is a bit
of an exaggeration—especially in light of his own work on identity—it nevertheless indicates his preference for recognition politics over identity politics. He
worries that identity politics degenerates into an "ideology of difference" that
only consolidates the differences among groups in a way that prevents dialogue,
reciprocity, and mutual understanding.

> The ideology of difference, by failing to differentiate among differ-
> ences, destroys the critical spirit which rests on shared common
> rules of discussion and on the participation of communities of argu-
> mentation recruited on bases other than the historical constitution
> of different group affiliations. The paradox is indeed that the praise
> of difference ends up reinforcing the internal identities of the
> groups themselves. (CC 56)

Recognition politics avoid the simplistic extremes of, on the one hand, the
ideology of integration that obliterates group differences, and, on the other
hand, the ideology of difference that fragments and disintegrates social life
beyond repair.

   While Ricoeur is sympathetic to the aims of the politics of difference as
a reaction to "the merciless leveling of the society of production, consumption, and leisure," he believes the attacks made on the idea of universality itself are misguided, self-defeating, and "potentially devastating" (CC 53–56).
The best way to address group membership, exclusion, and oppression, as well
as to redress wrongs inflicted on groups in the present or the past, is to retain
an ideal of universality underlying political liberalism that is dialectically opposed to the communitarian aim to take historic particularities into account.
This "to-and-fro" between universalists and communitarians proceeds "on
the basis of their recognized shortcomings" and produces the most "fruitful
mediations." We have already encountered a number of these mediations—
for example, between hermeneutics and the critique of ideology, the ethical
aim and moral norm, and critique and conviction. We have also seen that
these are interminable practical mediations with no theoretical outcome.
There will always be tensions between the universal and particular, the part
and the whole, and global and local. But at some point political action requires that we interrupt critique and adopt convictions that guide our actions,

policies, and laws, all the while understanding that they are always revisable, contestable, and fallible.[10]

Ricoeur, however, further complicates the politics of recognition with his claim that ideology and utopia are permanent features of our personal and collective identities. The very constitutive narratives we tell ourselves and inherit from others may also function as ideology or utopia, integrating and consolidating a society while legitimating a ruling authority, or disintegrating and challenging a society in the name of alternative possibilities. Gender, ethnicity, race, and sexuality are all narratively constituted social identities. As such they are highly interpretive, contestable constructions with no clear definition of who belongs, what membership consists of, what the relationship is between individual and group identity, who constructs identities, what the difference is between a legitimate group identity and a false stereotyped generalization, and why an identity is constructed and how it functions in relation to social inclusion and social justice. Even if we grant Taylor's notion of the "presumption of equal worth" of a tradition, how does recognizing a group further the Enlightenment project of freeing us from the domination concealed by tradition? How do we make sense of divisions within groups without retreating into liberal individualism? Are there important differences to identities based on gender, race, ethnicity, religion, and sexuality or do they all raise relevantly similar claims to legitimate recognition?

One of Ricoeur's most important contributions to the multiculturalism debates is his notion of collective memory. As part of the three related models designed to create new governing institutions for European nations, collective memory is at the heart of cultural understanding, or what he calls the "ethics of linguistic hospitality." By sharing the stories that constitute individual and group identities we learn how to experience things from the perspective of others. Exchanging memories, in the sense of recounting stories together, is "recognition considered in its narrative dimension."[11] Collective memory is at the crossroads of history, identity, and alterity; it mediates shared experiences and self-understanding, and is geared toward the practical level of ethical action.

> Memory exercises two functions: it ensures temporal continuity, by allowing us to move along the axis of time; it allows us to recognize ourselves and to say *I, my*. History in its turn contributes something other than the feeling of belonging to the same field of temporal consciousness, through its recourse to documents that have been preserved in a material form; this is what enables it to tell in other terms, to tell from the point of view of others. (CC 124)

Memory is both public and private, often constituted reciprocally, as people re-member events together and interpret them in terms of shared, historical events. Remembering together creates the bonds that hold social groups together—and just as often keeps groups apart. We often cannot help but rethink our own group membership(s) when confronted by the memories of and demand for recognition made by others. It is a complicated matter for many who may have only part of their identities tied up in those particular group memberships, or whose membership in these groups are the result of the perception of others, not of oneself.

Collective memory is very often intertwined with official state memory, commemorations, and celebrations that have a way of flirting with ideologically fixed interpretations that serve dominant group interests. Identities founded on memories not open to re-examination and reinterpretation fail to recognize and respect others. At best, such memories and identities should be tolerated, but never respected. Collective memory, however, is always debatable and revisable. Individuals and groups must be able to recount events in new ways, and hence remember themselves and constitute themselves differently. These memories and identities deserve recognition and respect. The task is to open dialogue, foster debate, and initiate exchanges of memories between and among the powerful and powerless to free ourselves from the grip of our fixed identities.

Opening the past to new interpretations and sharing these memories with each other creates the living traditions in which we all stand. As we reappraise the past we change the way the understand the present and the future. "Collec-tive memory," Ricoeur says, "is the place of humiliation, of demands, of guilt, of celebrations, hence of veneration as well as loathing" (CC 123). For individ-uals and groups who have suffered wrongs in the hands of other individuals and groups, revisiting the past and exchanging memories with others—including those who inflicted harm on us—is vital not only for a better self-understanding but also for the sake of setting the record straight, as well as for addressing and overcoming social and political exclusion, domination, violence, and oppression. That is why Ricoeur emphasizes a particularly healing form of mutual revision in the form of forgiveness. To forgive is to recognize harm inflicted and caused in order to be released from haunting memories and, perhaps, to be reconciled with an offender. A similar process of mutual recognition occurs in an apology, which also recognizes each party as guilty and suffering, allows for a reinterpre-tation of the past, and opens the possibility for reconciliation.

Ricoeur is careful to distinguish between the different calls for recogni-tion coming from different groups, on the basis of different identities, in differ-ent historical contexts. He explains that this is why he always returns to "the idea of incomparable histories, and consequently to the specificity of ethnic and political problematics. This is also why the universal, in this domain, cannot be constitutive but regulative" (CC 65). Because the historical contexts of the specific problems raised by particular groups are always different, Ricoeur says it would be irresponsible to determine in advance how problems of ethnic and political injustice should be addressed. In this respect he is like Habermas, who is also careful to differentiate among the struggles for recognition of disadvantaged groups.[12] The kind of discrimination incurred and the failure of cultural recognition experienced by each group needs to be considered in its historic specificity. For example, the struggles of women, homosexuals, the disabled, oppressed ethnic and cultural minorities, nationalist movements, and anticolonialists, are not only different from each other, but need to be further differentiated by historical context, political context, and intergroup divisions based on class, race, gender, and language. The specific goals of each group also must be considered given the different problems, strategies, and issues involved in, for example, the struggle for equal rights, social and political membership, multicultural education, preservation of identity, and political independence. Young's five faces of oppression are important for determining precisely what kind of social injustice is at issue so that it can be eliminated through the appropriate political, legal, institutional, or cultural changes. Ricoeur's notion of incomparable histories is his way of respecting difference without celebrating it for its own sake.

Closely related to the notion of incomparable histories is the idea that the universal must be regulative (providing rules for possible experience) not constitutive (of particular objects of experience). A regulative idea is not an object but a principle of understanding. As an example of a regulative political idea, Ricoeur cites Kant's notion (in "Perpetual Peace") that the law of world citizenship be limited to conditions of "universal hospitality." Hospitality, according to Kant, means the right of a stranger "not to be treated as an enemy upon his arrival in another's country." Strangers always have "the right to visit, to associate . . . for since the earth is a globe, they cannot scatter themselves infinitely, but must . . . tolerate living in close proximity."[13] Since no one originally owned the earth, Kant continues, no one has more right than another to any particular part of it. In other words, given the finite space we share we have the *right* to be treated with hospitality, not as strangers. It is not an argument for the rights of citizenship but an argument against xenophobia. It affirms the sovereignty of governments but insists that individuals have the right to live in its spaces of jurisdiction and be welcomed there. This is just one example of how a regulative idea can generate practical principles (CC 65–66).

According to Ricoeur, the mistake made by communitarians is to follow Hegel and thereby conflate the ideas of regulative and constitutive universality by attempting to deduce political power from geographical, cultural, ethnic, or other specific spaces of mutual recognition. Kant's argument hinges on the putatively coercive nature of the political realm, which he believes must be limited by a principle of reason that cannot be deduced from any culturally specific, communitarian considerations. Regulative ideas serve to limit the claims of particular political regimes. Echoing Habermas, Ricoeur states that the value and importance of universality cannot be challenged because, "one can regressively determine the conditions of the possibility of a minimal recognition in a space of exchange. And there one will again always find a universal prior to the regional operations of the spheres of recognition" (CC 67). Elsewhere Ricoeur calls it a "contextualized universal" that attempts to integrate the transcendental and empirical, universal and particular. Again and again he stresses that these oppositions have only practical, fragile resolutions—that is, practical wisdom as the desire to live well with and for others in just institutions.

Perhaps the ultimate contribution of Ricoeur's critical theory for the politics of identity and recognition is the requirement that social bonds be restored and reconciled in the face of conflicts. Justice must be restorative, not retributive, if we are to respect and fully recognize individuals and groups. The argument for restorative justice assumes that relationships of all sorts—personal, romantic, familial, social, and political—all involve conflicts from time to time; we would never be able to live together were we not capable of coping with and overcoming the bad things done to us by others. Restorative justice is one way to restore bonds after a conflict. Ricoeur proposes that we institutionalize the means for an ongoing public discourse geared toward exchanging memories, forgiving—and I would add apologizing—for past and ongoing oppression, violence, and suffering. It is a call for more public dialogue on the various racial, ethnic, gender, and other group differences that prevent us from living well together and respecting each other. The goal of these public dialogues can be anything from historical honesty, self-understanding, apology and restitution, reconciliation, reparations, among other ends.

There are examples of public debate over past and continuing offenses going on right now all around the world. In Germany, there is a continuing debate about its Nazi past, arguably stirred up following Reagan's visit to Bitburg in 1986, and continued by a series of books detailing the role of civilians in the holocaust. So far the results have been mixed. On the one hand, the government has paid more than 100 billion deutsche marks in reparations to more than 500,000 holocaust survivors, and there is a greater public recognition of past deeds through memorials, commemorations, and debate on their shared heritage, identity, and responsibility; on the other hand, there is an inevitable backlash, resentment, denial, and desire to put the past behind and move forward. Elsewhere the debates have a different character. In France, for example, the trials of Klaus Barbie in 1985 and Maurice Papon in 1998 have lead to a reexamination of the Vichy collaboration in Nazi atrocities. Japan is facing growing pressure to confront its wartime atrocities, including its use of sex slaves, cruel human medical experimentation, and the military invasion of Nanking, where an estimated 275,000 people were brutally killed in 1937. In the United States there is some public discussion over the genocide of Native-Americans, our heritage of slavery, Jim Crow apartheid, and our role in supporting oppressive regimes around the world. There is, however, no serious debate about the need to apologize, rethink our imperialist past and present, or make reparations for the victims of slavery and genocide. Perhaps the best example of exchange of memories, apology, and forgiveness is South Africa's Truth and Reconciliation Commission. Although it has polarized the country as much as it has healed it, and the offer of amnesty for disclosure violates the key element of memory in shaping identities and achieving recognition, the commission is another living example of a political body attempting to recognize others and seek restorative, not retributive justice.[14]

Owning up to past errors and offenses through apologies and requests for forgiveness and reconciliation are one way to reinterpret ourselves and recognize others. For example, in March, 2000, Pope John Paul XXIII issued a carefully worded apology and repentance for the Catholic Church's errors, including silence about participation in the Holocaust, and the Spanish Inquisition among other violent events over the last one-thousand years. Another way is through national and international conferences, councils, and panels, like President Clinton's President's Initiative on Race, and the World Conference on Racism sponsored by the United Nations. These are designed to build consensus, issue statements and positions, condemnations, and make policy and legal reforms. Another way to deal with the past is through the legal institutions like the International War Crimes Tribunals, held recently for those charged with the commission of atrocities in Yugoslavia and Rwanda. There are now increased calls for such tribunals to be held to address human rights violations in East Timor, Chile, Cambodia, as well as to assess number of U.S. violations of international law in such places as Iraq, Kosovo, Nicaragua, and Guatemala. To date the United States continues to oppose the United Nations' proposal for an International Criminal Court designed to deal specifically with war crimes, genocide, and crimes against humanity.[15]

The incomparable histories of different groups makes it difficult to generalize about the institutional, legal, and social implications of the politics of recognition. Groups face different forms of oppression and exclusion and so the challenges they face differ depending on their particular political contexts and their particular goals and agendas for action. There are, however, some common threads joining these different calls for recognition by various groups around the world that suggest some minimal political guidelines. (1) There have to be spaces of discourse where groups can raise claims to recognition, and where a public debate can occur that fosters understanding and an exchange memories; (2) there have to be institutional mechanisms in place that have the power to redress claims for recognition, and that are authorized to make changes affecting social, political, and economic practices; (3) criminal justice must be restorative, not retributive, so that the collective resolution of conflicts includes and thus recognizes everyone involved in an offense, its aftermath, and its implications for the future; and (4) public education should be geared toward teaching the virtues of citizenship implied in recognition politics and restorative justice, so that everyone will have the skills required to participate in public debate and political action. A critical theory can contribute to the politics of recognition by showing how conceptions of individual and group identities in conjunction with social, political, economic, and legal practices function to perpetuate or ameliorate injustice and domination.

TECHNOLOGY AND POLITICS

Philosophy of technology is a critical, reflective examination of the effects and transformation of technologies on human activities and societies. It aims to develop critical forms of thought so as to be able to understand, evaluate, appreciate, and criticize the ways in which technologies reflect as well as change human life, individually, socially, and culturally. The philosophy of technology of the first half of the twentieth century was dominated by philosophers who construed technology as a "technique" of knowledge that organizes both the natural and social worlds into neutral objects of control and manipulation. Philosophers like Heidegger, Marcuse, and Habermas adopted a transcendental critique of technology as a form of rationality based primarily on calculation and efficiency.[16] This technological rationality requires, legitimizes, and produces social domination by demanding that all life submit to its homogenizing techniques. They believed that technological rationality underlies the kind of thinking found in science, industry, economics, management, and bureaucracy. Anything that counters the rationality of efficiency is seen as irrational. Technological rationality consists of routine, mechanical, standardized rules for thought and action that have taken over advanced industrial societies to the point where every aspect of human life is "technicalized" and controlled by experts. Technology is amoral, blind to ends, and, above all, dehumanizing. So goes the critique by the forerunners of philosophy of technology.

Ricoeur falls squarely within this tradition. On more than one occasion, Ricoeur claims that both technology and economics are governed by a rationality of efficiency that links means to ends producing a social order governed only by the dictates of efficiency. He often opposes the realms of ethics and politics— or a kind of humanism, in general—to technology and the economy. Echoing Marcuse, he warns that "the conquest of the economy by . . . the same rationality that was previously at work in technology and in the sciences," will subordinate the social-political and culture dimensions to "dehumanizing calculation" and "technocracy" (PS 230). He concurs with Habermas that science and technology are forms of "knowledge for control" that function as ideology when such interests supersede an interest in communication. When "the primacy of accorded to calculation and efficiency" becomes "the new form of the sacred," responsible political action appears to impractical and unreasonable (TA 327). The task facing us is to begin a process that would subject the "dissolving action exerted by technology" over the economic sphere to democratic processes in order to restore our lost humanity and shattered cultural heritage. If we fail we will face increasing "anonymity and dehumanization," "barbaric forms of urbanism," and "the leveling of tastes and talents by the techniques of consumption and leisure" (PS 290–292).

The promise of technology, according to Ricoeur, is to harness its potential to serve the interests and needs of historic communities. The technological-economic order is an "abstract social mechanism" geared toward the "struggle against nature, the methodical organization of labor, and the rationalization of the relations between production, circulation, and consumption" (TA 326). The calculating efficiency of technological-economic rationality is a "universal rationality" detached from the historical-political contexts that inform the nontechnical realms of social life. As such it contains the potential to transform economic life into something genuinely universal, rational, and collective—in other words, uniformity in the good sense. Ricoeur follows Marx by characterizing the technological-economic realm as the "great educator" of individuals that is the key to developing our full, human capacities, as active, creative beings. Freeing ourselves from the struggle against nature is the minimal condition to achieving our full humanity. At the same time, the increasing autonomy of the technological-economic order has taken over and colonized the ethicopolitical

core of historical communities leaving us with only two choices: either we submit to the rationality of technocapitalism and let it govern our lives, or we recover our cultural and political life, tame the economy, and make it work for us,
not against us. Technology, on this reading, is a juggernaut that must be controlled or else it will swallow us whole.

In *Oneself as Another*, Ricoeur repeats this rather typical view of technology when he contrasts the different kinds of embodiment exhibited by literary
fiction and science fiction.[17] The former involve imaginative variations of our
embodied being-in-the-world, whereas the latter are variations on nonexperi-
enceable possibilities, usually involving things like cerebral traces, bionics, and
molecular teleportation. Ihde calls science fiction contrast of "technomyths,"
one utopian, the other dystopian. For example, Parfit's sci-fi, technological
thought experiments not only involve a reductionist notion of embodiment but
also a "technological dream" that my body become completely bionic through
technological intervention. The fantasy that technology will transform me, enhance me, and empower me is the hallmark of technological utopianism. By
contrast, the literary fiction that Ricoeur champions not only involves the notion of embodiment as being-in-the-world but also a fear of technology as
something that wrenches us away from the very "corporeal" and "terrestrial"
conditions that make experience meaningful. The notion that technology will
dominate me, control me, and separate me both from nature and face-to-face
encounters with other people is the hallmark of technological dystopianism.[18]
Ricoeur once again contrasts technology and technological rationality, this time
in the form of science fiction, with something more primordial, humane, and
connected to the natural and social worlds.

The problem with this interpretation of technology is not just that it is
old and tired, but that it is at best limited and at worst false. Both the utopians
and dystopians fail to recognize that not all technologies are the same. There is
no single essence of technological rationality, only a family resemblance of
overlapping devices, skills, knowledge, uses, and techniques. How can one
argue for an essence of technology in the face of the innumerably different
technologies, used in different contexts, in difference places and times, by different users, employing different skill sets, designed for different purposes, all of
which are open to conflicting interpretations? Some technologies are used like
tools, some are worn like clothes, some are ingested like medicine, some are
inhabited like houses, some are viewed like television, some are read like books,
some are in the background like air conditioning, some are played like the
piano. Some technologies are systems containing a number of different implements and skills, like a communication system, plumbing system, transportation

system, and agricultural systems. The notion of calculating rationality can hardly make sense of all of the different implements and skills required for entire technological systems to operate. The picture gets further complicated once we include the technologies of writing (e.g., books, maps, record keeping, mathematics) and other tools and skills of naming, dividing up and interpreting the world. Once we recognize that there are many different technologies, and that calculative-instrumental rationality poorly describes their use and function, then we can see that technologies are like anything else in the world having a social meaning, and must be interpreted against a cultural horizon just like any other social reality.

Feenberg makes a strong case against the understanding of technological rationality as singular and dystopic by showing how much in common it shares with the conventional, "instrumental" notion that technologies are neutral, value-free tools capable of being used for good or bad purposes. On the received view, technologies themselves are indifferent to the ends to which they are employed. They embody a universal, scientific rationality and thus are neutral with respect to particular use contexts, as well as other social-political contexts of application. Questions concerning technology are usually framed in terms of "trade-offs" between efficiency and other nontechnical values (e.g., the environment, bioethics, religion, and health). But the nature of technology itself as a neutral, efficient tool is never questioned; it can only be limited, not transformed by nontechnical values. In contrast to the instrumental theory, the "substantive" theory (of Heidegger, Marcuse, and Habermas) maintains that technology is a value-laden form of rationality that links means and ends producing a social world geared toward efficiency and control. Both views assume that technology is autonomous and resistant to change. Our only choice is to "take it or leave it," because it belongs to a different realm, governed by a different rationality, and is immune from transformation. All we can do is reject it, limit it, or control it; what we cannot do is change it. Yet both the instrumental and substantive theories of technology fail to see that humans can build or design tools and implements in a number of different ways, embodying different values, serving different ends, with the potential to control us, liberate us, and transform us. We have the potential to change the values designed into our technologies once we recognize that they are all too human, and thus no more or less oppressive than we are.[19]

Technologies are best seen as systems that combine techniques and activities with implements and artifacts, within a social context of organization in which the technologies are developed, employed, and administered. They alter patterns of human activity and institutions by making worlds that shape our culture and our environment. If technology consists of not only tools, implements and artifacts, but also whole networks of social relations that structure, limit, and enable social life, then we can say that a circle exists between humanity and technology, each shaping and affecting the other. Technologies are fashioned to reflect and extend human interests, activities, and social arrangements, which are, in turn, conditioned, structured, and transformed by technological systems. Critical theory can help us understand and evaluate this circular relationship only if we grant that technologies belong to the province of meaning. That way we can recognize them as human constructs that can be designed to reflect human needs and interests. Ricoeur's contribution to a critical theory of technology is a model of interpreting the meaning of technological devices, practices, and systems in a way that accounts for the many different possible experiences and conflicting interpretations of them, explains how they shape and influence individual and group identities, and provides with normative criteria capable of judging and evaluating the moral rightness and appropriateness of their use, development, and administration.

The most important aspect of Ricoeur's hermeneutics for a philosophy of technology is his notion of indirect, mediated experience. If human experience is always mediated by discourse, in particular texts, and discourse is materially embodied in the technologies of inscription, then it follows that human experience is also technologically mediated. The textual mediation of experience is also the technological mediation of experience. There would be no writing, no literary works, no recorded laws, no history, no literary genres at all were there no technologies like pens, paper, ink, typewriters, and word processors. Written works are the material embodiments of labor and action. There are a number of ways, as Ricoeur says, "of treating language as a material to be worked upon and formed. Discourse thereby becomes the object of a *praxis* and a *techne*. In this respect, there is not a sharp opposition between mental and manual labour" (TA 80). The circular relationship between narrating and experiencing embodied in writing brings together the realms of meaning, labor, and technology. As a result, the production and interpretation of written works requires that certain material conditions be met that allow for its creation, distribution, and comprehension. Ricoeur thus adds a material dimension to the Gadamerian notion of "effective history." The past that is operative in the present is a technologically mediated past. These material conditions also shape and form other kinds of experiences that are more recognizably mediated by technology, like reading maps, telling time through clocks, interpreting medical or scientific instruments, writing machine code, and a host of other implements that are read like texts.[20] The model of the text is also the model for the mediation of experience by technology.

Similarly, just as a text gains semantic autonomy with respect to its original author, context, and reader, any technology can be interpreted like a text, with a meaning open to interpretation apart from the original intentions of its creators or primary users. Like any object, technologies are given against a background in terms of which they gain meaning. Just as there is no thing in itself, there is no technology in itself apart from the social horizon in which it is embedded. A technology is what it is in relation to its use-context and broader cultural context. The meaning of a technology, therefore, is not determined only by experts, engineers, and inventors; any user, observer, or other interpreter determines the meaning and uses of things. Technologies are an inseparable part of human history, the interpretation of which belongs to no single privileged group. As a province of meaning, there are an indefinite number of questions to be asked concerning technology, including questions about use, purpose, and function, effects, risks, and consequences, as well as various *who* questions about who made it, who uses it, who paid for it, who benefits from it, and who suffers from it. In short, there is no single question concerning technology because there is no singular technological phenomenon.[21]

Like any other social phenomenon, the form of discourse used to address ourselves to various technological questions is narrative-argumentative. Technologies have histories. They are invented and developed over time, usually in collaboration with others, but always in a particular historical context to be applied in a particular use context. Understanding a technology involves an understanding of its past, the way that it interacts with and affects its users, and the vast network of activities, agents, and devices. What Latour calls "sociotechnical collectives" refers to the inseparably related network of relations between and among humans and machines. According to Latour, there has never been such a thing as humanity without technology nor technology without humanity. Sociality is material just as materiality is social. We are "sociotechnical animals," and so all of our interactions are also sociotechnical. Once we recognize how intertwined humans and nonhumans are, a number of modernist dichotomies blur: objectivity and subjectivity, realism and relativism, nature and society, scientific fact and social understanding. Too often Ricoeur takes over these dichotomies if only to link them dialectically, as he does with methodological explanation and historical understanding. But if Latour is right, then we must give up the illusion that technological understanding is somehow different from social understanding, and hence the illusion that science and technology are free and independent from ethics and politics.[22] To rescue Ricoeur from himself we need to extend his notion of narrative understanding beyond human action to include the natural and technical worlds as well. Science and technology are thoroughly human, social, and historical activities, and as such are to be understood in a narrative configuration of actions, events, intentions, devices, machines, and other technologies. If anything that takes place in time unfolds in a narrative, certainly the intertwined history of societies and their technologies also unfolds in a narrative.

The counterpole to humanizing technology is technologizing humans. If technological change patterns and shapes human history, and if Ricoeur is right that personal and political identities are formed by telling stories about ourselves that configure a history out of heterogeneous events, actions, decisions, and so on, then perhaps we have a way to explain how technologies enter into identity formation. Our technologically textured social environment forms the background and context within which individuals and groups constitute their identities. Technology is fundamental in the constitution of a social order. It establishes, organizes, maintains, and constrains social life by enabling, sustaining, and mediating our shared, sociotechnical experiences. Technology is not something that merely affects a society; it is a society. But unlike the substantive theorists, who believe that technology determines a social order, it is more accurate to say that it is influential in making a social order. As Winner says, technologies are forms of life. To make and implement a technology is not just to use a tool or an artifact; it is to make a world. Humans and technologies are interrelated by technological systems that shape our culture, alter patterns of human activity and institutions, and influence who we are, and how we live.[23]

There are many examples of tools, implements, devices and systems that play a role in the formation of one's identity. These may include the reading and writing implements I and others use to determine who I am; communication technologies, like telephones and e-mail I use to maintain my friendships and relationships; the medicine and medical technologies I need to stay alive or at least remain healthy; the enhancement technologies I use to alter my capacities or characteristics, like cosmetic surgery, and mood altering or performance enhancing drugs; official records, ID cards, photographs, DNA samples, and other things needed to identify me. More significantly are the technological practices I participate in to define my identity. I interpret who I am through my use of implements, devices, and artifacts within systems of social practices. For example, I may consider myself a painter, a writer, a basketball player, a musician, or a movie buff. As with a personal identity, the establishment of a political or group identity is also mediated by technological implements and practices. Identities are shaped by the materiality of where we live, how we live, and what economic opportunities are available to us. The historical conditions of our lives that influence our identities are also influence by our technological surroundings. Who we are is a matter of various technological considerations, having to do with economic practices, living conditions, communication and transportation systems, as well as various dangers from technologies that affect our lives like pollution, radiation, and hazardous working conditions.

All of the technologies that constitute our past and delimits our horizon of possibility can be understood in terms of Ricoeur's notion of traditionality, from *Time and Narrative*. Traditionality is the content of what is handed down from the past and constitutes our historical belonging. Among the things inherited from the past are the technologies that shape our world. They too become configured into the narratives we use to understand ourselves. The same dynamics of the text provide for a model for the technological mediation of experience.

Foucault's thesis that institutions function as techniques of control in the creation of subjects is helpful in thinking about how technologies affect us. In *Discipline and Punish*, where he focuses on institutions as the site of the production and control of (docile) bodies, Foucault includes physical spaces, design, and architecture as elements to power relations. He links technology, spatial relations, social relations, as being critical to the formation of identity. The section on "Panopticism" is especially insightful about the mechanisms and machinery of power.[24] Harvey's work on architecture, geography, and urbanization is also helpful in this connection. In various ways, our human capacities are embedded in a social and physical world of constraints and limitations. What Harvey calls "dialectical utopianism" is a search for spatiotemporal forms that would permit the full development of human potentialities. The design of a just society is inseparable from a critique of globalization, environmental degradation, and architectural processes that enable or hinder our ability to live together in a more equitable and ecologically sensible way. The "insurgent architect" respects universal human rights and ecological integrity in the design of utopian spaces.[25] The work of thinkers like Foucault and Harvey add content to Ricoeur's thesis that identities are narrative constructions of the practical field of action. They develop his idea that the spaces of political action, including the just institutions required for developing our capacities and living well with others, are actual, physical spaces, whose construction and design can either promote or undermine justice and happiness.

The political question concerning technological has to do with decisions about the design, development, management, and consequences of technological systems. The reason why technology is important for critical theory has to do with the powerful influence it has over the very nature of social life and its capacity to affect lasting changes on the environment. The kinds of technologies a society has determines how people live in the world and how they reproduce themselves materially, culturally, and symbolically. Ricoeur is sympathetic to the concerns of Jonas that the kinds of problems created by contemporary, global technologies requires a new kind of ethical reasoning corresponding to our new powers over the entire planet. This new notion of responsibility would be extended to consider future humanity and the environment as well. Although Ricoeur thinks that Jonas's imperative that responsibility extend into the unforeseeable future is problematic from the standpoint of moral imputation, he agrees that the "power that technology confers today on humankind over life" requires that we take responsibility for the consequences of technologies as they regard both the present and the future of the natural and social worlds (OA 272).

Unfortunately, there is very little public debate the United States over the design and choice of technologies. The way we determine which ones to adopt is through a combination of market forces and decisions made by elected officials. Most of us have little or no control over the former; even if I choose not to buy some things, my choices are determined by other people and circumstances beyond my control. I may still have to cope with technologies I would never choose—life filled with automobiles and traffic, pollution and noise, environmental hazards, unhealthy food additives, downtown ghost towns, and an unpredictable economy. It is hard to have faith in market mechanisms if my life and the choices available to me are exessively shaped and patterned by the decisions and choices of others. The same is true of decisions made by elected officials. Although we ostensibly have some say over the policies and practices of our representatives, when it cómes to technology policy they tend to favor market mechanism over long-term public interest considerations. Even worse is that many of these decisions are lasting and often irreversible. Among the crucial decisions are those made about systems of transportations, communication, agriculture, energy, medical care, and waste management. Too often these these decision are made by small groups of technically skilled peoples, who we have no choice but believe have our best interests in mind. Citizens have little or no say in decisions that shape and pattern our collective fate when market forces and undemocratic groups of people exercise illegitimate control over our lives.

The answer to the political question concerning technology is to allow for the participation of anyone affected by particular technologies and technological systems. Their design, choice, implementation, and administration must be democratic, if we truly respect the dignity and autonomy of individuals. The criteria for legitimate technologies should derive from the desire to live well with others in just institutions in exercising practical reasoning with respect to the role and the ends of government. All citizens should have a right to participate in the decisions that affect them in their capacity as citizens; since technologies affect my autonomy, freedom, opportunity, and the common good, we have a right to participate in decisions about them as well. In addition, since we all have a desire to live well, and since technologies affect our individual and collective notion of the good life, we should be able to determine how we want to live in communities, and hence determine which technologies foster the good life and which prevent it. The implication for political policy is to create the mechanisms that would enable people to accept or reject technologies wherever we determine that our autonomy and ability to live the good life is affected.[26]

One course of action would be to pressure political leaders to model their procedures for determining science and technology policy after existing European systems. In Sweden, for example, non-scientists represent the majority of the government's Council for Planning and Coordination of Research; in Denmark representatives from citizen, consumer, labor, and environmental groups have the opportunity to examine their science and technology policy recommendations, and then bring their findings both to Parliament and to the public in a nationally-televised press conference; citizen panels are also found in France, the Netherlands, Switzerland, Germany, and Japan. Decisions about technologies should be made in a democratic process that would include representatives from grassroots organizations, public interest groups, academics from the social and natural sciences, and community organizations. Technology policy already is political; the key is to make it serve public not private interests.

GLOBALIZATION AND DEMOCRACY

Throughout his political writings Ricoeur has argued for an international government as a federation of nations. A global government should respect human rights and foster the mutual recognition of people everywhere as free, equal, and responsible under a system of international laws. It should also protect the distinctive cultural heritage of groups and nations from the harmful, destructive effects of modernization, industrialization, and economic globalization. The universal element in globalization is paradoxical—the universal is a principle that assures that all persons are treated with dignity and respect as equal members of a world society and yet it takes the form of totalizing processes that require the conformity of everyone to a global economic order. The challenge facing advocates of global government is to maintain a balance between the push and pull of Enlightenment progress and the hope of attaining universal cosmopolitan citizenship, on the one hand, and conformity to the universal rationality of efficiency manifested in global consumer society, on the other. How is it possible to preserve a cultural heritage and respect universal human rights in the face of unavoidable globalization? Ricoeur's answer is socialism. Before making that argument, I will first discuss his conception of globalization to show how it relates to socialism. Then I will discuss the relevance of his works of the 1960s to the phenomenon of globalization we experience today.

In his 1961 article, "Universal Civilization and National Cultures," Ricoeur asks how we can work toward scientific, technological, and political progress for everyone while safeguarding cultural heritage. The contrast in this work is the familiar conflict between a universal rationality and the particular histories of nations and cultures.

On the one hand, a world civilization is something positive and progressive when it brings about the awareness and mutual recognition of ourselves as a single humanity with a shared, collective fate. Through science and technology, it makes possible things like medicine, labor-saving tools, and improvements in infrastructure that will free us from want and make life more comfortable and easy. In political institutions, a universal civilization would establish democracy, human rights, and other progressive, Enlightenment values. It would also make the recognition of human suffering possible through international governing bodies concerned with the fact that the majority of the world's population lives in poverty, with neither access nor the right to basic goods and services. Finally, at the level of the economy, a universal civilization is forced to act as an educator by fighting illiteracy, even if only as a means to perpetuate culture of consumption.

On the other hand, the universal standardization of rationality, technology, politics, and the economy also has a negative sense. Every potential benefit is contradicted by a number of actual negative affects. For every advancement brought about by globalization it

> at the same time constitutes a sort of subtle destruction, not only of traditional cultures, which might not be an irreparable wrong, but also of what I shall call for the time being the creative nucleus of great civilization and great cultures, that nucleus on the basis of which we interpret life, what I shall call . . . the ethical and mythical nucleus of mankind. (HT 276)

The kind of world civilization we are creating is "mediocre civilization" that is "wearing away" at the cultural resources of the truly great civilizations of the world by standardizing not only production but also "transportation, human relationships, comfort, leisure, and news programming. . . . Everywhere throughout the world, one finds the same bad movies, the same slot machines, the same plastic or aluminum atrocities, the same twisting of language by propaganda, etc." (HT 274–276). The triumph of the consumer culture, where everything is identical and everyone anonymous, would "represent the lowest degree of creative culture" and a danger "at least equal and perhaps more likely than that of atomic destruction" (HT 278).

The dilemma facing nations is that they have no choice but to participate in universal civilization, but at the same time, participation undermines "the creative nucleus" of each nation. The dilemma facing nations that were once European colonies is even more complicated. The struggles against colonialism were not only against economic exploitation but also social and cultural exploitation as well. Many of the ethnic, national, tribal, and religious conflicts that persist today in the postcolonial world are over the very identity and direction of a nation. The act of establishing a postcolonial identity that involves recovering and vindicating a past heritage conflicts with the demands of universal civilization—both in the good and bad senses. The dilemma facing the colonial world is to maintain and preserve a cultural identity when confronted by the plurality of cultures around the world. Without sounding like a conservative alarmist, Ricoeur observes that the experience of other cultures can shake confidence in one's own culture, and it may also lead to the worst kind of cultural relativism—that is, the refusal to see anything but differences among us. Above all, we may fail to recognize that there are indeed important differences between cultures created by consumerism and cultures created by historical traditions. It all becomes the same; nothing is better or worse than anything else.

Ricoeur addresses what he calls the "paradoxes" of universal civilization and national cultures as answers to three questions: "What constitutes the creative nucleus of a civilization? Under what conditions may this creativity be pursued? And how is an encounter with different cultures possible?" (HT 278). To the first question, one can respond that the creative nucleus of a nation is found in its traditional institutions. These institutions contain an "ethicomythical" core that underlies the images and symbols that both reflect and conceal the cultural resources of nation. Cultural traditions must be continually questioned, deciphered, reinterpreted, and re-created or else they will die. To the second question about the condition of creativity, Ricoeur says only cultures that can resist the "pressure and erosive influence" of universal civilization will be able to

renew themselves. To do so cultures must be able to assimilate universal rationality, using it to survive without letting it squelch cultural creativity. People
must also have faith in the historic value and importance of their culture to be
able to participate in systems of universalization without fear of losing their heritage. The point is not just to repeat the past but to be confident enough in our
ability to reinterpret ourselves with honesty and creativity so that we may continually reinvent ourselves—or else our fidelity to the past will be "nothing
more than a simple folkloric ornamentation" (HT 282).

The answer to the third question about the possibility of genuine encounters with different cultures is found in the conditions of cultural creativity.
Just as a living culture is able to renew itself without succumbing to the erosive
influences of universal civilization, it is also capable of encountering others
without the risk of "being swallowed up in a vague syncretism."

> Only a living culture, at once faithful to its origins and ready for
> creativity on the levels of art, literature, philosophy and spirituality,
> is capable of sustaining the encounter of other cultures—not merely
> capable of sustaining but also of giving meaning to that encounter.
> When the meeting is a confrontation of creative impulses, then it is
> itself creative. (HT 283)

Ricoeur concludes with a plea for more dialogue and understanding among nations and cultures as a way of opposing syncretism. The idea that national cultures can be obliterated by communicating with others misunderstands the
nature of both communication and identity. Genuine dialogue with the other
(whether it be a text, individual, or nation) is an exchange of questions and answers in which each is transformed by the other by taking the perspective of the
other. The great challenge facing nations and cultures is to confront each other
in the difficult task of open communication geared toward mutual understanding and recognition so that we may all rethink and renew the traditions that
shape who we are.

Ricoeur's reflections on global federalism were a part of a broader project
in the 1950s–1960s to reinterpret socialism as an economic, political, and social
philosophy. The task facing socialists at that time was to find a "third way" in between liberal capitalism, which respected human rights and liberties but failed to
meet human needs, and Marxist-Leninist communism, which met human needs
but failed to respect human rights and liberties. Above all, the challenge was to
show how socialism can respond to the globalization and rationalization of technology, politics, and economics. His attempt to balance universal civilization and

national cultures is based on the internationalist element of a socialist humanism concerned with political freedom, economic needs, and cultural expression.
Although Ricoeur has been silent on the subject of socialism since then, this has
less to do with a change in his political convictions as it does with a change in
the philosophical landscape. Rethinking Marxism no longer preoccupies him
the way it once he and his French contemporaries in the 1950s and 1960s.
Looking back, however, we can see how prescient he was to link the problems
of socialism, economic globalization, and culture. Although the face globalization has changed since then, the challenges it poses to socialism today are just as
pressing now as they were then.[27]

Ricoeur defines socialism as it relates to the economic, political, and cultural spheres. At the economic level it is "the transition from a market economy
to a planned economy that is responsive to human needs and that is characterized by a transfer of the ownership of the means of production to collective or
public entities" (PS 230). As opposed to a market economy governed by a distribution system based on profit, decisions in planned economy are made by organizations representing the public interest based on satisfying human needs in
order of their urgency. Socialist planning can exist along side a market economy
so long as the fundament needs of everyone are met. However, mixed
economies are intrinsically "incoherent," governed by contradictory ends: one
geared toward individual benefits, the other toward collective benefits. The danger inherent in mixed economies is that public enterprises tend to imitate private enterprises, especially when influenced by private sector representatives. To
prevent the public sector from privileging private sector interests, Ricoeur adds
the requirement that there be a change not only in the function of government
but in the structure and mentality of the economic planners. They must have a
"clear vision of priorities" and of the "large scale decisions" necessary to satisfy
human needs. The humanism in socialism is found even at the level of economic
planning. Another element of the economic sense of socialism is the collective
appropriation of the means of production. Private property is the biggest obstacle to satisfying human needs. The means of production must be democratized
and organized to serve the public interests, not private interest alone.

The goal of socialism is to increase democratic participation in both political and economic decisions. Even more than satisfying human needs, the
"vague aspiration toward a more just, egalitarian, and communal society is the
real soul of socialism" (PS 234). The practice of democratic management, however, even guided by egalitarian ideals is a difficult and intrinsically dangerous
task. Political power will not simply disappear when class antagonisms are eliminated, as Marx says in *The Poverty of Philosophy*.[28] Socialism has to guard against

the very real danger that planning will become centralized in the hands of the few—even if democratically elected—thereby concentrating power in a way that betrays its very egalitarian soul. Ricoeur says it is imperative to create mechanisms that would disperse power through representative bodies responsible for fundamental choices. Socialism "is the system in which a democracy of labor exists side-by-side with planning" (PS 237). A participatory economy requires a participatory democracy. It also requires other liberal safeguards that limit state powers and guarantee the rights of citizens.

> To advance along the path of the *socialist State*, we must continue the task of *liberal politics*, which has always consisted of two things: to divide power among powers, to control executive power by popular representation. (PS 213)

Among the features of divided political power in a socialist state would be an independent judiciary, a free press, labor unions, universities, and other institutions of learning and research. A socialist state needs to institute a separation of powers more than any other political arrangement precisely because of its concentration of economic powers.

Finally, the cultural sphere of socialism builds on the economic and political dimensions, and it is here "in the humanism of socialism that its most fundamental and most stable aim lies" (PS 238). The profound truth of Marx, according to Ricoeur, is to have exposed the dehumanizing conditions and consequences of labor that produces surplus value. The ongoing task for philosophers is to integrate the Marxist notion of alienation into a broader philosophical anthropology. Next, socialist humanism involves a transformation of all governing bodies by restoring human agency over all kinds of bureaucracy, administration, and other blind mechanisms of social control. The idea is to empower people to participate in whatever decisions affect them at the levels of government, work, and community. Finally, socialist humanism involves a transformation of the technical systems and rational techniques that govern our lives. The idea is to change how we live by replacing it with something better, not simply to substitute better techniques for achieving the same hedonistic ethics. "Socialism would then only be a more advanced and more rational industrialism pursuing the same dream of the Promethean conquest of well-being and of nature" (PS 240). To prevent its degeneration into a mere technique we must remember that, at its heart, socialism is based on solidarity and commitment to each other, especially with those who are underprivileged, poor, hungry, and oppressed.

The weakness of the welfare state is the lack of a human perspective. The strength of the socialist camp is precisely the feeling of collective work being done. The friendship, irrespective of border, for those who work and suffer and the deep feeling of belonging to a single human must not be lost. (PS 241)

The role of utopia is to establish hope where there is none so that someday we will overcome the causes of suffering and live together in a socialist society.

Unfortunately, Ricoeur's insightful and hopeful reflections on globalization and socialism suffer from the same shortcomings as his borrowed conception of technology. He remains bewitched by the Weberian the notion of "rationalization," the increasing presence of value-free, formalized procedures of reasoning that deprive both the social and natural world of meaning and purpose while subjecting them to scientific calculation and technological manipulation. Ostensibly, when reason is equated with formal techniques geared only toward efficiency, consistency, and profit our entire social, political, and aesthetic worlds are emptied of their meaning and purpose leaving us nothing but a bureaucratic, technocratic, amoral, and spiritless world.[29] Horkheimer, Adorno, Marcuse, and their colleagues at the Institute for Social Research continued to study the effects of rationalization by analyzing the totalitarian character of formal rationality that has become the dominant cultural logic of state capitalism, fascism, and bureaucratic state socialism.[30] Reason itself is seen as an autonomous cultural force that organizes social life into objects of manipulation, control, and domination. Even Habermas accepts the critique of rationalization as domination but makes it relative to and derivative of a more fundamental, communicative rationality geared toward mutual understanding. He does this by distinguishing between (bad) instrumental rationality and (good) communicative rationality. The aim of critical theory is to expose the influence of instrumental rationality insofar as it interferes with the ability of people to communicate with one another freely about their needs and interests.

Like Habermas, Ricoeur challenges the notion of rationalization by making it relative to a broader, hermeneutic model of social understanding. But he also gives too much credence to a conception of rationality that should have been discredited long ago. It is not at all clear that there even is such a thing as rationalization. Just as there is no single rationality of technology, there is no single rationality underlying science, bureaucracy, management, capitalism, and all the other places it supposedly operates. What Ricoeur calls "universal rationality" refers instead to an ideological self-misunderstanding of a number of techniques of measurement, precision, efficiency, standardization, and other seemingly inflexible rules of organization, administration, and reason. It is the ideology of expertise that attempts to justify procedures and rules to standardize behavior through seemingly objective techniques of reason. But it exists only as ideology. Both the advocates and critics of rationalization attribute a false universality to what is ultimately only an illusion of rationality pretending to be neutral and objective. Like technology, rationalization consists of a range of overlapping practices, meanings, uses, narratives, and machines that underlie a range of different activities and forms of life. Any conception of reason decontextualized from its actual use-contexts and historic contexts of application is a misunderstanding of rationality, not just a partial, limited, or incomplete understanding of it. Neither science, technology, nor universal rationality are ever actually severed from their historical hermeneutic conditions of meaning. Rather they are much more complex and communicative practices involving networks of relations among humans and machines, or sociotechnical collectives.[31]

I would suggest that instead of explaining globalization, or universal civilization, in terms the rationality it ostensibly manifests, we examine the policies, laws, practices, and sociotechnical systems that support it. Globalization does indeed require a pernicious form of standardization in order to achieve a reordering of the world's economic, political, and social arrangements. But it accomplishes its end by deregulating commercial activity, by restructuring economic and political regimes, and by transforming governmental agencies into vehicles serving corporate interests over public interests. In other words, globalization is caused by capitalism, not rationalization, and capitalism can be explained and criticized on strictly moral-political grounds. Such criticism is possible because the engine driving globalization is not some form of rationality but rather a capitalist growth economy fueled by the blind conviction that deregulation of corporate activity, in conjunction with the liberation of currency from national controls, will generate the most wealth for investors, currency speculators, employers, and employees. The ideas underlying economic globalization are not at all new; the only thing new about the "new economy" is its scope and effectiveness thanks to global institutions that support economic expansion. To understand these institutions we need Marx, not Marcuse.

The primary agents of globalization are transnational corporations (TNCs) and financial institutions working in conjunction with national governments and global institutions, like the World Bank, International Monetary Fund, and above all the World Trade Organization (WTO), the world's most powerful agent of global commerce. The WTO was established in 1995 to transform the Uruguay Round of the General Agreement on Tariffs and Trade

(GATT) into an enforceable world governing body. The WTO is currently the primary vehicle for the *corporate* globalization of the economy, politics, and culture. It established rules of commerce that require national governments to eliminate "non-tariff barriers to trade," which include food safety laws, workers' safety and public health laws, product standards and liability, environmental protections, use of tax revenues for public services, and other domestic laws regulating investment and trade that would limit the ability of TNCs to operate profitably. The WTO limits what kind of nontariff barriers to trade nations may implement and enforce. Through the WTO's Dispute Settlement Process, nations can challenge each others' laws as violations of its pro-industry, pro-corporate trade regulations. The result is that democratic political bodies have no choice but to conform WTO regulations under fear of economic sanctions. Cases are decided in highly secretive tribunals without due process by a small number of unelected, hence unaccountable officials. WTO tribunals thus far have systematically ruled against domestic laws in every case, giving precedence to global commerce over national sovereignty.[32]

Of all of the good reasons to oppose corporate globalization, I will mention just three.[33] First, globalization undermines the democratic process. International trade agreements place every government in the world at the mercy of global financial and commercial systems organized for the efficient mobility of capital and the maximization profit for the world's largest corporations. To date no environmental, health, food safety, or worker safety law challenged at the WTO has been upheld. Even though in each case these laws were established by democratic processes, they were all declared barriers to trade, hence illegal.[34] Private corporations have thus far very effectively used their governments to change the laws they do not like in other nations. The system is designed so that the interests of finance and commerce always win out over the interests of citizens and democracy. Even if it were true that deregulation and liberalization of the world economy will result in economic prosperity and other social benefits, the unjust and undemocratic means fail to justify the ends. Furthermore, even if it were true that GATT and the WTO were agreed to by democratically elected representatives throughout the world, the unjust and undemocratic character of the agreement is enough reason to oppose it, if not nullify it, on both moral and legal grounds.[35] Insofar as constitutional governments use public resources to promote WTO and GATT policies, they are open to legal challenges on the part of citizens whose rights and opportunities are limited.[36]

Second, globalization subjects basic goods and services to private monopoly control. The WTO agreement on Trade Related Aspects of Intellectual Property (TRIPs) states that food and medicine that was once under the public domain must now be privatized through global patent law. This allows food manufacturers to modify traditionally bred seeds, patent them, and then sell them back to people who had always used them for free. TRIPs covers not only seeds but also microorganisms such as cell lines, genes, and plant varieties, many of which are used for medicine. It allows for the private sector to own the diversity of nature itself. The United Nations Development Program (UNDP) criticized the TRIPs agreement in its 1999 Human Development Report as "undermining food security and public health in developing nations."[37] The UNDP reports that TRIPs rules make it much more costly for poor and developing countries to procure seeds for crops and to make medicine more accessible to the public. Food shortages in the developing world are already a problem for billions of people yet WTO regulations protect corporate property rights that undermine the ability of governments to respond to basic public needs. TRIPs have been also been evoked to prevent the development of generic versions of pharmaceuticals, most notably to stop African nations from developing generic drugs to treat AIDS patients. To make matters worse, if the Free Trade Area of the Americas (FTAA) is ratified by the thirty-four nations in the Western Hemisphere, it will allow for the privatization of basic services. National governments would be forbidden from preventing TNCs from delivering such services as health care, child care, elder care, education, postal service, waste management, sewer and water services, insurance, legal services, and all levels of municipal services. It is a conflict between the legitimate basic human right to food security and essential goods and services, and the illegitimate rights of private enterprises to privatize them.[38]

Third, globalization erodes diversity in favor of a homogenized global culture. The goal of globalization is to streamline economies into a single economic, political, and even cultural order to facilitate the accumulation of capital. Cultural diversity is an obstacle for the agents of globalization. It is more efficient to produce, distribute, and market goods and services if economic, political, and cultural conditions are the same everywhere. Global capitalism not only homogenizes modes and relations of production but it attempts to homogenize consumers and cultures as well. The trend in wealthy nations is toward the increased influence of TNCs on commerce, consumption, and culture. When poor, developing countries fall under control of TNCs and global financial institutions, what invariably happens is that modes of production and consumption that made sense in relation to the local resources and skills of indigenous people are replaced in favor of an economy geared toward maximizing the return on foreign investment. The most striking example is that when global agribusiness consolidates small farms into big ones they replace human labor with machinery thereby displacing millions of people every year while eradicating societies based on rural farming, where one half of the world's population still lives and works. These farms do not produce food for local people to eat, but instead grow single crops for export, usually luxury items like coffee, sugar, cotton, fruits, and flowers. As farming communities dwindle in the face of competition, people are driven off their land and into poverty, usually settling in urban centers. As communities, cultures, and traditions are destroyed, intergroup conflict and strife rises as a result of competition for resources and basic goods. The effects of globalization on culture ranges from the homogenization of mass culture in wealthy nations to the forced displacement and migrations of peoples and the rise of ethnic, religious, tribal, and racial violence in poor nations. While globalization, like the colonialism it replaced, is not directly responsible for regional violence, it is responsible for reshaping, if not determining, the social and economic conditions and opportunities available to people. Therefore, it plays a exceedingly large role in the fate of individuals and groups.

There are a number of ways that Ricoeur's works help us make sense of corporate globalization. First, his version of critical hermeneutics highlights the very contradictory forces between the past and future focusing our attention on universal civilization and particular, national cultures. Critical hermeneutics functions by recovering tradition and cultural heritage while anticipating consensus and the ideal of a liberated humanity. This interminable dialectic forces us to balance our dual allegiance to the universal and the particular. As such, we should recognize that both movements toward the global and the regional have positive and negative senses. The good sense of universal civilization should be fostered if it brings about a global recognition of our collective fate and makes universally available scientific and medical knowledge, technological advances, Enlightenment political institutions, and economic systems that attend to human needs. The bad sense of universal civilization should be rejected if it takes the form of a homogenous global economic-political-ecological order that tends toward the satisfaction of private, corporate interests over public interests. Similarly, the good sense of national cultures refers to traditions that foster continual self-interpretation, promote the creative renewal of the past, and lead to genuine dialogue and exchange with other cultures. The bad sense of national cultures refers to frozen, ossified traditions that prevent plural and alternative interpretations. Ricoeur provides a framework for understanding how the economic, political, and cultural effects of globalization are situated between excesses and deficiencies of universality of civilization and the particularity of culture. Finding the just mean is an act of practical wisdom.[39]

Second, critical hermeneutics is also a narrative-argumentative practice. Therefore corporate globalization can only be understood in terms of the overlapping stories and conflicting interpretations that describe and explain it. The many different aspects of globalization—in all of its dimensions, in all of the places and incomparable histories it affects, and all of the different actors and agents it touches—only make sense as stories told from different perspectives, making up parts of a whole. Globalization is the central story of our day, and it would be negligent for activists and critical theorists to fail to address how it figures into the story of social justice at the levels of universal civilization and national cultures. There are three particular aspects of the narratives on globalization worth highlighting.

One, perhaps because the institutions of globalization are relatively new, the discourses surrounding globalization are especially ideological and utopian. Its proponents evoke a rhetoric of "free trade," "free markets," and "free choice," while they label critics of globalization as "protectionists" and "isolationists." Global utopianism is expressed in typically liberal terms of "progress," "prosperity," and the connection between free markets and "open societies."[40] Critics of globalization advance their own utopian agenda, projecting an imagined, better world characterized by "fair trade," "living democracy," "democratic community," "sustainable development," and other ideals. Antiglobalization ideology consists of anticapitalist sloganeering that oversimplifies the complex relationship between political and economic institutions. In the process, critics too often fail to appreciate the virtues of globalization that often foster social and cultural exchanges. Ricoeur helps us makes sense of how ideology and utopia shape the discourses on globalization, how they relate to dominant power structures by affecting political action and influencing the construction of our identities. There is still a need for a critique of ideology to counter the pro-globalization agenda espoused by most U.S political leaders and the mainstream media. Consequently, there is also a need for utopian alternatives that would challenge globalization. So long as one is criticizing illegitimate power and authority, it is a good thing to be utopian without the fear of being labeled "impractical," or "unrealistic." Following Ricoeur, we need less realism and more utopianism.[41]

Two, narratives on globalization are intrinsically moral and political, and as such belong in part to the realm of testimony and conviction with its correspondingly appropriate notions of argument and evidence. Although expert, technical discourses are perfectly legitimate and often necessary to make a compelling a case, they should be used to compliment and not replace citizen participation in the decision-making process over issues affecting the general welfare. As philosophers and activists, we can call attention to the political character of our laws, policies, institutions, and forms of life to show that economic practices also involve political choices, embody political ideas, and are thus open to political deliberation and transformation. So long as our political and legal decisions are made on the basis of rational convictions, open to deliberation and revision, and subject to continual reinterpretation and critique, we do not need to rely on anything but our own best sense of what kind of world we would like to create. Ricoeur believes that

> we cannot eliminate from a social ethics the element of risk. We wager on a certain set of values and then try to be consistent with them; verification is therefore a question of our whole life. No one can escape this. (IU 312)

All we can do is to make our convictions known by communication, testimony, and collective action. Ricoeur admits that his wager is "fideist," but he says, "I do not see how we can say that our values are better than all others except that by risking our whole life on them we expect to achieve a better life, to see and to understand better than others" (IU 312). Of all of the convictions motivating critics of globalization the most basic is belief that there are some things that should not be privatized. The challenge is to present matters of conscience in a convincing fashion in order to effect change. Since the discourses of liberalism and science carry the most weight, critical theory should co-opt their vocabularies to make the strongest case possible against corporate globalization.

Three, narratives about globalization are inherently political, hence rhetorical, fallible, and fragile. The fragility of political discourse stems from the fragility of everything political. Any institution or regime conferred with the authority to use force is inherently dangerous. Ricoeur wisely links the fragility of everything political with the political responsibility held by every member of society to exercise prudence and judgment given the enormous powers of governments. Political societies render us responsible because they are ultimately based on a "fiduciary bond." Citizens should "feel particularly responsible for the constitutive horizontal bond of the will to live together. In short, he or she must ascribe public safety to the vitality of the associate life which regenerates the will to live together."[42] The intuition here is that because we all live together, rely on each other, and have to trust to each other in order to survive and flourish we are also responsible for each other. We need to be especially vigilant about the powers we confer onto political institutions precisely because of the vital role they play in holding us together. Consequently, any global political institutions or federation among nations that would protect universal civilization and national cultures would only heighten the already fragile nature of governing bodies, as well as demand even more responsibility on the part of us all. Even the most progressive, egalitarian, and utopian alternatives to capitalist globalization involve governing institutions, and as such they should be viewed with caution and suspicion even as we endorse them.[43] Owning up to the fragility of politics means that we do our best to find a reflective equilibrium in between critique and conviction, individual rights and the debt owed to historical communities. Ricoeur implores us to be at once more ambitious and more humble in our political aspirations. We should work equally to develop global political institutions and limit their powers.

A third way Ricoeur's works helps us makes sense of corporate globalization is through socialism. Our world appears irrational and unjust when measured against the standards of a socialist society that would best maintain the fragile balance between universal civilization and national cultures by democratizing political, economic, and cultural institutions. At the political level, socialism is opposed to the influence of money in politics and political institutions geared toward protecting only the interests of capitalism. There is a growing consensus in the United States that capitalism perverts the political process as representatives serve the interests of their contributors instead of their constituents.[44] There is also a growing concern among watchdog organizations that the impartiality of the United Nations, the primary international governing body, is being compromised by its growing number of parterships with private sector interests.[45] The socialist response would be to restore integrity to regional, national, and international democratic institutions in a participatory democracy that respects human rights, civil liberties, and the rule of law.

At the economic level, socialism would democratize the means of production through publicly owned and operated businesses and collectives, allocating resources to people according to their needs. It is debatable whether market socialism or communism is the form of socialism Ricoeur endorses. Market socialism eliminates wage labor and private ownership of the means of production but retains a market system for the production and distribution of nonbasic goods and services; communism seeks to eliminate the production of all surplus value, and hence end the reign of market imperatives—regardless of whether they are democratically or collectively managed.[46] Even though he endorses state planning in the economy, given Ricoeur's concern to disperse power, his version of socialism is arguably closer to market socialism than to communism.

Finally, at the level of culture, socialism is a humanism that aims to foster autonomy, community, creativity, and solidarity. It is a plea for humanity in the face of the class and social conflicts, violence, and hatred that prevents us from living well together. Above all, it affirms our responsibility and commitment to alleviate the suffering of others, not only within our communities and borders but throughout the world, especially in poor nations where suffering is the worst. If Ricoeur is right, to achieve a fully democratic political economy and community that would balance universal civilization and national cultures we would all have to do a much better job of communicating and acting together. That means we should engage one another in discourse geared toward reinterpreting our past in anticipation of a liberated future; it also means we should aim at the good life, with and for others, in just institutions.

NOTES

INTRODUCTION

1. Don Ihde, *Hermeneutic Phenomenology: The Philosophy of Paul Ricoeur* (Evanston: Northwestern University Press, 1970). Patrick L. Bourgeois, *Extension of Ricoeur's Hermeneutic* (The Hague: Martinus Nijhoff, 1975). David Rassmussen, *Mythic-Symbolic Language and Philosophical Anthropology: A Constructive Interpretation of the Thought of Paul Ricoeur* (The Hague: Martinus Nijhoff, 1971).

2. John Dicenso, *Hermeneutics and the Disclosure of Truth: A Study in the Work of Heidegger, Gadamer, and Ricoeur* (Charlottesville: University Press of Virginia, 1990). David Klemm, *The Hermeneutical Theory of Paul Ricoeur: A Constructive Analysis* (Lewisburg: Bucknell University Press, 1983). Patrick Bourgeois and Frank Schalow, *Traces of Understanding: A Profile of Heidegger's and Ricoeur's Hermeneutics* (Amsterdam: Rodopi, 1990).

3. Domenico Jervolino, *The Cogito and Hermeneutics: The Question of the Subject in Ricoeur,* trans. Gordon Poole (Dordrecht: Kluwer Academic Publishers, 1990). J. Van den Hengel, *The Home of Meaning: The Hermeneutics of the Subject of Paul Ricoeur* (Washington: University Press of America, 1982). Henry Isaac Venema, *Identifying Selfhood: Imagination, Narrative, and Hermeneutics in the Thought of Paul Ricoeur* (Albany: SUNY Press, 2000).

4. Pamela Sue Anderson, *Ricoeur and Kant: Philosophy of the Will* (Atlanta: Scholars Press, 1993).

5. P. J. Albano, *Freedom, Truth and Hope: The Relationship of Philosophy and Religion in the Thought of Paul Ricoeur* (Lanham: University Press of America, 1987). Loretta Dornisch, *Faith and Philosophy in the Writings of Paul Ricoeur* (Lampeter-Dyfed: Edwin Meller Press, 1990). K. J. Vanhoozer, *Biblical Narrative in the Philosophy of Paul Ricoeur: A Study in Hermeneutics and Theology* (Cambridge: Cambridge University Press, 1990). T. M. Van Leeuwen, *The Surplus of Meaning: Ontology and Eschatology in the Philosophy of Paul Ricoeur* (Amsterdam: Rodopi, 1981).

6. Patrick L. Bourgeois, *Philosophy at the Boundary of Reason: Ethics and Postmodernity* (Albany: SUNY Press, 2001). S. H. Clark, *Paul Ricoeur* (London: Routledge, 1990). Dennis Lawlor, *Imagination and Chance* (Albany: SUNY Press, 1992).

7. Charles E. Reagan, *Paul Ricoeur: His Life and His Work* (Chicago: The University of Chicago Press, 1996). Francois Dosse, *Paul Ricoeur: Les sens d'une vie* (Paris: La Découverte, 1997).

8. See Mary Gerhart, *The Question of Belief in Literary Criticism: An Introduction to the Hermeneutical Theory of Paul Ricoeur* (Stuttgart: Akademischer Verlag. 1979). Lewis Edwin Hahn, ed., *The Philosophy of Paul Ricoeur* (Chicago: Open Court, 1995). Richard Kearney, ed., *Paul Ricoeur: The Hermeneutics of Action* (London: SAGE Publications, 1996). Charles Reagan, ed., *Studies in the Philosophy of Paul Ricoeur* (Athens: Ohio University Press, 1979). T. Peter Kemp and David Rassmussen, ed., *The Narrative Path: The Later Works of Paul Ricoeur* (Cambridge: The MIT Press, 1989). David E. Klemm and William Schweiker, ed., *Meanings in Texts and Actions: Questioning Paul Ricoeur* (Charlottesville: University Press of Virginia, 1993). David Wood, ed., *On Paul Ricoeur: Narrative and Interpretation* (London: Routledge, 1991).

9. John B. Thompson, *Critical Hermeneutics: A Study in the Thought of Paul Ricoeur and Jürgen Habermas* (Cambridge: Cambridge University Press, 1981).

10. Bernard Dauenhauer, *Paul Ricoeur: The Promise and Risk of Politics* (Lanham: Rowman & Littlefield Publishers, 1998).

11. For Ricoeur's mediation of the Habermas-Gadamer debate see PS, pp. 153–165. HHS, pp. 270–307.

12. For Habermas's critique of Gadamerian hermeneutics, see Jürgen Habermas, *On the Logic of the Social Sciences*, trans. Shierry Weber Nicholson and Jerry A. Stark (Cambridge: The MIT Press, 1988), p. 143–175. Habermas, "The Hermeneutic Claim to Universality," trans. Josef Bleicher in Bleicher, *Contemporary Hermeneutics* (London: Routledge, 1980), pp. 181–211. For Gadamer's response, see Hans-Georg Gadamer, "The Universality of the Hermeneutical Problem," *Philosophical Hermeneutics*, trans. and ed. David E. Linge (Berkeley: University of California Press, 1976), pp. 3–17. Gadamer, "The Scope and Function of Reflection," in *Philosophical Hermeneutics*, pp. 18–43.

13. For faithful accounts of this tradition, see Hans-Georg Gadamer, *Truth and Method*, 2nd. ed., trans. Joel Weinsheimer (New York: Continuum, 1975). Richard E. Palmer, *Hermeneutics* (Evanston: Northwestern University Press, 1969). Josef Bleicher, *Contemporary Hermeneutics*.

14. For faithful accounts of this tradition, see Jürgen Habermas, *Knowledge and Human Interests*, trans. Jeremy J. Shapiro (Boston: Beacon Press, 1972). Seyla Benhabib, *Critique, Norm and Utopia. A Study of the Foundations of Critical Theory* (New York: Columbia University Press, 1986). Martin Jay, *The Dialectical Imagination. A History of the Frankfurt School and the Institute for Social Research, 1923–1950* (Boston: Little, Brown and Company, 1973).

15. For a statement of the debate, see *The Communicative Ethics Controversy*, ed. Seyla Benhabib and Fred Dallmayr (Cambridge: MIT Press, 1990). See also *Universalism vs. Communitarianism: Contemporary Debates in Ethics*, ed. David Rassmussen (Cambridge: MIT Press, 1990).

16. The central text that evoked the communitarian challenge to liberalism is John Rawls, *A Theory of Justice* (Cambridge: Harvard University Press, 1971). The main communitarian works include the following: Alisdair MacIntyre, *After Virtue* (South Bend: University of Notre Dame Press, 1981). Michael Sandel, *Liberalism and the Limits of Justice* (Cambridge: Cambridge University Press, 1982). Charles Taylor, *Sources of the Self* (Cambridge: Cambridge University Press, 1990). Michael Walzer, *Spheres of Justice* (New York: Basic Books, 1983).

17. Ricoeur, Foreword to Ihde, *Hermeneutic Phenomenology*, p. xiv.

18. See J. L. Austin, *How to Do Things with Words* (Oxford: Oxford University Press, 1962). John R. Searle, *Speech Acts* (Cambridge: Cambridge University Press, 1969).

19. "Interview with Charles Reagan, July, 1991," in Reagan, *Paul Ricoeur: His Life and His Work*, p. 133.

20. Ibid., p. 87.

21. Ricoeur, "The Creativity of Language." Interview by Richard Kearney (Paris, 1981), in *A Ricoeur Reader: Reflection and Imagination*, ed. Mario J. Valdes (Toronto: University of Toronto Press, 1991), p. 465.

22. See, for example, CI, pp. 412–416, TA pp. 197–204, 221, TN III, p. 215.

23. "Interview with Charles Reagan, October 26, 1988," in Reagan, *Paul Ricoeur: His Life and His Work*, p. 112.

24. For the ethical character of Ricoeur's method of mediation that respects differences, see Olivier Abel, "Ricoeur's Ethics of Method," *Philosophy Today*, Spring 1993, 23–30.

CHAPTER 1. HERMENEUTICS

1. See, Rudolf Bernet, "Husserl and Heidegger on Intentionality and Being," *Journal of the British Society for Phenomenology* 21 (1990): pp. 136–152. John Caputo, "Husserl, Heidegger, and the Question of a 'Hermeneutic Phenomenology,'" *Husserl Studies* 1 (1984): pp. 157–178. Friedrich Elliston, "Phenomenology Reinterpreted: From Husserl to Heidegger," *Philosophy Today* 21 (1977): pp. 273–283. Timothy J. Stapleton, *Husserl and Heidegger: The Question of a Phenomenological Beginning* (Albany: SUNY, 1983).

2. For the most complete discussion of the problem, see, Burt C. Hopkins, *Intentionality in Husserl and Heidegger: The Problem of the Original Method and Phenomenon of Phenomenology* (Dordrecht: Kluwer Academic Publishers, 1993). See also, J. N. Mohanty, "Transcendental Philosophy and the Hermeneutic Critique of Consciousness," in *Phenomenology and the Human Sciences*, ed. J. N. Mohanty (The Hague: Martinus Nijhoff, 1985), pp. 96–120.

3. For his early phenomenology of signification, see, Edmund Husserl, *Logical Investigation, I*, trans. J. N. Findlay (London: Routledge and Kegan Paul, 1970). For his later egological philosophy, see, Edmund Husserl, *Cartesian Meditations*, trans. Dorion Cairns (Dordrecht: Martinus Nijhoff, 1960).

4. Ricoeur, Foreword to Ihde, *Hermeneutic Phenomenology*, pp. xv–xvi.

5. Martin Heidegger, *Being and Time*, trans. John Macquarrie and Edward Robinson (New York: Harper & Row, 1962), pp. 188–195.

6. Edmund Husserl, "Origin of Geometry," in *The Crisis of European Sciences and Transcendental Phenomenology*, trans. David Carr (Evanston: Northwestern University Press, 1970), pp. 353–378.

7. Ricoeur is concerned that Husserlian idealism tends to forget that intentionality can be considered either in the direction from subjectivity to object, or in the direction from object to subjectivity. Husserl's reflective methodology priviledges the ego and act of constitution because he chose to make it appear last, as the fundamental level of consciousness. Subjectivity constitutes the world. At the same time, Husserl recognizes that the (intersubjective, social) world is always given to a subject, so that the subject cannot know itself without the world. Sometimes Ricoeur claims that Husserlian

phenomenology "entails a methodological rather than a doctrinal idealism"; other times he goes further and claims that phenomenology does indeed entail a doctrinal idealism (H 36, 89, 176).

8. Similarly, recourse to interpretation is needed in order to distinguish between occasional and nonoccasional meanings, and between the perception of objects and sensory data that gives rise to the logical operations that produce meaningful statements.

9. The moment of culmination and crisis occurs in §33 of *The Cartesian Meditations*. "Since the monadically concrete ego includes also the whole of actual and potential conscious life, it is clear that the problem of *explicating (Auslegung) this monadic ego phenomenologically* (the problem of his constitution for himself) must include *all constitutional problems without exception*. Consequently the phenomenology of this *self-constitution* coincides with *phenomenology as a whole*." Husserl, *Cartesian Meditations*, p. 68, cited in TA 48.

10. Ricoeur, "Interview with Charles Reagan, June 19, 1982," in Charles E. Reagan, *Paul Ricoeur: His Life and His Work*, p. 104.

11. "So one can ask whether Heidegger really broke through the immanentism of the Husserlian description of consciousness and self-consciousness by replacing it with care—or whether he simply concretized consciousness by care and temporality? I think that, because the answer is unclear, it was possible, when *Being and Time* had just come out, for readers like Oskar Becker to see it as simply a new variation and extension within the framework of phenomenology." Hans-Georg Gadamer, "The Hermeneutics of Suspicion," in *Hermeneutics: Questions and Prospects*, ed. Gary Shapiro and Alan Sica (Amherst: University of Massachusetts Press, 1984), p. 61.

12. For a similar criticism of Ricoeur's interpretation of the recourse to *Auslegung*, see, Hopkins, *Intentionality in Husserl and Heidegger*, pp. 236–238.

13. Paul Ricoeur, "Husserl and Wittgenstein on Language," in *Phenomenology and Existentialism*, ed. E. N. Lee and M. Mandelbaum (Baltimore: Johns Hopkins Press, 1967), p. 209.

14. Ibid., p. 213.

15. H. P. Grice, "Meaning," *Philosophical Review* 66 (1957): pp. 377–388. "Utterer's Meaning, Sentence-Meaning, and Word-Word-Meaning," *Foundations of Language* 4 (1968): pp. 225–245.

16. See, J. L. Austin, *How to Do Things with Words*, pp. 14–45.

17. Gottlob Frege, "On Sense and Reference," trans. Max Black, in *Translations from the Philosophical Writings of Gottlob Frege*, ed. Peter Geach and Max Black (Oxford: Basil Blackwell, 1970), pp. 56–78.

18. In a rare reference to Derrida, Ricoeur writes that to hold as Derrida does "that writing has a root distinct from speech and that this foundation has been misunderstood due to our having paid excessive attention to speech, its voice, and its *logos*, is to overlook the grounding of both modes of the actualization of discourse in the dialectical constitution of discourse" (INT 26). For a summary of the differences between Ricoeur and Derrida, see, Lawlor, *Imagination and Chance*, pp. 123–129.

19. Wilhem Dilthey, *Selected Writings*, ed. and trans. H. P. Rickman (Cambridge: Cambridge University Press, 1976), pp. 66–105.

20. See, Jürgen Habermas, *The Theory of Communicative Action, Vol. I, Reason and the Rationalization of Society,* trans. Thomas McCarthy (Boston: Beacon Press, 1984).

21. Ibid.

22. Jürgen Habermas, "What Is Universal Pragmatics?," in *Communication and the Evolution of Society*, trans. Thomas McCarthy (Boston: Beacon Press, 1979), p. 3.

23. Thompson, *Critical Hermeneutics*, pp. 163–165.

24. Karl Otto Apel, "Is the Ethics of the Ideal Communication Community a Utopia? On the Relationship between Ethics, Utopia, and the Critique of Utopia," in *The Communicative Ethics Controversy*, pp. 23–59.

CHAPTER 2. NARRATIVE

1. Paul Ricoeur, "Creativity in Language: Word, Polysemy, Metaphor," in *The Philosophy of Paul Ricoeur: An Anthology of His Work*, ed. Charles E. Reagan and David Stewart (Boston: Beacon Press, 1978), p. 132–133.

2. Monroe Beardsley, *Aesthetics: Problems in the Philosophy of Criticism* (New York: Harcourt, Brace and World, 1958).

3. Ricoeur, "Narrated Time," in *A Ricoeur Reader*, p. 339.

4. Ricoeur, "The Metaphorical Process as Cognition, Imagination, and Feeling," *Critical Inquiry* 5 (1978): p. 148.

5. Ricoeur, "Intellectual Autobiography," in *The Philosophy of Paul Ricoeur*, ed. Lewis Edwin Hahn (Chicago: Open Court, 1987), p. 44.

6. Narrative also involves "syntactic features" that function like Kantian schemas to configure events into a whole. Ricoeur explains the relation between the conceptual network of action and the rules of narrative composition by the distinction between the "paradigmatic order" and the "syntagmatic order." The paradigmatic order refers to the synchronic elements of a story; the syntagmatic to the diachronic character of a story that unfolds in time. The paradigmatic elements in a narrative are the interchangeable and even reversible relations of intersignification among means, ends, agents, and circumstances. Narratives are constituted by paradigms that are synchronic and repeatable. But because every narrated story is irreducibly diachronic, the syntagmatic character of a narrative is the key to understanding the link between narrativity and temporality. Actions receive their meaning through the sequential interconnections of the plot, which confers on the agents their deeds and their sufferings, as a story take place and unfold in time during the act of reading. The result is that understanding a narrative involves a familiarity with both the conceptual network of the semantics of action, as well as the rules of composition that order events into a diachronic narrative. A plot, then, is "the literary equivalent of the syntagmatic order the narrative introduces into the practical field" (TN1 56).

7. Clifford Geertz, *The Interpretation of Cultures* (New York: Basic Books, 1973).

8. Heidegger, *Being and Time*, pp. 364–380.

9. For a similar account of the phenomenological grounding of narrative discourse, see, David Carr, *Time, Narrative and History* (Bloomington: Indiana University Press, 1986). Carr's links narrative with pre-predicative experience in a far more thorough and satisfying way than Ricoeur does. His discussion of the temporal structure of experience, action, and narrative establishes the relationship between our historical belonging and historical understanding in a far more thorough and satisfying way, as well. Ricoeur and Carr share the central thesis that experience and narrative form a circle based on the prenarrative quality of experience and the temporal structure of narrative. Carr states that

a continuity exists between narrative and everydayness because a "narrative structure pervades our very experience of time and social existence, independently of our contemplating the past as historian" (p. 9). Carr claims that Ricoeur separates experience and narrative, and imposes a narrative structure onto otherwise intelligible experience. Such a claim would make the connection between experience and narrative inessential, rather than essential. But Ricoeur clearly argues for an essential connection between life and narrative in what he calls the "pre-narrative quality of human experience." Perhaps the difference between the two is that Carr is the more faithful phenomenologist, suspicious of nonphenomenologically grounded structures of experience. Ricoeur's narrative theory continues his debates with the structuralists, and so he treats it as both an intentionality of subjective consciousness and an objective and impersonal structure of experience, as the structuralists maintain. For an excellent discussion of the similarities and differences between Ricoeur and Carr, see, David Pellauer, "Limning the Liminal: Carr and Ricoeur on Time and Narrative," *Philosophy Today* 35 (1991), pp. 51–62.

10. Ricoeur, "Mimesis and Representation," in *A Ricoeur Reader*, p. 150.

11. Ricoeur, "Interview with Charles Reagan, June 19, 1982," in *Paul Ricoeur*, p. 108.

12. Carl Hempel, "The Function of General Laws in History," in *Aspects of Scientific Explanation and Other Essays in the Philosophy of Science* (New York: The Free Press, 1942), pp. 231–243. Carl Hempel and Paul Oppenheim, "Studies in the Logic of Explanation," in *Scientific Knowledge*, ed. Janet A. Kourany (Belmont: Wadsworth Publishing Company, 1987), pp. 30–43.

13. W. B. Gallie, *Philosophy and Historical Understanding* (New York: Schocken Books, 1964).

14. Paul Ricoeur and Hans-Georg Gadamer, "The Conflict of Interpretations," in *A Ricoeur Reader*, pp. 229–230.

15. Paul Ricoeur, "Narrative Time," in *On Narrative*, ed. W. J. T. Mitchell (Chicago: The University of Chicago Press, 1981), pp. 165–186.

16. "To follow a trace, to trace back a trace, is to effect practically the fusion of two sides of the trace, to constitute it as effect-sign. The temporal implication is considerable: to follow a trace is to effect the temporal mediation between the *no-longer* of the passage and the *still* of the mark. At this price we now no longer have to say that the past is something over and done with in any negative sense but can say that it is something that has been and, because of this, is now preserved in the present. Ricoeur, "Narrated Time," in *A Ricoeur Reader*, p. 345.

17. Ricoeur, "The Creativity of Language," in *A Ricoeur Reader*, p. 464.

18. Ibid.

19. Ibid.

20. Ricoeur, "Interview with Charles Reagan, June 19, 1982," in *Paul Ricoeur*, pp. 104–105.

21. Wilhem Dilthey, *Selected Writings*, ed. and trans. H. P. Rickman (Cambridge: Cambridge University Press, 1976).

22. Ricoeur, "Intellectual Autobiography," p. 31.

23. E. D Hirsch, *Validity in Interpretation* (New Haven: Yale University Press, 1967).

24. Karl Popper, *The Logic of Scientific Discovery* (New York: Harper & Row, 1968).

25. Ronald Dworkin, *A Matter of Principle* (Cambridge: Harvard University Press, 1985).

26. Robert Alexy, *A Theory of Legal Argumentation: The Theory of Rational Discourse as Theory of Legal Justification*, trans. R. Adler and N. MacCormick (Oxford: Clarendon Press, 1989). Jürgen Habermas, *Between Facts and Norms: Contributions to a Discourse Theory of Law and Democracy*, trans. William Rehg (Cambridge: MIT Press, 1996).

27. For a similar criticism of the lack of a theory of evidence in communicative action, see, John B. Thompson, "Universal Pragmatics," in *Habermas: Critical Debates*, ed. John B. Thompson and David Held (Cambridge: The MIT Press, 1982), pp. 116–134. See also, Mary Hesse, "Science and Objectivity," in *Habermas: Critical Debates*, pp. 98–115. In response to these critics Habermas concedes the importance of evidence in a theory of truth. "I regard as justified the admonition that I have hitherto not taken the 'evidential dimension' of the concept of truth adequately into account." Jürgen Habermas, "A Reply to My Critics," in *Habermas: Critical Debates*, p. 275.

28. Karl-Otto Apel, "C. S. Peirce and the Post-Tarskian Problem of an Adequate Explication of the Meaning of the Truth: Towards a Transcendental-Pragmatic Theory of Truth, Part II," *Transactions of the Charles S. Pierce Society*, 18 (1982): p. 8.

29. Others have noted the complementarity of phenomenology and the theory of communicative action as well. See, for example, James L. Marsh, *Post-Cartesian Meditations* (New York: Fordham University Press, 1988), pp. 239–258.

CHAPTER 3. SELFHOOD

1. See, Bernard Dauenhauer, *Paul Ricoeur: The Promise and Risk of Politics* for the clearest explanation of the connection between Ricoeur's early philosophical anthropology and his recent works on ethics, politics, and the law. See also, Henry Isaac Venema, *Identifying Selfhood: Imagination, Narrative, and Hermeneutics in the Thought of Paul Ricoeur* for an excellent clarification of Ricoeur's early and recent conceptions of the self.

2. Husserl, *Ideas Pertaining to a Pure Phenomenology and a Phenomenological Philosophy, First Book*, trans. F. Kersten (Dordrecht: Kluwer Academic Publishers, 1982), pp. 157–160.

3. Ricoeur, "Philosophy of Will and Action," in *The Philosophy of Paul Ricoeur*, p. 67.

4. "To consent is less to state a necessity than to adopt it; it is to say 'yes' to what is already determined. It represents converting, within myself, the hostility of nature into the freedom of necessity. Consent is the asymptotic progress of freedom towards necessity" (FN 346).

5. Ricoeur, "Methods and Tasks of a Phenomenology of the Will," in *Husserl*, p. 228.

6. Ibid., p. 216.

7. See, Hubert L. Dreyfus, *Being-in-the-World: A Commentary of Heidegger's Being and Time, Division I* (Cambridge: MIT Press, 1991). Charles B. Guignon, *Heidegger and the Problem of Knowledge* (Indianapolis: Hackett Publishing Company, 1983).

8. Michel Foucault, *The History of Sexuality*, vol. I, trans. Robert Hurley (New York: Vintage Books, 1980). Gilles Deleuze and Felix Guattari, *Anti-Oedipus: Capitalism and Schizophrenia* (Minneapolis: University of Minnesota Press, 1983).

9. "False needs are those which are superimposed upon the individual by particular social interests in his repression: the needs which perpetuate toil, aggressiveness, mis-
ery, and injustice." Herbert Marcuse, *One-Dimensional Man: Studies in the Ideology of
Advanced Industrial Society* (Boston: Beacon Press, 1964), p. 5.

10. Ricoeur, "Intellectual Autobiography," in *The Philosophy of Paul Ricoeur*,
p. 32.

11. For Ricoeur's attempt to link speech-act theory with identity, interpreted in
terms of Husserl's notion of intersubjectivity, see, David Rasmussen, "Rethinking Subjectivity," in *Philosophy and Social Criticism*, 21 (5/6) (1995): pp. 159–172.

12. For example, Anscombe frames the question in terms of what distinguishes
intentional action from unintentional action. An acceptable answer is one that explains
why someone acted by offering relevant reasons. The answer to the question "Why?" is
"Because . . ." Such explanations may be either causal or motivational since it also belongs to ordinary language to ask "What caused you to do that?" One advantage of emphasizing the causal-objective side of action that results from asking Why? is that the
meaning of an action is freed from the intentions of the actor. Reasons can either be true
or false, depending on how adequately they describe an action. See, G. E. M. Anscombe,
Intention (London: Basil Blackwell, 1979).

13. Like Anscombe, Donald Davidson also adopts an adverbial definition of intention (X does A intentionally) in order to determine what counts as an action. An
event is an action if it is done intentionally. To give an explanation for an action is to
give a description of it, which is to explain the reasons why it was done, or what caused
it to occur without making reference to mental events like motives and volition. An intentional action is an action done for a reason; to know the reason why someone acted
is to know an intention of an action. This claim satisfies the ordinary language practice
of answering the question why someone did something by offering a reason that explains what caused someone to act. Causal explanations of intentions also satisfy the requirement that all events are entities that belong to a single, non-dualistic universe that
is shared and public. See, Donald Davidson, *Essays on Actions and Events* (Oxford:
Clarendon Press, 1980).

14. G. Von Wright, *Explanation and Understanding* (London: Routledge and
Kegan Paul, 1971).

15. Ricoeur, "Life in Quest of Narrative," in *On Paul Ricoeur*, p. 32.

16. Paul Ricoeur, "Reflections on a New Ethos for Europe," *Philosophy and Social
Criticism*, 21 (5/6) (1995): p. 6.

17. Derek Parfit, *Reasons and Persons* (Oxford: Oxford University Press, 1986).

18. "This addition is so essential that it governs a large part of the reflections on
power as it is exerted by someone on someone, as well as the reflections on violence as
the destruction by someone else of a subject's capacity to act; by the same token, it leads
to the threshold of the idea of justice, as the rule aiming at the equality of the patients and
agents of action " (OA 157).

19. For an excellent discussion of Ricoeur's conception of attestation, see Jean
Greisch, "Testimony and Attestation," in *Philosophy and Social Criticism*, 21 (5/6) (1995):
pp. 81–98. Greisch shows how the presence of the notion of attestation functions at each
level of analysis in *Oneself as Another*, at the levels of speaking, acting, narrating, and
assuming responsibility.

20. Emmanuel Levinas, *Totality and Infinity*, trans. Alphonso Lingis (Pittsburgh: Duquesne University Press, 1969).

21. For an excellent discussion of Ricoeur's reading of Levinas, see, Patrick Bourgeois, *Philosophy at the Boundary of Reason*, pp. 157–183.

22. Ricoeur, "Interview with Reagan, July 8, 1991," in *Paul Ricoeur*, p. 125.

23. Ricoeur, "Intellectual Autobiography," in *The Philosophy of Paul Ricoeur*, p. 53.

24. Ricoeur, "Reflections on a New Ethos for Europe," in *Philosophy and Social Criticism*, 21 (5/6) (1995): p. 7.

25. See, Bernard Dauenhauer, "Ricoeur and Political Identity," *Philosophy Today*, 39 (1) (1995).

26. Ricoeur, "Reflections on a New Ethos for Europe," in *Philosophy and Social Criticism*, 21 (5/6) (1995): p. 7.

27. Ibid., p. 12.

28. Martha C. Nussbaum, *Poetic Justice: The Literary Imagination and Public Life* (Boston: Beacon Press, 1995). See also, Nussbaum, *Cultivating Humanity: A Classical Defense of Reform in Liberal Education* (Cambridge: Harvard University Press, 1997).

29. Ricoeur, "Reflections on a New Ethos for Europe," in *Philosophy and Social Criticism*, 21 (5/6) (1995): p. 8.

30. Ibid., p. 10.

31. Ibid., p. 12.

CHAPTER 4. PRACTICAL WISDOM

1. Aristotle, *The Nicomachean Ethics*, trans. Terence Irwin (Indianapolis: Hackett Publishing, 1985), 1094a.

2. Alasdaire MacIntyre, *After Virtue: A Study in Moral Theory* (South Bend: University of Notre Dame Press, 1981).

3. Attestation appears at this stage "when the certainty of being the author of one's own discourse and of one's own acts becomes the conviction of judging well and acting well in a momentary and provisional approximation of living well" (OA 180).

4. Aristotle, *The Nicomachean Ethics*, 1166a10–1166b1, p. 227.

5. Hannah Arendt, *The Human Condition* (Chicago: University of Chicago Press, 1958), p. 7.

6. Aristotle, *The Nicomachean Ethics*, 1128b35–1134a12, pp. 106–122.

7. Immanuel Kant, *Grounding for the Metaphysics of Morals*, trans. James W. Ellington (Indianapolis: Hackett Publishing, 1981).

8. John Rawls, *A Theory of Justice* (Cambridge: Harvard University Press, 1971).

9. Rawls concedes this point but reminds his critics that the original position is merely a "device of representation" for thinking about ourselves as members of a political society. Furthermore, our prior conceptions of goods says nothing about the requirement of impartiality and universality in social justice. See, John Rawls, *Political Liberalism* (New York: Columbia University Press, 1993).

10. Sophocles, *Antigone*, trans. Elizabeth Wyckoff (Chicago: University of Chicago Press, 1960).

11. G. W. F. Hegel, *Philosophy of Right*, trans. T. M. Knox (Oxford: Clarendon, 1973).

12. "The practical wisdom we are seeking aims at reconciling Aristotle's *phronesis*, by way of Kant's *Moralität*, with Hegel's *Sittlichkeit*. . . . In this way "critical" *phronesis* tends . . . to be identified with *Sittlichkeit*. The latter, however, has been stripped of its pretension to mark the victory of Spirit over the contradictions that it itself provokes. Reduced to modesty, *Sittlichkeit* now joins *phronesis* in moral judgment in situation. In return, because it has crossed through so many mediations and so many conflicts, the *phronesis* of moral judgment in situation is saved from any temptation of anomie. It is through public debate, friendly discussion, and shared convictions that moral judgment in situation is formed. Concerning the practical wisdom suited to this judgment, one can say that *Sittlichkeit* 'repeats' *phronesis* here, to the extent that *Sittlichkeit* 'mediates' *phronesis*" (OA 290–291).

13. Karl-Otto Apel, "Is the Ethics of the Ideal Communication Community a Utopia? On the relationship between Ethics, Utopia, and the Critique of Utopia," in *The Communicative Ethics Controversy*, p. 41.

14. Habermas, "Discourse Ethics: Notes on a Program of Philosophical Justification," in *Moral Consciousness and Communicative Action*, trans. Christian Lenhardt and Sheirry Weber Nicholson (Cambridge: MIT Press, 1990), p. 65.

15. Ibid., p. 66.

16. Ibid., p. 82.

17. Discursive will formation, which produces generalizable interests, is the "bridge principle" between need interpretation and the principle of universalization (U). "This bridging principle, which makes consensus possible, ensures that only those norms are accepted as valid that express a *general will*. As Kant noted time and again, moral norms must be suitable for expression as 'universal laws.'" Ibid., p. 63.

18. Habermas, "Discourse Ethics: Notes on a Program of Philosophical Justification," p. 104.

19. "Moral questions can in principle be decided rationally, i.e., in terms of *justice* or the generalizability of interests. Evaluative questions present themselves at the most general level as issues of the *good life* (or of self-realization); they are accessible to rational discussion only *within* the unproblematic horizon of a concrete historical form of life or the conduct of an individual life." Ibid., p. 108.

20. Habermas, "Morality, Society, and Ethics: An Interview with Torben Hviid Nielsen," in *Justification and Application: Remarks on Discourse Ethics*, trans. Ciaran P. Cronin (Cambridge: The MIT Press, 1993), p. 151.

21. Ibid., p. 158.

22. Habermas, "Remarks on Discourse Ethics," in *Justification and Application*, p. 36.

23. Ibid., p, 38.

24. For Ricoeur's theory of practical wisdom compared to communicative ethics, see, Mara Rainwater, "Refiguring Ricoeur: Narrative Force and Communicative Ethics" *Philosophy and Social Criticism*, 21 (5/6) (1995): 99–110.

25. Hans Jonas, "Technology and Responsibility: Reflections on the New Tasks of Ethics," in *Philosophical Essays: From Ancient Creed to Technological Man* (Englewood Cliffs: Prentice Hall, 1974), pp. 3–20.

26. See, for example, Mark S. Muldoon, "Ricoeur's Ethics: Another Version of Virtue Ethics? Attestation Is Not a Virtue," *Philosophy Today*, Fall (1998).

CHAPTER 5. POLITICS

1. Arendt, *The Human Condition*. Eric Weil, *La philosophie politique* (Paris: Vrin, 1956).

2. Max Weber, "Politics as a Vocation," in *From Max Weber: Essays in Sociology*, trans. and ed. by H. H Gerth and C. Wright Mills (New York: Galaxy Books, 1958), pp. 77–79.

3. Weber, "Politics as a Vocation," p. 120–128.

4. "Modern democratic society seems to me . . . like a society in which power, law and knowledge are exposed to a radical indetermination, a society that has become the theatre of an uncontrollable adventure, so that what is instituted never becomes established, the known remains undermined by the unknown, the present proves to be undefinable, covering many different social times which are staggered in relation to one another within simultaneity—or definable only in terms of some fictitious future; an adventure such that the quest for identity cannot be separated from the experience of division. This society is historical society par excellence." Claude Lefort, *The Political Forms of Modern Society: Bureaucracy, Democracy, Totalitarianism*, ed. John B. Thompson (Cambridge: The MIT Press, 1986), p. 305.

5. Ibid., p. 288.

6. Paul Ricoeur, "The Fragility of Political Language," *Philosophy Today*, Spring 1987, pp. 35–44. Dauenhauer's discussion of political fragility is especially good. See, Dauenhauer, *Paul Ricoeur*, pp. 211–244.

7. Karl Marx, *Economic and Philosophical Manuscripts of 1844*, ed. Dirk J. Struik, trans. Martin Milligan (New York: International Publishers, 1968).

8. Marx and Engels, *The German Ideology*, Part I. ed. C. J. Arthur (New York: International Publishers, 1970).

9. Louis Althusser, *For Marx*, trans. Ben Brewster (New York: Vintage Books, 1970); *Lenin and Philosophy*, trans. Ben Brewster (New York: Monthly Review Press, 1971).

10. Althusser further argues that to elucidate and explain the real economic base of a society we need a conception of "science" that is free from ideological distortion. Such a science would require an "epistemological break" from humanism and from dialectics in general. For Althusser, Marx's image of an inversion is still too caught up in Hegelian dialectics. What is needed is a model of understanding that completely severs all ties from ideology, not just the inversion or negation of ideology.

Ricoeur finds at least five main problems with Althusser's concept of ideology. (1) What is the historic and epistemology status of Althusser's proposed conception of scientific Marxism? (2) What would constitute an epistemological break, and how would we know if we have achieved one? (3) In the structural model of an economic base and a derivative superstructure, how does the base cause ideology? (4) How does this model explain different ideologies that emerge from similar economic conditions? (5) How can an economic model explain how ideology distorts human action if it rejects any conception of anthropology as nonscientific and, therefore, already ideological? See IU 103–158 for Ricoeur's reading of Althusser.

11. Weber, *Economy and Society*, ed. Guenther Roth and Claus Wittich (Berkeley: University of California Press, 1978).

12. In *Oneself as Another* Ricoeur says that the three conflicts internal to demo-cratic political institutions are conflicts over the priority of goods to be distributed, the ends of good government, and the legitimation of democracy itself. In the 1987 article "The Fragility of Political Language," he describes the conflicts in a democratic society, which take place both inside and outside of political institution. These conflicts of polit-ical discourse are over political deliberation itself, the ends of good government, and over the nature and meaning of the "good life."

13. John Stuart Mill, *On Liberty* (Indianapolis: Hackett Publishers, 1978).

14. Ricoeur, "The Fragility of Political Language," p. 39.

15. Ibid., p. 41.

16. Ibid., p. 43.

17. Ibid.

18. Ibid.

19. Charles Taylor, *Sources of the Self: The Making of the Modern Mind* (Cambridge: Harvard University Press, 1989).

20. Ricoeur also recommends that the resocialization and incarceration of pris-oners be managed by different personnel. The reeducation to sociability include all mat-ters that have to do with their health, work, schooling, leisure, visitation rights, and sexual activities. All of these aspects of a prisoner's life should be performed by people who have nothing to do with security.

CHAPTER 6. CRITICAL THEORY

1. Theodore Adorno, *Negative Dialectics*, trans. John Cummings (New York: Continuum Press, 1973).

2. Iris Marion Young, *Justice and the Politics of Difference* (Princeton: Princeton University Press, 1990).

3. Ibid., pp. 99–102.

4. Ibid., pp. 39–65.

5. Ibid., p. 168.

6. Charles Taylor, "The Politics of Recognition," in *Multiculturalism*, edited by Amy Gutmann (Princeton: Princeton University Press, 1994), pp. 25–73.

7. Ibid., p. 39.

8. Michael Walzer, "Comment," in *Multiculturalism*, pp. 99–103.

9. Taylor, "The Politics of Recognition," p. 73.

10. For a more thorough and complete appreciation of Ricoeur's mediation of liberalism and communitarianism, see Dauenhauer, *Paul Ricoeur: The Promise and Risk of Politics*, pp. 303–319.

11. Ricoeur, "New Ethos for Europe," in *Philosophy and Social Criticism*, 21 (5/6) (1995): p. 7.

12. Jürgen Habermas, "Struggles for Recognition in the Democratic Constitu-tional State," in *Multiculturalism*, pp. 107–122.

13. Kant, "Perpetual Peace," p. 118.

14. For a good discussion of how nations lie to themselves and attempt to deal with their histories, see, Erna Paris, *Long Shadows: Truth, Lies, and History* (New York: Bloomsbury, 2001).

15. See, Noam Chomsky, *Year 501: The Conquest Continues* (Boston: South End Press, 1993).

16. See, for example, Martin Heidegger, "The Question Concerning Technology," in *The Question Concerning Technology and Other Essays*, trans. William Lovitt (New York: Harper Torchbooks, 1977), pp. 3–35. Herbert Marcuse, *One-Dimensional Man* (Boston: Beacon Press, 1965), pp. 1–18, 144–169, 247–257. Jürgen Habermas, "Technology and Science as 'Ideology,'" in *Toward a Rational Society*, trans. Jeremy Shapiro (Boston: Beacon Press, 1970), pp. 81–122.

17. See, Don Ihde, *Expanding Hermeneutics* (Evanston: Northwestern University Press, 1998), pp. 55–120.

18. Ihde calls it the contradictory desire for, on the one hand, total transparency of technology that will become me and be seamlessly absorbed into my activities, but, on the other hand, the desire that technology will be different from me, empower me, and enhance my activities. Both the utopian and dystopian views of technology share this contradictory desire for technological embodiment. The difference is one fears it while the other celebrates it. "The desire," Ihde explains "is simultaneously a desire for a change in situation—to inhabit the earth, or even to go beyond the earth—while sometimes inconsistently wishing that this movement could be without the mediation of the technology." Ihde, *Technology and the Lifeworld* (Bloomington: Indiana University Press, 1990), p. 75.

19. Andrew Feenberg, *Critical Theory of Technology* (Oxford: Oxford University Press, 1991), pp. 3–20.

20. For a discussion of hermeneutic technologies, see, Idhe, *Technology and the Lifeworld*, pp. 80–97.

21. Latour undermines the putative objectivity and rationality of the idea of efficiency by studying the activities of scientific discovery and technological invention as they are in the process of creating theories and machines. That way we get to see how ideas of "nature," "objectivity," and "efficiency" are social constructions resulting from settled controversies; they do not stand outside of controversies as standards by which to determine the truth of a theory or the efficiency of a machine. Latour reverses the usual order. Efficiency, he argues, is never something determined beforehand, but rather results from the choice of machine, which is then determined to be more efficient than its competitor. Efficiency is the consequence of whatever machine is adopted; it does not help us decide which model is better or worse. Machines work when the relevant people say they work. See, Latour, *Science in Action* (Cambridge: Harvard University Press, 1987).

22. Latour, "A Collective of Humans and Non-Humans," in *Pandora's Hope: Essays on the Reality of Science Studies* (Cambridge: Harvard University Press, 1999), pp. 174–215.

23. Langdon Winner, *The Whale and the Reactor* (Chicago: University of Chicago Press, 1986), pp. 3–18.

24. Michel Foucault, *Discipline and Punish: The Birth of the Prison*, trans. Alan Sheridan (New York: Vintage Books, 1975), pp. 135–230.

25. David Harvey, *Spaces of Hope* (Berkeley: University of California Press, 2000), pp. 182–196, 213–255.

26. On democratizing decisions about technologies, see Richard E. Sclove, *Democracy and Technology* (New York: Guilford Press, 1995), pp. 25–57.

27. For Ricoeur's socialist politics, see, Dauenhauer, *Paul Ricoeur: Promise and Risk of Politics*, pp. 36–93.

28. Marx, *The Poverty of Philosophy* (Moscow: Progress Publishers, 1973), pp. 91–110.

29. Weber, *From Max Weber*, edited by H. H. Gerth and C. W. Mills (Oxford: Oxford University Press, 1969).

30. See, for example, Theodore Adorno and Max Horkheimer, *Dialectic of Enlightenment*, trans. John Cumming (New York: Seabury Press, 1972).

31. My argument is similar to the one Feenberg makes against rationalization. He endeavors to expose the contextual horizon of technologies to remove the illusion of necessity and reveal the relativity of technical choices. He construes technology dialectically; it is both a technical system and something embedded in nontechnical, social contexts. I want to take it a step farther and reject entirely any notion of neutrality and objectivity of scientific-technical rationality. It is simply a myth that they are the embodiment of an abstract logic or calculative-reasoning. Such a conception of technological rationality should be rejected rather than integrated dialectically. See Andrew Feenberg, *Critical Theory of Technology*, pp. 163–198.

32. For an assessment of the World Trade Organization published by Public Citizen, the leading not-for-profit public interest research and advocacy group in the United States, see Lori Wallach and Michelle Sforza, *Whose Trade Organization? Corporate Globalization and the Erosion of Democracy* (Washington: Public Citizen Foundation, 1999).

33. For a full discussion of the impacts of corporate globalization, see, *The Case Against the Global Economy*, edited by Jerry Mander and Edward Goldsmith (San Francisco: Sierra Club Books, 1996). See also, Richard Barnet and John Cavanagh, *Global Dreams: Imperial Corporations and the New World Order* (New York: Simon and Schuster, 1994).

34. Wallach and Sforza, *Whose Trade Organization?*, pp. 195–209.

35. Even mainstream business journals have been critical of corporate globalization. In particular, criticism has been focused on the putative productivity of globalization as well as the negative effects of the trend. As *Business Week* reported, "The plain truth is that market liberalization by itself does not lift all boats, and in some cases, it has caused severe damage to poor nations. What's more, there's no point denying that multinationals have contributed to labor, environmental, and human-rights abuses as they pursue profit around the globe. . . . The downside of global capitalism is the disruption of whole societies, from financial meltdowns to practices by multinationals that would never be tolerated in the West. Industrialized countries have enacted all sorts of worker, consumer, and environmental safeguards since the turn of the century, and civil rights have a strong tradition. But the global economy is pretty much still in the robber-baron age." Pete Engardio and Catherine Belton, "Global Capitalism: Can It Be Made to Work Better?" *Business Week*, November 6, 2000, pp. 6–7.

36. WTO regulations have been subject to constitutional challenges in India, Canada, France, and the United States. See, for example, Vandana Shiva, *Protect or Plunder? Understanding Intellectual Property Rights* (New York: Zed Books, 2001). For examples of oppositions to GATT biotechnology regulations in the United States and Canada, see, Andrew Pollack, "Farmers Joining State Efforts Against Bioengineered Crops," *New York Times*, March 24, 2001.

37. United Nations Development Programme (UNDP), *Human Development Report 1999*, Geneva (1999), p. 68.

38. On the connection between globalization and food security, see, Wallach and Sforza, *Whose Trade Organization?*, pp. 101–130. On the privatization of services, see, Barry Appelton, *Navigating NAFTA: A Concise User's Guide to the North American Free Trade Agreement* (Toronto: Carsewell Books, 1994); see also, Sherri M. Stephenson, ed., *Services and Trade in the Western Hemisphere: Liberalization, Integration and Reform* (Washington: Brookings Institute, 2000).

39. Barber details the two bad senses of universalization civilization and national cultures in terms of a dialectic of globalism and tribalism, or what he calls "Jihad vs. Mc-World." Globalization homogenizes economic, political, and cultural life in nondemocratic ways that privilege corporate over public interests; tribalism is a reaction to globalism but is equally undemocratic in its reactionary affirmation of the regional, ethnic, and religious values over the universal political values. Globalism and tribalism share an indifference to civil liberties, human rights, democratic institutions, and the sovereignty of nation-states. See, Barber, *Jihad vs. McWorld: How Globalism and Tribalism Are Reshaping the World* (New York: Ballentine Books, 1995). For another version of how globalization affects nations and cultures primarily for the sake for the accumulation of capital but with occasionally beneficial consequences for people, especially women, in oppressive, patriarchal societies, see, William Greider, *One World, Ready or Not: The Manic Logic of Global Capitalism* (New York: Simon & Schuster, 1997).

40. For an optimistic account of how globalization will lead to opportunity and democracy, see, Thomas L. Friedman, *The Lexus and the Olive Tree: Understanding Globalization* (New York: Anchor Books, 2000).

41. Even some of the most trenchant and pessimistic analyses of globalization conclude by suggesting utopian possibilities in the face of the most entrenched structures of power. See, for example, David C. Korten, *When Corporations Rule the World*, 2nd edition (San Francisco: Kumarian Press, 2001); Noami Klein, *No Logo: Taking Aim at the Brand Bullies* (New York: Picador, 1999). Jeremy Brecher, Tim Costello, and Brendan Smith, *Globalization from Below: The Power of Solidarity* (Cambridge: South End Press, 2000).

42. Ricoeur, "Fragility and Responsibility," in *Philosophy and Social Criticism*, 21 (5/6) (1995): p. 21.

43. For example, former Serbian leader Slobodan Milosevic was not entirely mistaken when he denounced his prosecution as "victor's justice" at the 2002 International War Crimes Tibunal in the Hague. It is very unlikely that any international tribunal would ever hold Russia accountable for its crimes in Chechnya, China for its crimes against Tibet, or the United States for its war crimes in Iraq. Ian Fisher and Marlise Simons, "Defiant, Milosevic Begins His Defense by Assailing NATO." *New York Times*, February 15, 2002.

44. *Business Week* editorialized about excessive corporate influence over American political life. A poll of its readers found that 72 percent believed that corporations have too much power over too many aspects of our lives. See, Aaron Bernstein, "Too Much Corporate Power," *Business Week*, September 1, 2000, pp. 145–158.

45. Kenny Bruno and Joshua Karliner, "Tangled Up in Blue: Corporate Partnerships at the United Nations," *CorpWatch*, September 2000.

46. For the pros and cons of market socialism, see Bertell Ollman, ed. *Market Socialism: The Debate Among Socialists* (New York: Routledge, 1998).

BIBLIOGRAPHY

Abel, Olivier. "Ricoeur's Ethics of Method," *Philosophy Today*, Spring 1993.

Adorno, Theodore and Max Horkheimer. *Dialectic of Enlightenment*. Trans. John Cumming. New York: Seabury Press, 1972.

———. *Negative Dialectics*. Trans. E. B. Ashton. New York: Seabury Press, 1973.

Althusser, Louis. *Lenin and Philosophy*. Trans. Ben Brewster. New York: Monthly Review Press, 1971.

———. *For Marx*. Trans. Ben Brewster. New York: Vintage Books, 1970.

Anderson, Pamela Sue. *Ricoeur and Kant: Philosophy of the Will*. Atlanta: Scholars Press, 1993.

Anscombe, G. E. M. *Intention*. London: Basil Blackwell, 1979.

Apel, Karl-Otto. "Is the Ethics of the Ideal Communication Community a Utopia? On the Relationship between Ethics, Utopia, and the Critique of Utopia," in ed. Seylas Benhabib and Fred Dallmayr. *The Communicative Ethics Controversy.*

———. *Toward a Transformation of Philosophy*. Trans. Glyn Adey and David Frisby. London: Routledge & Kegan Paul, 1980.

Appelton, Barry. *Navigating NAFTA: A Concise User's Guide to the North American Free Trade Agreement*. Toronto: Carsewell Books, 1994.

Arendt, Hannah. *The Human Condition*. Garden City: Anchor Books, 1959.

Aristotle. *The Complete Works of Aristotle, vols. 1 and 2*. Ed. Jonathan Barnes. Princeton: Princeton University Press, 1984.

———. *The Nicomachean Ethics*. Trans. W. D. Ross. Oxford: Oxford University Press, 1980.

Austin, J. L. *How to Do Things with Words*. Oxford: Oxford University Press, 1962.

Barber, Benjamin. *Jihad Vs. McWorld: How Globalism and Tribalism Are Reshaping the World*. New York: Ballentine Books, 1995.

Baynes, Ken. *The Normative Grounds of Social Criticism: Kant, Rawls, Habermas*. Albany: SUNY Press, 1992.

Beardsley, Monroe. *Aesthetics: Problems in the Philosophy of Criticism*. New York: Harcourt, Brace and World, 1958.

Beiner, Ronald. *What's the Matter with Liberalism?* Berkeley: University of California Press, 1992.

Benhabib, Seyla. *Critique Norm and Utopia: A Study of the Foundations of Critical Theory*. New York: Columbia University Press, 1986.

————, ed. *Democracy and Difference: Contesting the Boundaries of the Political*. Princeton: Princeton University Press, 1996.

————. "The Generalized and the Concrete Other: The Kohlberg-Gilliagan Controversy and Feminist Theory," in *Feminism as Critique*. Ed. S. Benhabib and Drucilla Cornell. Minneapolis: University of Minnesota Press, 1987, 77–95.

————. *Situating the Self*. New York: Routledge, 1991.

———— and Fred Dallmayr, ed. *The Communicative Ethics Controversy*. Cambridge: MIT Press, 1990.

Barnet, Richard and John Cavanagh. *Global Dreams: Imperial Corporations and the New World Order*. New York: Simon and Schuster, 1994.

Bernet, Rudolf. "Husserl and Heidegger on Intentionality and Being," *Journal of the British Society for Phenomenology* 21 (1990).

Bernstein, Aaron. "Too Much Corporate Power." *Business Week*, September 1, 2000.

Bernstein, Richard J. *Beyond Objectivism and Relativism: Science, Hermeneutics, and Praxis*. Philadelphia: The University of Pennsylvania Press, 1991.

————. *The New Constellation: The Ethical-Political Horizons of Modernity/Postmodernity*. Cambridge: The MIT Press, 1992.

Black, Max. *Models and Metaphors: Studies in Language and Philosophy*. Ithaca: Cornell University Press, 1962.

Blaug, Ricardo. *Democracy, Real and Ideal: Discourse Ethics and Radical Politics*. Albany: SUNY Press, 1999.

Bohman, James. *New Philosophy of Social Science*. Cambridge: MIT Press, 1991.

Bourgeois, Patrick L *Extension of Ricoeur's Hermeneutic*. The Hague: Martinus Nijhoff, 1975.

————. "From Hermeneutics of Symbols to the Interpretation of Texts," in *Studies in the Philosophy of Paul Ricoeur*. Ed. Charles E. Reagan. Athens: Ohio University Press, 1979.

————. *Philosophy at the Boundary of Reason: Ethics and Postmodernity*. Albany: SUNY Press, 2001.

————. and Frank Schalow. *Traces of Understanding: A Profile of Heidegger's and Ricoeur's Hermeneutics*. Amsterdam: Rodopi, 1990.

Bowles, Samuel and Herbert Gintis. *Democracy and Capitalism*. New York: Basic Books, 1986.

Brecher, Jeremy, Tim Costello, and Brendan Smith, ed. *Globalization From Below: The Power Of Solidarity*. Cambridge: South End Press, 2000.

Bruno, Kenny and Joshua Karliner. "Tangled Up in Blue: Corporate Partnerships at the United Nations," *CorpWatch*, September 2000.

Calhoun, Craig. *Critical Social Theory*. Oxford: Blackwell, 1995.

Caputo, John. "Husserl, Heidegger, and the Question of a Hermeneutic Phenomenology," *Husserl Studies* 1 (1984).

Carr, David. *Time, Narrative and History*. Bloomington: Indiana University Press, 1986.

Chomsky, Noam. *Year 501: The Conquest Continues*. Boston: South End Press, 1993.

————. *Deterring Democracy*. London: Verson, 1991.

Clark, S. H. *Paul Ricoeur*. London: Routledge, 1990.

Danto, Arthur. *Analytical Philosophy of History*. Cambridge: Cambridge University Press, 1964.

Dauenhauer, Bernard. *Paul Ricoeur: The Promise and Risk of Politics*. Lanham: Rowman & Littlefield Publishers, 1998.

———. "Ricoeur and Political Identity," *Philosophy Today*, Vol. 39, no. 1, 1995.

Davidson, Donald. *Essays on Actions and Events*. Oxford: Clarendon Press, 1980.

Deleuze, Giles and Felix Guattari. *Anti-Oedipus: Capitalism and Schizophrenia*. Trans. Robert Hurley, Mark Seem, and Helen R. Lane. Minneapolis: University of Minnesota Press, 1983.

Derrida, Jacques. *Of Grammatology*. Trans. Gayatri Chakrovorty Spivak. Baltimore: Johns Hopkins University Press, 1970.

———. *Writing and Difference*. Chicago: University of Chicago Press, 1982.

Dicenso, John. *Hermeneutics and the Disclosure of Truth: A Study in the Work of Heidegger, Gadamer and Ricoeur*. Charlottesville: University Press of Virginia, 1990.

Dilthey, Wilhem. *Selected Writings*. Ed. and trans. H. P. Rickman. Cambridge: Cambridge University Press, 1976.

Dosse, Francois. *Paul Ricoeur: Les sens d'une vie*. Paris: La Découverte, 1997.

Dreyfus, Hubert L. *Being-in-the-World: A Commentary of Heidegger's Being and Time, Division I*. Cambridge: MIT Press, 1991.

——— and Stuart E. Dreyfus, "What Is Morality? A Phenomenological Account of the Development of Ethical Expertise," in *Universalism and Communitarianism*.

Dworkin, Ronald. *Taking Rights Seriously*. Cambridge: Harvard University Press, 1977.

Engardio, Pete and Catherine Belton. "Global Capitalism: Can It Be Made to Work Better?" *Business Week*, November 6, 2000.

Elliston, Friedrich. "Phenomenology Reinterpreted: From Husserl to Heidegger," *Philosophy Today* 21 (1977).

Feenberg, Andrew. *Critical Theory of Technology*. Oxford: Oxford University Press, 1991.

———. *Questioning Technology*. London: Routledge, 1999.

Foucault, Michel. *Discipline and Punish: The Birth of the Prison*. Trans. Alan Sheridan. New York: Vintage Books, 1979.

———. *The History of Sexuality, vol. I*. Trans. Robert Hurley. New York: Vintage Books, 1980.

———. *Michel Foucault: Politics, Philosophy, Culture*. Ed. Lawrence D. Kritzman. New York: Routledge, 1988.

Fraser, Nancy. *Unruly Practices: Power, Discourse and Gender in Contemporary Social Theory*. Minneapolis: University of Minnesota Press, 1989.

Frege, Gottlob. "On Sense and Reference," in *Translations from the Philosophical Writings of Gottlob Frege*. Trans. Max Blac. Ed. Peter Geach and Max Black. Oxford: Basil Blackwell, 1970), 56–78.

Friedman, Thomas L. *The Lexus and the Olive Tree: Understanding Globalization*. New York: Anchor Books, 2000.

Freud, Sigmund. *The Ego and the Id*. Trans. Joan Riviere, ed. James Strachey. New York: W. W. Norton & Company, 1960.

Gallie, W. B. *Philosophy and Historical Understanding*. New York: Schocken Books, 1964.

Gadamer, Hans-Georg. "The Hermeneutics of Suspicion," in ed. Gary Shapiro and Alan Sica. *Hermeneutics: Questions and Prospects*. Amherst: University of Massachusetts Press, 1984

————. *Philosophical Hermeneutics*. Trans. and ed. David E. Linge. Berkeley: University of California Press, 1976.

————. *Reason in the Age of Science*. Trans. Frederick G. Lawrence. Cambridge: The MIT Press, 1982.

————. "The Scope and Function of Reflection," in ed. David E. Linge. *Philosophical Hermeneutics*.

————. *Truth and Method*, 2d. ed. Trans. Joel Weinsheimer. New York: Continuum, 1975.

————. "The Universality of the Hermeneutical Problem," in ed. David E. Linge. *Philosophical Hermeneutics*. Berkeley: University of California Press, 1976.

Geertz, Clifford. "From a Native's Point of View: On the Nature of Anthropological Understanding," in *Interpretive Social Science: A Reader*. Ed. Paul Rabinow and William M. Sullivan. Berkeley: University of California Press, 1979.

————. *The Interpretation of Cultures*. New York: Basic Books, 1973.

Gerhart, Mary. *The Question of Belief in Literary Criticism: An Introduction to the Hermeneutical Theory of Paul Ricoeur*. Stuttgart: Akademischer Verlag, 1979.

Gilligan, Carol. *In a Different Voice: Psychological Theory and Women's Development*. Cambridge: Harvard University Press, 1982.

Gramsci, Antonio. *Prison Notebooks*. Ed. and trans. Quentin Hoare and Geoffrey Nowell Smith. New York: International Books, 1971.

Greider, William. *One World, Ready or Not: The Manic Logic of Global Capitalism*. New York: Simon & Schuster, 1997.

————. *Who Will Tell the People: The Betrayal of American Democracy*. New York: Simon & Schuster, 1992.

Greisch, Jean. "Testimony and Attestation," *Philosophy and Social Criticism*, vol. 21, no. 5/6, 1995.

Grice, H. P. "Meaning," *Philosophical Review*, 66 (1957).

————. "Utterer's Meaning, Sentence-Meaning, and Word-Word-Meaning," *Foundations of Language*, 4 (August 1968), 225–245.

Guignon, Charles B. *Heidegger and the Problem of Knowledge*. Indianapolis: Hackett Publishing Company, 1983.

Gutmann, Amy, ed. *Multiculturalism*. Princeton: Princeton University Press, 1994.

Habermas, Jürgen. *Between Facts and Norms: Contributions to a Discourse Theory of Law and Democracy*. Trans. William Rehg. Cambridge: The MIT Press, 1996.

————. *Communication and the Evolution of Society*. Trans. Thomas McCarthy. Boston: Beacon Press, 1979.

————. "The Hermeneutic Claim to Universality," in Josef Bleicher, *Contemporary Hermeneutics*. London: Routledge, 1980.

————. *Justification and Application: Remarks on Discourse Ethics*. Trans. Ciaran P. Cronin. Cambridge: The MIT Press, 1993.

————. *Knowledge and Human Interests*. Trans. Jeremy J. Shapiro. Boston: Beacon Press, 1972.

————. *Legitimation Crisis*. Trans. Thomas McCarthy. Boston: Beacon Press, 1975.

————. *Moral Consciousness and Communicative Action*. Trans. Christian Lenhardt and Shierry Weber Nicholson. Cambridge: MIT Press, 1990.

————. "Morality, Society, and Ethics: An Interview with Torben Hviid Nielsen," trans. Ciaran P. Cronin, in *Justification and Application: Remarks on Discourse Ethics*. Cambridge: The MIT Press, 1993.

————. *On the Logic of the Social Sciences*. Trans. Shierry Weber Nicholson and Jerry A. Stark. Cambridge: The MIT Press, 1988.

————. *The Philosophical Discourse of Modernity*. Trans. Frederick Lawrence. Cambridge: The MIT Press, 1990.

————. *Postmetaphysical Thinking: Philosophical Essays*. Trans. William Mark Hohengarten. Cambridge: The MIT Press, 1992.

————. "A Reply to My Critics," in ed. John B. Thompson and David Held. *Habermas: Critical Debates*. Cambridge: The MIT Press, 1982.

————. "Struggles for Recognition in the Democratic Constitutional State," in ed. Amy Gutmann. *Multiculturalism*.

————. *The Theory of Communicative Action, Vol. I, Reason and the Rationalization of Society*. Trans. Thomas McCarthy. Boston: Beacon Press, 1984.

————. *Toward a Rational Society*. Trans. Jeremy Shapiro. Boston: Beacon Press, 1970.

Hahn, Lewis Edwin, ed. *The Philosophy of Paul Ricoeur*. Chicago: Open Court, 1995.

Harvey, David. *Spaces of Hope*. Berkeley: University of California Press, 2000.

Heidegger, Martin. *Being and Time*. Trans. John Macquarrie and Edward Robinson. New York: Harper & Row, 1962.

————. *The Question Concerning Technology and Other Essays*. Trans. William Lovit. New York: Harper and Row, 1977.

Hegel, G. W. F. *Philosophy of Right*. Trans. T. M. Knox. Oxford: Clarendon, 1973.

Held, David. *Democracy and the Global Order: From the Modern State to Cosmopolitan Governance*. Stanford: Stanford University Press, 1995.

Hempel, Carl. "The Function of General Laws in History," in *Aspects of Scientific Explanation and Other Essays in the Philosophy of Science*. New York: The Free Press, 1942.

———— and Paul Oppenheim, "Studies in the Logic of Explanation," in *Scientific Knowledge*. Ed. Janet A. Kourany. Belmont: Wadsworth Publishing Company, 1987.

Hesse, Mary B. *Models and Analogies in Science*. South Bend: University of Notre Dame Press, 1966.

————. "Science and Objectivity," in *Habermas: Critical Debates*. Ed. John B. Thompson and David Held. Cambridge: The MIT Press, 1982.

Hirsch, E. D. *Validity In Interpretation*. New Haven: Yale University Press, 1967.

Hopkins, Burt C. *Intentionality in Husserl and Heidegger: The Problem of the Original Method and Phenomenon of Phenomenology*. Dordrecht: Kluwer Academic Publishers, 1993.

Horkheimer, Max. *Critique of Instrumental Reason*. Trans. Matthew O'Connell. New York: Seabury Press, 1974.

————. *Eclipse of Reason*. New York: Seabury Press, 1974.

Husserl, Edmund. *Cartesian Meditations*. Trans. Dorion Cairns. Dordrecht: Martinus Nijhoff, 1960.

————. *The Crisis of European Sciences and Transcendental Phenomenology*. Trans. David Carr. Evanston: Northwestern University Press, 1970.

————. *Ideas Pertaining to a Pure Phenomenology and a Phenomenological Philosophy, First Book*. Trans. F. Kersten. Dordrecht: Kluwer Academic Publishers, 1982.

————. *Logical Investigation, vols. I, II*. Trans. J. N. Findlay. London: Routledge and Kegan Paul, 1970.

————. *Phenomenological Psychology*. Trans. John Scanlon. The Hague: Martinus Nijhoff, 1977.

Ihde, Don. *Expanding Hermeneutics*. Evanston: Northwestern University Press, 1998.

———. *Hermeneutic Phenomenology: The Philosophy of Paul Ricoeur*. Evanston: Northwestern University Press, 1970.

———. *Technology and the Lifeworld: From Garden to Earth*. Bloomington: Indiana University Press, 1990.

———. "Text and the New Hermeneutics," in *On Paul Ricoeur: Narrative and Interpretation*. Ed. David Wood. London: Routledge, 1991.

Ingram, David. *Critical Theory and Philosophy*. New York: Paragon House, 1990.

———. *Habermas and the Dialectic of Reason*. New Haven: Yale University Press, 1987.

———. *Reason, History, and Politics: The Communitarian Grounds of Legitimation in the Modern Age*. Albany: State University of New York Press, 1995.

Jackobson, Roman. "Closing Statement: Linguistics and Poetics," in *Style in Language*. Ed. T. A. Sebeok. Cambridge: MIT Press, 1960.

Jay, Martin. *The Dialectical Imagination*. Boston: Little, Brown and Company, 1973.

Jervolino, Domenico. *The Cogito and Hermeneutics: The Question of the Subject in Ricoeur*. Trans. Gordon Poole. Dordrecht: Kluwer Academic Publishers, 1990.

Jonas, Hans. "Technology and Responsibility: Reflections on the New Tasks of Ethics," in *Philosophical Essays: From Ancient Creed to Technological Man*. Englewood Cliffs, NJ: Prentice Hall, 1974.

Kant, Immanuel. *Critique of Practical Reason*. Trans. T. K. Abbott. Amherst, NY: Prometheus Books, 1996.

———. *Critique of Pure Reason*. Trans. Norman Kemp Smith. New York: St. Martin's Press, 1965.

———. *Grounding for the Metaphysics of Morals*. Trans. James W. Ellington. Indianapolis: Hackett Publishing Company, 1981.

Kearney, Richard, ed. *Paul Ricoeur: The Hermeneutics of Action*. London: SAGE Publications, 1996.

Kemp, T. Peter and David Rassmussen, ed. *The Narrative Path: The Later Works of Paul Ricoeur*. Cambridge: The MIT Press, 1989.

Klein, Noami. *No Logo: Taking Aim at the Brand Bullies*. New York: Picador, 1999.

Klemm, David. *The Hermeneutical Theory of Paul Ricoeur: A Constructive Analysis*. Lewisburg: Bucknell University Press, 1983.

——— and William Schweiker, ed. *Meanings in Texts and Actions: Questioning Paul Ricoeur*. Charlottesville: University Press of Virginia, 1993.

Kohlberg, Lawrence. "From Is to Ought: How to Commit the Naturalistic Fallacy and Get Away with It in the Study of Moral Development," in ed. Theodore Mischel, *Cognitive Development and Epistemology*. New York: Academic Press, 1971.

Korten, David C. *When Corporations Rule the World*, 2d ed. San Francisco: Kumarian Press, 2001.

Kymlicka, Will. *Liberalism, Community and Culture*. Oxford: Clarendon Press, 1989.

Laclau, Ernest and Chatal Mouffe. *Hegemony and Socialist Strategy: Towards a Radical Socialist Politics*. New York: Verso Books, 1985.

Latour, Bruno, "A Collective of Humans and Non-Humans," in *Pandora's Hope: Essays on the Reality of Science Studies*. Cambridge: Harvard University Press, 1999.

———. *Science in Action*. Cambridge: Harvard University Press, 1987.

Lawlor, Dennis. *Imagination and Chance*. Albany: SUNY Press, 1992.

Lefort, Claude. *The Political Forms of Modern Society: Bureaucracy, Democracy, Totalitarianism*. Ed. John B. Thompson. Cambridge: The MIT Press, 1986.

Levinas, Emmanuel. *Totality and Infinity*. Trans. Alphonso Lingis. Pittsburgh: Duquesne University Press, 1969.

MacIntyre, Alasdaire. *After Virtue: A Study in Moral Theory*. South Bend: University of Notre Dame Press, 1981.

———. *Whose Justice? Which Rationality?* South Bend: University of Notre Dame Press, 1988.

Mander, Jerry and Edward Goldsmith, ed. *The Case Against the Global Economy*. San Francisco: Sierra Club Books, 1996.

Marcuse, Herbert. *Essays on Liberation*. Boston: Beacon Press, 1969.

———. *Eros and Civilization*. New York: Vintage, 1961.

———. *One-Dimensional Man: Studies in the Ideology of Advanced Industrial Society*. Boston: Beacon Press, 1964.

Marsh, James L. *Critique, Action and Liberation*. Albany: State University of New York Press, 1995.

———. *Post-Cartesian Meditations*. New York: Fordham University Press, 1988.

Marx, Karl. *Economic and Philosophical Manuscripts of 1844*. Ed. and intro. Dirk J. Struik, trans. Martin Milligan. New York: International Publishers, 1968.

——— and Frederick Engels, *The German Ideology*. Ed. and intro. C. J. Arthur. New York: International Publishers, 1970.

———. *The Poverty of Philosophy*. Moscow: Progress Publishers, 1973.

McCarthy, Thomas. *The Critical Theory of Jürgen Habermas*. Cambridge: The MIT Press, 1978.

Mill, John Suart. *On Liberty*. Indianapolis: Hackett Publishers, 1978.

Mohanty, J. N. "Consciousness and Existence: Remarks on the Relation between Husserl and Heidegger," *Man and World* 11 (1978).

———. "Transcendental Philosophy and the Hermeneutic Critique of Consciousness," in *Phenomenology and the Human Sciences*. Ed. J. N. Mohanty. The Hague: Martinus Nijhoff, 1985.

Muldoon, Mark S. "Ricoeur's Ethics: Another Version of Virtue Ethics? Attestation Is Not a Virtue," *Philosophy Today*, Fall (1998).

Mulhall, Stephen and Adam Swift. *Liberals and Communitarians*. Oxford: Blackwell, 1992.

de Muralt, André. *The Idea of Phenomenology: Husserlian Exemplarism*. Trans. Garry L. Breckon. Evanston: Northwestern University Press, 1974.

Nussbaum, Martha C. *Cultivating Humanity: A Classical Defense of Reform in Liberal Education*. Cambridge: Harvard University Press, 1997.

———. *Poetic Justice: The Literary Imagination and Public Life*. Boston: Beacon Press, 1995.

Ollman, Bertell, ed. *Market Socialism: The Debate Among Socialists*. New York: Routledge, 1998.

O'Neill, Shane. *Impartiality in Context: Grounding Justice in a Pluralistic World*. Albany: SUNY Press, 1997.

Palmer, Richard E. *Hermeneutics*. Evanston: Northwestern University Press, 1969.

Parfit, Derek. *Reasons and Persons*. Oxford: Oxford University Press, 1986.

Paris, Erna. *Long Shadows: Truth, Lies and History*. New York: Bloomsbury, 2001.

Peffer, R. G. *Marxism, Morality, and Social Justice*. Princeton: Princeton University Press, 1990.

Pellauer, David. "Limning the Liminal: Carr and Ricoeur on Time and Narrative," *Philosophy Today* 35 (1991).

———. "The Significance of the Text in Paul Ricoeur's Hermeneutical Theory," in ed. Charles E. Reagan. *Studies in the Philosophy of Paul Ricoeur*. Athens: Ohio University Press, 1979.

Polkinghorne, Donald E. *Narrative Knowing and the Human Sciences*. Albany: SUNY Press, 1988.

Pollack, Andrew. "Farmers Joining State Efforts Against Bioengineered Crops," *New York Times*, March 24, 2001.

Popper, Karl. *The Logic of Scientific Discovery*. New York: Harper & Row, 1968.

Rainwater, Mara. "Refiguring Ricoeur: Narrative Force and Communicative Ethics." *Philosophy and Social Criticism*, vol. 21, no. 5/6, 1995.

Rassmussen, David. *Mythic-Symbolic Language and Philosophical Anthropology: A Constructive Interpretation of the Thought of Paul Ricoeur*. The Hague: Martinus Nijhoff, 1971.

———. "Rethinking Subjectivity," *Philosophy and Social Criticism*, vol. 21, no. 5/6, 1995.

———, ed. *Universalism vs. Communitarianism: Contemporary Debates in Ethics*. Cambridge: MIT Press, 1990.

Rawls, John. *Political Liberalism*. New York: Columbia University Press, 1993.

———. *A Theory of Justice*. Cambridge: Harvard University Press, 1971.

Reagan, Charles E. *Paul Ricoeur: His Life and His Work*. Chicago: The University of Chicago Press, 1996.

———, ed. *Studies in the Philosophy of Paul Ricoeur*. Athens: Ohio University Press, 1979.

——— and David Stewart. *The Philosophy of Paul Ricoeur: An Anthology of His Work*. Boston: Beacon Press, 1978.

Rehg, William. *Insight and Solidarity: The Discourse Ethics of Jürgen Habermas*. Berkeley: University of California Press, 1994.

Richards, I. A. *Principles of Literary Criticism*. New York: Harcourt & Brace, 1925.

Ricoeur, Paul. *The Conflict of Interpretation: Essays in Hermeneutics*. Trans. Willis Domingo et al., ed. Don Ihde. Evanston: Northwestern University Press, 1974.

———. "The Creativity of Language." Interview by Richard Kearney (Paris, 1981), in ed. Mario J. Valdes. *A Ricoeur Reader: Reflection and Imagination*. Toronto: University of Toronto Press, 1991.

———. *Critique and Conviction*. New York: Columbia University Press, 1998.

———. *Fallible Man*. Trans Charles Kelbley. New York: Fordham University Press, 1986.

———. *Freedom and Nature: The Voluntary and the Involuntary*. Trans Erazim Kohak Evanston: Northwestern University Press, 1966.

———. *Freud and Philosophy: An Essay on Interpretation*. Trans. Dennis Savage. New Haven: Yale University Press, 1970.

———. "From Existentialism to the Philosophy of Language," *Criterion* 10 (1971), Spring, 14–18.

———. *From Text to Action: Essays in Hermeneutics, II*. Trans. Kathleen Blamey and John B. Thompson Evanston: Northwestern University Press, 1991.

————. *Hermeneutics and the Human Sciences: Essays on Language, Action, and Interpretation*. Ed. and trans. John B. Thompson. Cambridge: Cambridge University Press, 1981.

————. *History and Truth*. Trans. Charles A. Kelbley, Evanston: Northwestern University Press, 1965.

————. "The Human Being as the Subject Matter of Philosophy," in *The Narrative Path: The Later Works of Paul Ricoeur*. Ed. T. Peter Kemp and David Rasmussen. Cambridge: The MIT Press, 1989.

————. *Husserl: An Analysis of His Phenomenology*. Trans. Edward E. Ballard and Lester G. Embree. Evanston: Northwestern University Press, 1967.

————. "Husserl and Wittgenstein on Language," in *Phenomenology and Existentialism*. Ed. E. N. Lee and M. Mandelbaum. Baltimore: Johns Hopkins Press, 1967.

————. "Ideology and Utopia as Cultural Imagination," in *Being Human in a Technological Age*. Ed. Donald M. Borchert and David Stewart. Athens: Ohio University Press, 1979.

————. "Ideology, Utopia, and Faith," *The Center for Hermeneutical Studies* 17 (1976).

————. "Intellectual Autobiography," in *The Philosophy of Paul Ricoeur*. Ed. Lewis Edwin Hahn. Chicago: Open Court, 1987.

————. *Interpretation Theory: Discourse and the Surplus of Meaning*. Fort Worth: Texas Christian University Press, 1976.

————. "Interview with Charles Reagan, June 19, 1982," in *Paul Ricoeur: His Life and His Work*. Charles E. Reagan. Chicago: The University of Chicago Press, 1996.

————. "Interview with Charles Reagan, July 8, 1991," in *Paul Ricoeur: His Life and His Work*.

————. *Lectures I: Autour du politique*. Paris: Seuil, 1991.

————. *Lectures on Ideology and Utopia*. Ed. George H. Taylor. New York: Columbia University Press, 1986.

————. "Life in Quest of Narrative," in *On Paul Ricoeur: Narrative and Interpretation*. Ed. David Wood. London: Routledge, 1991.

————. "The Metaphorical Process as Cognition, Imagination, and Feeling," *Critical Inquiry* 5 (1978), Fall, 143–159.

————. "Narrative Identity," in *On Paul Ricoeur: Narrative and Interpretation*. Ed. David Wood. London: Routledge, 1991.

————. "Narrative Time," in *On Narrative*. Ed. W. J. T. Mitchell. Chicago: The University of Chicago Press, 1981, 165–186.

————. *Oneself as Another*. Trans. Kathleen Blamey, Chicago: The University of Chicago Press, 1992.

————. "Poetry and Possibility: An Interview with Paul Ricoeur Conducted by Philip Fried," *Manhattan Review* 2 (1982), no. 2, 6–21.

————. *Political and Social Essays*. Ed. David Stewart and Joseph Bien. Athens: Ohio University Press, 1974.

————. "The Power of Speech: Science and Poetry," *Philosophy Today* 29 (1985), Spring.

————. "Reflections on a New Ethos for Europe," *Philosophy and Social Criticism*, vol. 21 (1995), no. 5/6.

————. *A Ricoeur Reader: Reflection and Imagination*. Ed. Mario J. Valdes. Toronto: University of Toronto Press, 1991.

————. *The Rule of Metaphor. Multi-Disciplinary Studies of the Creation of Meaning in Language*. Trans Robert Czerny, Kathleen McLaughlin and John Costello, SJ. Toronto: University of Toronto Press, 1977.

————. *The Symbolism of Evil*. Trans Emerson Buchanan Boston: Beacon Press, 1967.

————. *Time and Narrative*, vol. I. Trans. Kathleen McLaughlin and David Pellauer. Chicago: University of Chicago Press, 1984.

————. *Time and Narrative*, vol. II. Trans. Kathleen McLaughlin and David Pellauer. Chicago: University of Chicago Press, 1985.

————. *Time and Narrative*, vol. III. Trans. Kathleen McLaughlin and David Pellauer. Chicago: University of Chicago Press, 1988.

————. *The Just*. Trans. David Pellauer. Chicago: University of Chicago Press, 2000.

———— and Hans-Georg Gadamer, "The Conflict of Interpretations," in *Phenomenology: Dialogues and Bridges*. Ed. Ronald Bruzina and Bruce Wilshire. Albany: State University of New York Press, 1982.

Rouse, Joseph. "Interpretation in Natural and Human Science," in *The Interpretive Turn: Philosophy, Science, Culture*. Ed. David R. Hiley, James F. Bohman, Richard Shusterman. Ithaca: Cornell University Press, 1991.

Roth, Paul A. "Interpretation as Explanation," in *The Interpretive Turn: Philosophy, Science, Culture*.

Sandel, Michael J. *Liberalism and the Limits of Justice*, 2d ed. Cambridge: Cambridge University Press, 1998.

de Saussure, Ferdinand. *Course in General Linguistics*. Trans. Wade Baskin, ed. Charles Bally and Albert Sechehaye. New York: McGraw-Hill, 1959.

Searle, John R. *Speech Acts*. Cambridge: Cambridge University Press, 1969.

Schlosser, Eric. *Fast Food Nation: The Dark Side of the All-American Meal*. New York: Houghton Mifflin, 2001.

Sclove, Richard E. *Democracy and Technology*. New York: Guilford Press, 1995.

Shiva, Vandana. *Protect or Plunder? Understanding Intellectual Property Rights*. New York: Zed Books, 2001.

Sklar, Holly. *Chaos or Community? Seeking Solutions, Not Scapegoats for Bad Economics*. Boston: South End Press, 1995.

Sophocles. *Antigone*. Trans. Elizabeth Wyckoff. Chicago: University of Chicago Press, 1960.

Stapleton, Timothy J. *Husserl and Heidegger: The Question of a Phenomenological Beginning*. Albany: State University of New York Press, 1983.

Strawson, P. F. *Individuals: An Essay in Descriptive Metaphysics*. London: Methuen & Co., 1959.

Stephenson, Sherri M., ed. *Services and Trade in the Western Hemisphere: Liberalization, Integration and Reform* Washington: Brookings Institute, 2000.

Taylor, Charles. *Hegel*. Cambridge: Cambridge University Press, 1975.

————. *Philosophy and the Human Science: Philosophical Papers 2*. Cambridge: Cambridge University Press, 1985.

————. "The Politics of Recognition," in ed. Amy Gutmann. *Multiculturalism*.

————. *Sources of the Self: The Making of the Modern Identity*. Cambridge: Harvard University Press, 1989.

Thompson, John B. *Critical Hermeneutics: A Study in the Thought of Paul Ricoeur and Jürgen Habermas*. Cambridge: Cambridge University Press, 1981.

————. *Studies in the Theory of Ideology*. Berkeley: University of California Press, 1984.

————. "Universal Pragmatics," in *Habermas: Critical Debates*. Ed. John B. Thompson and David Held. Cambridge: The MIT Press, 1982.

United Nations Development Programme. *Human Development Report 1999*, Geneva (1999).

Van Leeuwen, T. M. *The Surplus of Meaning: Ontology and Eschatology in the Philosophy of Paul Ricoeur*. Amsterdam: Rodopi, 1981.

Van den Hengel, J. *The Home of Meaning: The Hermeneutics of the Subject of Paul Ricoeur*. Washington: University Press of America, 1982.

Venema, Henry Isaac. *Identifying Selfhood: Imagination, Narrative, and Hermeneutics in the Thought of Paul Ricoeur*. Albany: SUNY Press, 2000.

Von Wright, G. *Explanation and Understanding*. London: Routledge and Kegan Paul, 1971.

Wallach, Lori and Michelle Sforza. *Whose Trade Organization? Corporate Globalization and the Erosion of Democracy*. Washington: Public Citizen Foundation, 1999.

Walzer, Michael. "Comment," in ed. Amy Gutmann. *Multiculturalism*.

————. *Spheres of Justice: A Defense of Pluralism and Equality*. New York: Basic Books, 1983.

Weber, Max. *Economy and Society*, 2 vols. Ed. Guenther Roth and Claus Wittich. Berkeley: University of California Press, 1978.

————, ed. H. H. Gerth and C. W. Mills. *From Max Weber*. Oxford: Oxford University Press, 1969.

————. "Politics as a Vocation," trans. and ed. H. H Gerth and C. Wright Mills. *From Max Weber: Essays in Sociology*. New York: Galaxy Books, 1958.

Weinsheimer, Joel C. *Gadamer's Hermeneutics: A Reading of Truth and Method*. New Haven: Yale University Press, 1985.

Wellmer, Alberecht. *Critical Theory of Society*. Trans. John Cumming. New York: Continuum, 1971.

Winner, Langdon. *The Whale and the Reactor*. Chicago: University of Chicago Press, 1986.

Wittgenstein, Ludwig. *Philosophical Investigations*. Trans. G. E. M. Anscombe, 3rd. ed. New York: Macmillan Publishing, 1968.

Wood, David, ed. *On Paul Ricoeur: Narrative and Interpretation*. London: Routledge, 1991.

Young, Iris. *Justice and the Politics of Difference*. Princeton: Princeton University Press, 1990.

INDEX

Printed in the United States
1541500002B/357-502